SIMPLY AIX

SIMPLY AIX

Casey Cannon,
Carolyn Jones,
and Scott Trent

To join a Prentice Hall PTR internet mailing list, point to:
http://www.prenhall.com/register

Prentice Hall PTR
Upper Saddle River, New Jersey 07458
http://www.prenhall.com

Library of Congress Cataloging-in-Publication Data

Casey, Cannon
    Simply AIX / Casey Cannon.
        p.   cm.
    Includes index.
    ISBN 0–13–568882–5
    1. AIX (Computer file)   2. Operating systems (Computers
    I. Title.
    QA76.76.063T748   1996
    005.4'469—dc20

                                            96–27759
                                                CIP

Acquisitions editor: Greg Doench
Cover designer: Design Source
Cover design director: Jerry Votta
Manufacturing manager: Alexis R. Heydt
Compositor/Production services: Pine Tree Composition, Inc.

© 1997 by Prentice Hall PTR
Prentice-Hall, Inc.
A Simon & Schuster Company
Upper Saddle River, New Jersey 07458

The publisher offers discounts on this book when ordered in
bulk quantities. For more information contact:

> Corporate Sales Department
> Prentice Hall PTR
> One Lake Street
> Upper Saddle River, New Jersey 07458
>
> Phone: 800-382-3419
> Fax: 201-236-7141
> email: corpsales@prenhall.com

Printed in the United States of America
10 9 8 7 6 5 4 3 2

ISBN: 0-13-568882-5

Prentice-Hall International (UK) Limited, *London*
Prentice-Hall of Australia Pty. Limited, *Sydney*
Prentice-Hall Canada Inc., *Toronto*
Prentice-Hall Hispanoamericana, S.A., *Mexico*
Prentice-Hall of India Private Limited, *New Delhi*
Prentice-Hall of Japan, Inc., *Tokyo*
Simon & Schuster Asia Pte. Ltd., *Singapore*
Editora Prentice-Hall do Brasil, Ltda., *Rio de Janeiro*

Trademarks

1-2-3 is a trademark of Lotus Development Corporation.

386SX is a trademark of Intel Corporation.

3Com is a trademark of 3Com Corporation.

486 is a trademark of Intel Corporation.

486SX is a trademark of Intel Corporation.

AFS is a trademark of Transarc Corporation.

AIX is a trademark of International Business Machines Corporation.

AIX 3278/79 Emulation/6000 is a trademark of International Business Machines Corporation.

AIX/370 is a trademark of International Business Machines Corporation.

AIX/6000 is a trademark of International Business Machines Corporation.

AIX InfoCrafter/6000 is a trademark of International Business Machines Corporation.

AIXwindows is a trademark of International Business Machines Corporation.

AIXwindows Interface Composer/6000 is a trademark of International Business Machines Corporation.

Encina is a trademark of Transarc Corporation.

GL is a trademark of Silicon Graphics, Inc.

Gradient is a trademark of Gradient Technologies, Inc.

graPHIGS is a trademark of International Business Machines Corporation.

HP is a trademark of Hewlett-Packard Company.

HP LaserJet+ is a trademark of Hewlett-Packard Company.

HP-UX is a trademark of Hewlett-Packard Company.

IBM is a registered trademark of International Business Machines Corporation.

INed is a trademark of INTERACTIVE Systems Corporation.

InfoCrafter is a trademark of International Business Machines Corporation.

InfoExplorer is a trademark of International Business Machines Corporation.

Intel is a trademark of Intel Corporation.

Lotus is a trademark of Lotus Development Corporation.

Macintosh is a trademark of Apple Computer Corp.

Motif is a trademark of Open Software Foundation, Inc.

Motorola is a trademark of Motorola, Inc.

MS-DOS is a trademark of Microsoft Corporation.

NetLS is a trademark of Apollo Computer, Inc.

NetView is a trademark of International Business Machines Corporation.

NetView/6000 is a trademark of International Business Machines Corporation.

NetWare is a trademark of Novell Corporation.

NFS is a trademark of Sun Microsystems, Inc.

Novell is a trademark of Novell Corporation.

OpenDoc is a trademark of Apple Computer Corp.

OpenGL is a trademark of Silicon Graphics, Inc.

Open Software Foundation is a trademark of Open Software Foundation, Inc.

OS/2 is a trademark of International Business Machines Corporation.

OSF is a trademark of Open Software Foundation, Inc.

OSF/Motif is a trademark of Open Software Foundation, Inc.

PostScript is a trademark of Adobe Systems Incorporated.

POWER Architecture is a trademark of International Business Machines Corporation.

PowerOpen is a trademark of International Business Machines Corporation.

PowerPC is a trademark of International Business Machines Corporation.

PowerPC Architecture is a trademark of International Business Machines Corporation.

POWERserver is a trademark of International Business Machines Corporation.

POWERstation is a trademark of International Business Machines Corporation.

PS/2 is a trademark of International Business Machines Corporation.

RISC System/6000 is a trademark of International Business Machines Corporation.

RS/6000 is a trademark of International Business Machines Corporation.

Sun is a trademark of Sun Microsystems, Inc.

Sun OS is a trademark of Sun Microsystems, Inc.

ThinkPad is a trademark of International Business Machines Corporation.

ToolTalk is a trademark of Sun Microsystems, Inc.

Transarc is a trademark of Transarc Corporation.

Ultimedia is a trademark of International Business Machines Corporation.

UNIX is a registered trademark in the United States and other countries, licensed exclusively through X/Open Company Limited.

Wabi is a trademark of Sun Microsystems, Inc.

Windows is a trademark of Microsoft Corporation.

Windows NT is a trademark of Microsoft Corporation.

X11 is a trademark of Massachusetts Institute of Technology.

X.desktop is a trademark of IXI Limited.

X/Open is a trademark of X/Open Company Limited.

X Window System is a trademark of Massachusetts Institute of Technology.

Contents

Preface

Welcome to *Simply AIX!* AIX customers have been asking us for a book that has a little bit of everything in it (from installing a system to connectivity) but is written in a friendly style. You've asked for a book that enables you to get started but can also enable you to keep your system up and running. *Simply AIX* is for you!

UNIX usage and popularity is at an all-time high (with no end in sight). UNIX systems are becoming the system of choice in schools, small businesses, Fortune 500 corporations, and on the Internet. A lot of these folks are using AIX for the first time. This book is easy to read and understand; it'll make you a *respectable* and *productive* user in short order!

Who Should Use This Book?

Our goal in writing this book is to help our customers enjoy AIX as much as we do! We have written about topics that will be useful to all users, including system administrators, programmers, and end users. Cheat sheets, useful tables, technical tidbits, an easy, fun, plain English, writing style, and pertinent, straightforward information make this book useful to novices as well as the seasoned UNIX user.

Use this book to find out about AIX; use this book to administer your AIX network; use this book to manage your AIX PowerPC. We're not kidding—whether you've tunneled around AIX or have only recently mastered MS-DOS, we'll familiarize you with the basics and amaze you with the functionality of an industrial-strength operating environment.

This book is designed for both new users and more advanced users. A hot pepper icon within chapters indicates the level of information in the chapter is hot stuff and looks like the following:

The hot pepper icon is used to mark sections that are more advanced. Power users (gurus) may want to read these sections first. New users can become gurus after learning these sections.

How This Book Is Organized

The overview explains the history of AIX, details the information provided in each chapter, and gives you a general introduction to the AIX environment.

Chapter 1, "Customizing Your Environment," shows you how to use the Common Desktop Environment (CDE) tools and launchpad to make yourself feel right at home.

Chapter 2, "Using AIX," teaches you AIX commands, file system structure, shell usage, and additional tricks that will make you a genuine AIX user.

Chapter 3, "I Know Windows/DOS, What's AIX?" compares and contrasts the Windows/DOS and AIX worlds. It gives you the inside information on running Windows on AIX.

Chapter 4, "Editors," gives you an overview and cheat sheets for your favorite AIX editor.

Chapter 5, "Installing AIX," provides easy, fast GUI (graphical menu) tools and instructions for what is often perceived as the most difficult part of a UNIX operating system—getting it up and running.

Chapter 6, "Setting Up Peripherals," tells you how to set up printers, CD-ROM drives, and other devices you'd like to attach to your system.

Chapter 7, "Communicating with the World," describes what you need to know to survive the alphabet soup of AIX-supported communication protocols, including the use of AIX Net Browsers on the Internet.

Chapter 8, "SMIT Happens! Administering AIX," enables you to manage, do simple or complex tasks, and administer your system and/or any other systems on your network using either GUI applications or command line combinations.

Chapter 9, "AIX Speaks Your Language: Internationalization," tells you how to get AIX to speak your language—look in this chapter for information on how to communicate globally in a different language.

Chapter 10, "All the Help You Need," describes how to use InfoExplorer, the AIX on-line hypertext information library (50,000 pages on-line); AIX developer help available through the Internet; 1-800 numbers and fax sheets; and URL addresses and descriptions for IBM Internet sites.

Chapter 11, "Gathering Up the Pieces," wraps up our journey into AIX with information on performance tools, file system management, the AIX development environment, security, as well as special tools that help you learn how to resolve common AIX problems, as well as obtain the latest bug fixes from the Internet.

Chapter 12, "IBM Developer Connection for AIX CD-ROM" describes the CD goodies included in this book, how to install them, and how to get more!

Acknowledgments

We would like to thank our families for putting up with us while we worked on this book night and day. We promise to do more around the house now.

Also, thanks to our managers that supported us during this endeavor—Jeri Hilsabeck, Cal Killen, Dave Robertson, Cora Scurlock, Pam Spann, Donna Van Fleet, Chris Albury, and Dave Higgins.

Many thanks to Team AIX for their technical help: Carlos Ayala, Katie Barrett, Raymond Bauer, Davin Bentti, Rick Bowers, Ed Bradford, Gena Brown, Nick Camillone, Faye Dedrick, Doug Woestendiek, Randy Greenberg, Carolyn Greene, Enrique Gomez, Jesse Haug, George Icossipentarhos, Dennis Lee, Tracey Porter, Barbara Rignew, Frank Rojas, Melanie Rose, Jim Shaffer, Marvin Toungate, I-Hsing Tsao, Ed Williams, Becky Wood, and Juan Zalles and also Niels Christiansen and John Sullivan deserve thanks for suggesting the title "Simply AIX".

Special thanks to Charlie Cree, Jerome Kruemke, Syed Pasha, and others for making it possible for us to include the IBM Developers Connection for AIX CDROM.

We are deeply indebted to the folks we worked with at Prentice Hall and the people we worked with at Pine Tree Composition—Greg Doench, Leabe Berman, Beth Sturla, Daniel Boilard, and Patty Sawyer—for making this book the polished product it is today.

Foreword by Donna Van Fleet, Vice President of AIX Development

We've had a guiding vision that AIX would be a tool to make your work easier—not a tool that makes work for you. To that end, we have designed AIX to be not just easy, but even intuitive for the novice while at the same time, we have preserved the classical Unix look for sophisticated Unix-trained users.

It's a tremendous pleasure to welcome you to AIX. It and we are here to make your job easier, even more fun!

Donna

Foreword by Cal Killen, Director of AIX Development, Leader of Team AIX

AIX enables scalability from palmtops to terraflops. It is *the* operating system for UniProcessors, symmetric MultiProcessors, embedded OEM systems, cluster and massively parallel systems. AIX is used in many commercial and technical applications including client, entry, mid-range, and high-end server applications.

AIX has been accepted as the provider of business and mission-critical solutions (including mainframe-centric applications) and the transition to client/server. It leads the industry with exploitation of PowerPC and RS/6000 hardware; high availability servers; software graphics; support of new, emerging devices; integration into PC networks; enterprise management; and the emerging IBM technologies including objects, human-centrics, network centric, interactive broadband services, and parallelism.

AIX has a reputation for quality with our customers. We have achieved ISO 9000 certification and high scores on rigorous internal assessments based on Malcom Baldrige criteria. Our quality program objective is to have ever increasing customer satisfaction. We will continue our evolution to total quality management.

This book will help you get the most from your AIX systems and from your other systems, too, and that will save you time and money. You and your co-workers will learn AIX faster and you will be in a good mood while you're doing it!

Cal

Overview

This book can be used by itself if you don't know anything about AIX or UNIX. It can also be used if you know UNIX but want to also understand the unique features of AIX. This book will focus on the latest and greatest AIX goodies delivered in AIX Version 4 (and there are lots of them).

Why AIX?

Scalability

AIX runs on high-performance machines which make it very fast and powerful. This software/hardware combo allows folks to run heavy-duty applications on affordable systems. AIX also runs on non-IBM machines (such as those from Apple, Motorola, and Bull) which gives it a strong future. AIX runs on machines from PCs up to symmetric multiprocessor systems.

AIX is a high quality, IBM-tested operating system. It has been tuned and improved with many performance enhancements. AIX has IBM-backed service and support with goodies like Internet fixes and information as well as personal contact.

AIX speaks many languages! It has multinational support for a variety of languages and locales and characters across the world. AIX can connect in a variety of ways with nearly any machine or software. It supports a long list of different communication protocols and devices. This keeps you connected to your colleagues and the world.

Standards

AIX supports many of the commands and library calls from the old versions of UNIX that have been around since the beginning (such as Berkley and System V) as well as the newer standards such as NIST (National Institute of Standards and

Technology), XTI (X/Open Transport Library Interface), FIPS, XPG4, X/Open, POSIX, UNIX 95, and other standards. Why do you care? If you learn AIX, you can use UNIX just about anywhere and still know what you're doing. You'll also get more applications that run on AIX (standards make programmers' lives much simpler).

Simplicity

IBM has added functions to make AIX much easier for people to use. It's fast and easy to install and administer (unlike typical UNIX systems). AIX teaches you AIX commands as you use graphical interfaces, so you can become a guru as you go. AIX has on-line hypertext (multimedia) documentation so that you can search across many books and get to exactly what you're after.

Solutions

AIX has many applications from IBM and vendors. Related applications and hardware have been grouped into solutions as a one button orderable item that solves the customer's needs.

Style

AIX has the style and personality of UNIX while remaining on the leading edge of technology. AIX has alot of sizzling software to keep customers up to date with the Internet, objects, multimedia, and more.

Why Simply AIX?

You've heard of UNIX. You now have or may want an AIX machine. So, how do you get started? BUY THIS BOOK!!! If you want to learn about and get more out of your AIX system, then you need this book. Even if you only use an AIX system occasionally at school or work, then you will want to have this book. We cover topics such as installation and configuration, cool graphic interfaces, and hot tips that improve your productivity as either a user or an administrator. We discuss advanced topics such as how to make your computer do Japanese or other languages.

We've included pullout cheat sheets, useful tables, technical tidbits, hot tips, fun, and a CD-ROM loaded with goodies. This book has it all—from A to Z.

How Did AIX Grow Up?

First of all, what does AIX stand for anyway? It's the Advanced Interactive Executive. You didn't know you were in the executive class, did you?

We needed an operating system that would blow users socks off with the new processor performance. The AIX operating system didn't start in someone's garage, but it did have its beginning in a small strip center down the street from the IBM plant in Austin in the early 1980s. There was a project using the beginnings of a RISC processor from research, a compiler that took advantage of it, and a layer of software called the VRM (virtual resource manager) to isolate the software from the hardware.

The project blossomed when it converged with teams from early word processor systems such as the 5520, the DisplayWriter, and the 5280. The commercial UNIX version out in the world at the time was from Interactive Systems Corporation so that's what we started with. Unix is very popular because it was and is an "open architecture" which allows flexible applications and system extendability

But when we really started using it, whoah! Can you see a banker "grepping for it?" We recognized that it was a programmer's heaven but everyone else would find it . . . complex. In response, a new user interface was written and we added easier system management.

There are also lots of programmers that grew up with UNIX so we incorporated many UNIX standards so the same command can be used no matter where you grew up! AIX uses standards from System V, Berkeley, OSF, NIST, and others.

The file system was improved and the virtual resource manager and virtual memory managers were created. An exciting idea for the time was a virtual terminal, which allowed multiple "screens" on a single display. AIX also included a DOS 3.0 (yes, that was a long time ago!) emulator.

AIX was then enhanced to support almost every protocol customers were using, both IBM protocols like SNA and protocols gaining momentum from universities, like TCP/IP. We could list them all but it would fill the page with alphabet soup!

We really worked on improving the quality of the UNIX operating system while keeping its universal appeal. AIX was enhanced to be more reliable and robust for continuous operation so our commercial customers could count on it. The installation and system management were greatly improved. A friendly and powerful on-line publication tool was created to help folks learn the system. AIX went world-wide with messages and menus in many languages.

We have worked on AIX so that it can be the fastest gun in the west! (It was developed in Texas so it has to be.) The AIX software and compilers work hand in hand with the hardware to optimize the performance of your applications. AIX performance is very important to us!

Then came more standards! There were lots of "UNIXs" floating around and they weren't close enough for an application to simply recompile when moving from one platform to the next, so several standards were developed in the industry that AIX participated in. AIX also brought in commands and libraries that were available including AT&T's System V and the Berkeley versions of UNIX. Other defacto standards for X Windows, multiple shells, mailers, and postscript printer output format were adopted as well.

AIX Version 4 came up another level in usability and functionality with the Common Desktop, a visual graphics system management tool, symmetric multiprocessing and support for a wide range of hardware systems and I/O adapters. It's the best UNIX yet!

If you're a history buff, you might enjoy the following articles from the early days of AIX and the RISC family of workstations written by the original architects:

1. *IBM RT Personal Computer Technology* SA23-1057, 1986

2. *IBM Tech PC Journal,* Volume 4, Number 12, December 1986 devoted to the RT PC.

3. *The IBM Systems Journal,* Volume 26, Number 4, 1987.

4. *IBM Journal of Research and Development,* Volume 34, Number 1, January 1990.

I'd Like to See How It Ends First!

If you like to read the end of the book first (did the butler do it?), you can use this book from the back, using the index or the chapters that you need first. Or, start from the beginning. The chapters flow so that you can use it right away and get more proficient as you keep on reading—what a concept! We assume the following:

- You have the CDs or tapes and are ready to install, or you have a pre-installed machine.

- Your hardware is put together and running.

- You don't have to know anything about AIX.

- You know how to use a mouse and keyboard.

How Do I Find What I Need?

We use an icon in this book to give you a quick perspective of the type of information that is included in a chapter or section. The "hot pepper" icon is HOT STUFF and indicates information that, when mastered, will enhance your standing with AIX wizards and make you an AIX hot shot!

Chapter 1   Customizing Your Environment

Getting Started with the Desktop

CDE, Common Desktop Environment, hides the complexity of AIX—it is designed for end users. The Front Panel (resembles a launch pad) enables any user to sit down and immediately start using the desktop. CDE makes applications easy to use—the Style Manager (located on the Front Panel) enables you to increase or decrease the font size, change fonts, turn off that annoying beep, and enables you to select color combinations and backdrops.

Using the Front Panel

This section explains all the icons on the Front Panel of the common desktop. You can have multiple desktops running at one time—like you have several virtual desks in your office. You can also bring up an editor, a calendar, your mail, and help.

Using Style Manager

This section tells all on customizing the colors, fonts, character sizes, backdrops, keyboard, mouse, that darn BEEP, terminals, and desktop startup.

Using File Manager

The File Manager is great for folks that are still a little queasy about using the command line. Through this application, you can get to your files and directories through a set of menus and action selections. The files are listed right in front of you so that you can pick them out.

Using Application Manager

This section describes how you can bring up applications and add additional applications to the Application Manager—such as multimedia demos, the online publications, tools, printers, and sample programs.

Getting Help

The Help Manager is a super way to learn about the desktop! It gives you the basic skills and allows you to search through the information. On-line help is available for each of the standard applications in CDE. Whether you are using File Manager, Calendar, or Mailer for example, you request and display help topics in the same way. You can also browse help information on your system using the desktop Help Manager.

Chapter 2   Using AIX

Commands—Are These Real Words?

If you want to be a *real* UNIX user, you need to learn some shell commands. This section describes a small subset that will give you the ability to get around the directories, list files and print them, as well as clue you in on more interesting commands like "grep" which searches a set of files for something you're looking for. We'll tell you our favorite commands and demystify some of the acronyms associated with them.

Shells

This section explains what a "shell" is and the differences between those available on AIX so you can pick the best one for you. The shell is very powerful—you can do lots when you put commands together with pipes and redirection! You will also learn about pattern matching and other good guru tricks.

File and User Permissions—What's a Root?

UNIX systems have a security system built into the filesystem. This section explains file permissions, the "root" user, and users and groups.

I'd Rather Call it Sam—Links

If you would rather have your own names for commands and directories instead of the real thing (it's easier to remember), read about aliases.

Paper Dolls—Cutting and Pasting

It's really useful to take a paragraph from the memo from your boss and put it into a memo from you! There are many uses of the cut and paste capability and this section will tell you how to do it.

Where Did My Files Go?

Have you ever lost a file? You know it's in there somewhere, but you can't find it! The directories look like files to you and it's hierarchical so you can't see them all. This section will give you some tricks to find lost files.

Fun Commands

There are a few fun commands that you might like. They're not the CD-ROM multimedia games we play now, they're just some lightweight little programs like fish, blackjack, and tic-tac-toe that can give you a break in the day from your work (but it still looks like you're working!).

Chapter 3   *I Know Windows & DOS, What's AIX?*

OK, Give Me Some Hints!

Many folks know DOS commands but are just learning AIX. This section explains the overall similarities and differences of Windows/DOS and AIX.

Crib Notes: DOS to AIX

This part of the book is a "crib note set" to AIX if you know DOS. It's a list of DOS commands and some parameters translated into the AIX commands and parameters. The whole list is in the book twice, so you can cut the list out and keep it handy but you'll still have a copy in the book.

DOS Functions in AIX

This section describes how you can move files to and from DOS and AIX. It can be real handy to get a list of files on that DOS diskette while you're using AIX. Or you can take that AIX file home to your PC.

Wow! AIX Windows Are Easy, Too!

If you are a Microsoft Windows user, you know the basics about using windows user interfaces. Using AIX CDE Windows will be a snap! You can also run many of the Microsoft Windows applications on AIX with other software, called Wabi and SoftWindows.

SoftWindows Runs Microsoft Windows and App's!

There's a separate product you can install to run Windows 3.11 and Windows applications from your AIX system. That will come in handy if you have some favorites. It could also save you some money if you have invested in a bunch of applications.

AIX Connections Brings Them All Together

This software will allow you to connect NT, OS/2, Macintosh, and other systems to your AIX systems. You'll be able to share files, printers, terminals, and other services.

Chapter 4 *Editors*

There are lots of different editors available on AIX. This section gives you a how-to that gets you in the file with a few necessary functions (like adding a line, changing the text), and then how to save it and get out. Just a few basics to get you by. There are many good books completely devoted to one editor that we list so you can become an expert. There's also a handy list of commands that you can cut out of the book and keep handy.

Editor FAQs

This section describes some clever key-strokes you can learn; multiple functions in a few keys, for example, or changing all occurrences of "evrone" to "everyone" in your file. Some of the key-strokes are quite cryptic, but that's what impresses the gurus.

Chapter 5 *Installing AIX*

How to Get AIX Up and Running

Installing an operating system can be intimidating, so this chapter keeps the instructions simple. AIX is organized into small, installable filesets. You can install only what you need!

All Right! Installation Assistance!

Install Assistant is displayed when you first start-up your system. It walks you through the tasks needed to install and configure the system for use. You can also bring up the Installation Assistant by entering install_assist on the command line.

Network Installation Manager

You can install AIX using tape or CD-ROM or by using the Network Installation Manager (NIM). NIM is not only an excellent tool for installing multiple machines over a network, it can also be used for software maintenance and machine customizations. Using NIM, you can set up an installation once for machines with identical requirements or customize the specific needs of specific machines.

Chapter 6 *Setting Up Peripherals*

Using SMIT to Install Devices

Setting up CD-ROM drives and other devices can be frustrating. This section gets you straight to it and gives you the steps to take.

Printers

Printers are a special case because they are so critical to getting work completed. How can you hand in your report when it can't be printed? This section gives you a lot of good printer information, such as setting up the devices, the queues, and the commands available to print. Another essential piece of information is how to fix and get status on the printer queues and processes (there's a daemon back there!). It will explain the mysteries of different file types and how to print them.

Chapter 7   Communicating with the World

Communicating from your system to the outside world is essential in today's work environment. This section describes what you need to know to survive the alphabet soup of communication protocols.

You will learn how to send and receive files and log into someone else's machine. E-mail will be described so that you can pick the mail program that fits your needs the best and you can get up to speed quickly. This section also explains the mysteries behind local and distributed file systems.

We also discuss the power and ease of the Internet Web Browsers that are available for AIX such as the AIX WebExplorer, Netscape, and Mosaic.

Chapter 8   SMIT Happens! Administering AIX

System Management Interface Tool (SMIT)

System administration can be time consuming and complex. The SMIT (Systems Management Interface Tool) application eases that work by providing menus and help screens to allow you to do things like add new users or set up a new printer.

I've Fallen and I Can't Get Up!—The "Running Man" icon is the SMIT indicator of command success or failure. While the command is still processing, an icon at the top of the window will show a man running and running and running . . . If the running man falls down, the command failed. If the running man stops running in place and stands up triumphantly, the command worked!

Distributed System Management (Or Why Just Worry About One Machine When You Can Multitask?!)

The Distributed System Management Interface Tool (DSMIT) adds functionality to SMIT by enabling the SMIT interface to build commands for system management and distribute them to other clients on a network. DSMIT has most of the functionality of the SMIT program, such as fast paths, log files, and flags.

Visual System Manager

Visual System Manager (VSM) is a graphical interface that lets you conduct system management by selecting pictures! Most of the tasks performed in VSM consist of drag and drop actions. The VSM application user interfaces are similar in design so if you know how to use one, you'll know how to use them all. Each application has a template area, actions area, work area, and information area.

Backup—and make restore an option!

AIX Version 4 provides multiple ways of backing up your systems. If you backup regularly, you'll have the option of restoring files you lose! You can use SMIT or the command line. Backup commands available include `cpio`, `tar`, `pax`, `dd`, `backup`, `restore`, and `mksysb`. SMIT also provides a menu-driven method of backing up and restoring AIX files or the entire rootvg volume group. After restoring your files using SMIT, you can use the `fsck` command to check the integrity of the file system after you have restored your files.

Chapter 9   AIX Speaks Your Language: Internationalization

An internationalized and localized computer system should be taken for granted. Messages are displayed in the native language of the user. Date and time formats are familiar and understandable. Lists of sorted data are ordered so that people can find stuff. In other words, the computer works "right" no matter who is using it or which country they are in.

Why Should I Care About Speaking Your Language?

Well, if you live in the United States, English is your only language, and your customers live in the United States and only speak English, and this will never change, then you probably don't need to care.

But if you don't live in the United States, or if you don't want to use your computer in English, or if your customer wants information processed such that it can be used in another country, then you should care deeply. As an English speaking person, what would you think if your computer only spoke Japanese?

This becomes an even bigger issue when it comes to selling software and other products overseas.

I'm Convinced! How Do I Get AIX to Speak My Language?

This is the simple part, all you need to do is to make sure that the right parts were installed.

Next, with our help, configuration will be a total snap, and we will have you on the way to editing Japanese files, getting messages in German, reading French, and sending e-mail in Korean!

This is Interesting! Tell Me More!

Did you know that over 50% of the information technology market is found outside of the United States? Look in this section for tidbits about internationalization, additional sources for more information, and even a couple of interesting anecdotes.

Chapter 10 All the Help You Need

Now that you know your way around AIX some, here's a way to get more info. Get ready to access 50,000 pages of on-line AIX documentation through InfoExplorer, a hypertext information retrieval system. And after you've exhausted the on-line documentation, call 1-800-IBM-FAX to have documents faxed directly to you from a menu including RISC/6000, AIX, networking, and SP2 information. We have also provided a list of Internet references to get to AIX information that is currently available on the Net such as product descriptions, forums, newsgroups, service information, and more! The amount of Internet information is growing by the day so this list will only get you started.

Chapter 11 Gathering Up the Pieces

Performance Tools for System Management

Who doesn't want to know what's going on under the covers? This section describes tools that keep track of memory, disk space usage, processes, and so on.

The AIX Development Environment

Are you curious about what tools and programs AIX provides for programmers? Does AIX have RCS, SCCS? What is CMVC? Can I write C++ programs with AIX? Read on for the answers!

Security and System Management

AIX provides features and tools you can use to ensure that your system is secure. Plus we tell you where the log files are so that you can see what happened on your system over the weekend.

FixDist—How to Get the Latest Bug Fixes from the Internet

Use these fantastic tools to obtain the latest fixes from the Internet, as well as learn how to resolve problems.

Chapter 12 IBM Developer Connection for AIX CD-ROM

This section describes the CD included in this book.

This CD-ROM is packed full of interesting graphic demos you can run with a click of a mouse, technical documentation, and sample code you can read. See this appendix for a complete list of what's on this CD-ROM, as well as installation instructions.

Appendix: Handy Command Details

The most frequently used commands are described in this section so you can find exactly what parameter you need when you need it and how to use it. It's not the entire set of commands, but it will get you most of what you need!

The command descriptions are long enough to get details on how to type in the right flags without being overwhelming.

AIX for Busy Managers

Some of you (managers especially) are too busy to learn how to set up your AIX system. If you have the time, do it yourself. If you just won't get to it, don't keep using that old system. You won't be respectable! Here's a way to get your system customized to what you need in your environment. Read this section through completely so you can talk the lingo and then execute the plan.

Here's the plan. First, go buy some really good chocolate chip cookies to share. Then ask your friendly techie guru to help you install and customize your system. You want the latest level of AIX that the office is using, the common desktop environment (CDE), local printers, local networks, DOS compatibility if you need it, local applications added to the CDE application manager, any cool tools the guru uses and likes, CDE customization the guru uses, and e-mail initialized. If you'll have private files stored here (like personnel records), turn off the read/write for group and others. Get access to the on-line publications so you can be self-sufficient.

When the system is ready, ask the guru to demo the system to you so you can see what cool tools they have and see the general usage if you're not used to the windows. Discuss connecting to your e-mail system, especially if you have been using something else before now.

Whew! After that, you'll have to give your guru a raise! Chocolate chip cookies will help and a free lunch wouldn't hurt either!

Read the CDE chapter, it's what you'll need to be functional. CDE is very easy to use so it will be a breeze! If you're not used to the windowing environment, you'll need to play with window resizing, iconifying, and other actions. Spend a few minutes to see what the help screens are like: indices, searches, hypertext links to more help, and so on, so you'll know where to look when you're in a crunch! Check out the CDE e-mail program, the file manager, the application manager, the calendar, and printing. They're what you'll use every day.

You might want to show the guru the CD that comes with this book. They will love it!

Keep this book on hand and look up specific sections when you need to perform different tasks. The back sections have a lot of information and references you should browse through also. There's a lot more you can learn.

AIX for System Managers

If you manage AIX systems, you'll want to go straight to the SMIT chapter to install and set up a system. Then read the chapters "Installing AIX" and "Setting Up Peripherals" to customize and get printers and devices set up. The chapter "Gathering Up the Pieces" will give you the tools you need to find out whether the file system is getting full and how its performing. The chapter "All the Help You Need" is a wealth of information such as FAQs (frequently asked questions), Internet web addresses with home pages on IBM, AIX, Talk Radio to exchange information with IBM developers, and other references.

Read the chapter describing the CD so you can check it out. You may also need to read about Internationalization to get the right language running.

AIX for Novices

If you're a UNIX guru "wanna-be," start by reading the Common Desktop Environment—that's the quickest startup. You can get your work done using the CDE text editor, but to be a guru, you need to learn the "vi" editor. It's the de-facto standard for editors for UNIX systems. It's very cryptic, so you'll need to practice! There are tables in the "Editors" chapter to show you the different operations for the editors available.

The "Customizing Your Environment" chapter will show you how to change the background to something cool and other stuff to get CDE just like you want.

You'll also want to get on the Internet, so read part of the "Connecting to the World" chapter and the parts of the "All the Help You Need" chapter for the html addresses. There are book references throughout the book if you want to become an expert in a specific area.

You'll need to read the "Using AIX" chapter to get acquainted with the commands, file system, shell, and other systemwide functions. Cut out the "cheat-sheet" list of commands and put it next to your computer for reference

AIX for Windows/DOS Users

If you have been using a DOS computer with or without Windows, you should read the chapter specifically written for you, "AIX for Windows/DOS Users." Keep the "cheat sheet" handy and set up aliases to get you up and running right-away. Read the CDE chapter and use the "Customizing Your Environment." You'll have no trouble using it if you know Windows. Read the "All the Help You Need" "Customizing Your chapter to find out about the on-line publications, Internet html addresses, and other very useful references. You'll also need the Editors chapter to learn about changing file contents.

SIMPLY AIX

CHAPTER 1

Customizing Your Environment

The Common Desktop Environment (CDE) is a graphical user interface for open systems, jointly developed by IBM, Hewlett-Packard, Sun, and Novell. The desktop was developed to hide the complexities of UNIX and to provide a common user interface for the UNIX environment.

In this chapter we'll highlight how the desktop works and what functions you can perform using the desktop. However, we don't have the space to convey the unlimited functionality the desktop makes available to users, developers, and system administrators. When you're ready to really exploit the desktop, see the Common Desktop Environment 1.0 documentation available through Addison Wesley.

End user titles include

- *Common Desktop Environment 1.0: User's Guide*
- *Common Desktop Environment 1.0: Programmer's Overview*
- *Common Desktop Environment 1.0: Advanced User's and System Administrator's Guide*

Development environment titles include:

- *Common Desktop Environment 1.0: Application Builder's Guide*
- *Common Desktop Environment 1.0: Programmer's Guide*
- *Common Desktop Environment 1.0: ToolTalk Messaging Guide*
- *Common Desktop Environment 1.0: Desktop KornShell User's Guide*
- *Common Desktop Environment 1.0: Help System Author's and Programmer's Guide*

- *Common Desktop Environment 1.0: Style Guide and Certification Checklist*
- *Common Desktop Environment 1.0: Internationalization Programmer's Guide*

Getting Started with the Desktop

CDE hides the complexity of AIX—it is designed for end users. The front panel (resembles a launch pad) enables any user to sit down and immediately start using the desktop. CDE applications look and feel the same—smart applications running on CDE follow the same Motif style and design guidelines. (This means that application menus and window characteristics are similar, enabling you to use the applications without wasting time figuring out how to cut and paste or exit. You complete these types of functions the same way within each application.)

CDE makes applications easy to use—the Style Manager (located on the Front Panel) enables you to increase or decrease the font size, change fonts, and select color combinations and backdrops. With CDE, help is always available.

Upon startup, users can immediately begin using the desktop and applications or can customize the desktop for a more personal configuration. VSM, SMIT, and InfoExplorer can by launched directly from the desktop.

Desktop services, productivity tools, and applications are available through the

- Front Panel
- Style Manager
- File Manager
- Application Manager
- Workspace Objects
- Trash Can
- Mailer

Starting and Ending a Desktop Session

To log into the desktop, enter your login id and password and press Return. Session Manager is started after Login Manager authenticates your login and password. Session Manager provides the ability to manage sessions—to remember the state of your most recent session and return you there the next time you log in. Session Manager saves and restores

- The appearance and behavior settings—for example, fonts, colors, and mouse settings;

- The window applications that were running—for example, your File Manager and Text Editor windows.

To log out, either click the Exit control on the Front Panel, or choose Log Out from the Workspace menu.

When you log out of a regular desktop session, Session Manager saves information about your current session so that it can be restored the next time you log in. Information about non-desktop applications might not be saved.

Ready to Speak Another Language?

1. Choose Language from the Options menu on the login screen.

2. Choose the language group that includes the language you need.

3. Select a language.

4. Log in.

The default language for your system is set by your system administrator. The Options menu enables you to access other languages. Choosing a language in the Options menu sets the LANG environment variable for your session. The default language is restored at the end of the session.

Using the Front Panel

Let's start with the Front Panel, the horizontal window at the bottom of the display as shown in Figure 1–1.

The Front Panel provides direct access to the Style Manager, File Manager, Application Manager, Workspace Objects, Trash Can, Text Editor, Print Manager, Mailer, and Help. The Front Panel continuously displays the time, date, and if you have new mail. Dragging and dropping objects onto the File Manager, Print Manager, Mailer, or Text Editor enables you to copy, print, mail, or edit your files immediately. You can also throw anything away at any time by simply dragging and dropping the object onto the Trash Can. The Front Panel moves with you as you switch workspaces (switch workspaces by selecting the workspace buttons—identified as One, Two, Three, and Four in the Front Panel illustration).

Figure 1–1   Common Desktop Environment Front Panel

Many of the controls in the Front Panel start applications when you click them— for example, the File Manager and Style Manager controls. Some controls are drop zones—for example, the Printer and Trash Can controls. You can drag a file from File Manager or Application Manager to the Printer or Trash Can icons.

Certain icons, such as the clock and busy light, are indicators that tell you something about the state of your system. Other icons have a dual purpose; for example, the Calendar and Mailer icons are both indicators (showing today's date and the arrival of new mail, respectively) and buttons for starting applications.

Subpanels.   If a control in the Main Panel has an arrow button on top of it, then that control has a subpanel. Subpanels always contain

- An Install Icon—use the Install Icon to customize the subpanel;
- A labelled copy of the icon in the Main Panel.

Workspace Switch.   The workspace switch contains the buttons you use to change from one workspace to another. Each workspace occupies the entire display, as though your display has several layers. Workspaces simply multiply the amount of display area available for windows. You can customize your workspaces and label each workspace button accordingly as shown in Figure 1–2.

Using Style Manager

Tired of your backdrop or backdrops? Double-click on Style Manager, select the backdrop icon, select the backdrop you're willing to stare at all day, and select apply. (Note that you can select a unique backdrop for each workspace.)

Is your beep too high, too loud, or just generally annoying? Select the Beep icon, change the volume, tone, or duration of the beep, then click OK.

Figure 1–2   Workspace Switch

Figure 1–3   Style Manager Icon

Can't read your font? Click on the Style Manager Font icon, select a new font, and change your font size, click OK. Isn't this great? The Style Manager icon is located on the right side of the Front Panel (Figure 1–3).

CDE is totally customizable—change your colors, modify the color palette, and/or delete any color palette that is really annoying. You can also modify window behavior by clicking on the Window icon—either select Point In Window To Make Active (makes a window active when the mouse pointer enters it) or select Click In Window to Make Active (makes a window active when the mouse enters it and you click on the left mouse button).

Start Style Manager by clicking on the Style Manager icon located on the Front Panel. Use Style Manager to customize your desktop

- Colors

- Workspace backdrops

- Font size

- Keyboard, mouse, and window behavior

The Style Manager panel is depicted in Figure 1–4.

Figure 1–4   Style Manager Panel

Figure 1-5   File Manager Icon

Using File Manager

File Manager displays the files, folders, and applications on your system as icons. Working with File Manager icons saves you from having to learn complex commands or typing long file names. To open a File Manager view of your home folder, click the File Manager control in the Front Panel. Click on the File Manager icon on the Front Panel (Figure 1–5). Do you see your folders and files?

The File Manager main window as shown in Figure 1–6 is a view of a folder on your system. The folder you are currently viewing is called the current folder.

Ready to use File Manager? Some actions to try include the following:

1. Move a file to another folder (or directory). Drag and drop the file icon on the new folder icon. Your file is now located in a new directory (and you didn't have to know the AIX mv or cp commands to do this).

2. Place an icon for a file or folder on the backdrop of your current workspace (remember the workspace switch?). Drag and drop the file or folder icon outside of any window. Note that any changes you make in the file located on your workspace will be reflected in the copy of your file located in the File Manager.

3. Print a file. Drag and drop the file icon onto the Printer icon. Or, if you have multiple printers, open your Printer subpanel and drop the file on the printer of your choice.

4. Delete a file. Drag and drop your unwanted file to the Trash Can icon (you can clean up your files and directories without knowing the delete, remove, or erase AIX commands).

You can get help with your files by selecting the file or folder and pressing F1; or by putting the mouse pointer on the object and selecting help from the object's

Figure 1–6   My files displayed using File Manager

pop-up window; or by choosing On Item from the Help menu, then clicking on the file or folder's icon.

Once you start piling up lots of files, you might need help tracking them down. File Manager's Find function is just what you need. Select Find from the File Menu, enter the name of the file or folder you want to find, determine where you want the search to start by editing the Search Folder field, and click on Start. Figure 1–7 shows the results after I searched my home directory for a document with the word *network* in the document title.

Figure 1–7   Search Using File Manager Find Option

Using Application Manager

Application Manager provides access to applications you use in your everyday work through action icons. Clicking on action icons starts applications. Action icons are stored in special folders called application groups.

When you click on Application Manager, you'll see the icons for the Desktop_Apps, Desktop_Tools, Information, and System_Admin application groups. The desktop provides these built-in application containers for tools and utilities available with AIX. To run any application within Application Manager, you just double-click on the application icon.

If there are choices within the application, when you double-click on the application icon, the icon will display its contents and you can then choose the specific application function you want to start.

Figure 1–8   Front Panel Control for Application Manager

To open Application Manager, click its Front Panel control (Figure 1–8).

You can place the files, folders, and actions you use frequently on the workspace backdrop as icons (so you don't have to search File Manager or Application Manager for a file, folder, or application). To place an object on the workspace, drag its icon from a File Manager or Application Manager window and drop it directly on the workspace backdrop.

Note that the object you've placed on your workspace is a reference to the actual object, not a copy. Any changes you make to the object will be reflected in the actual object within File Manager or Application Manager.

If you find yourself frequently using a certain application, you can add the application to a Front Panel subpanel. Simply drag the application icon from the Application Manager to the Install Icon control in the Text Editor subpanel.

I frequently use the Edit Resources function (found in the Application Manager System_Admin group as shown in Figure 1–9). So I installed the Edit Resources icon on the Front Panel Personal Applications subpanel (Figure 1–10).

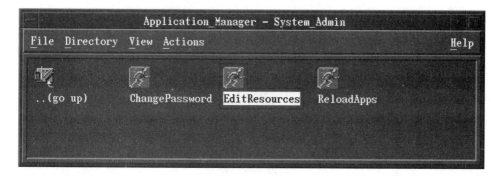

Figure 1–9   Application Manager System_Admin Group

Figure 1–10   Customized Personal Applications Sub-panel

Using the Trash Can

The Trash Can collects the files and folders that you delete. They are not actually removed from the file system until the trash is "emptied." You can only change your mind and *restore* a file you've put in the Trash Can if the Trash Can hasn't been emptied.

Click on the Trash Can icon Figure 1–11) on the Front Panel to open the Trash Can window. To put an object in the Trash Can follow these steps:

- Choose Put in Trash from the object's pop-up menu (displayed by pressing Shift+F10 or mouse button 3).

- *Or*, select the object's icon, then choose Put in Trash from the selected menu.

Figure 1–11   Trash Can Icon

- *Or*, drag and drop the object's icon onto the Trash Can control in the Front Panel.

- *Or*, drag an object's icon to the open Trash Can window.

To put back a file or folder from the Trash Can drag the object from the Trash Can window to File Manager.

Using Mailer

Mailer is a desktop application that enables you to send, receive, and manage your electronic mail (e-mail) messages. Click on the Mailer icon to bring up the Mailer main window as shown in Figure 1–12.

Once you've started Mailer, you can read, sort, find, delete, file, and send mail. Select a message to read it—the text will be displayed in the Message view area. If the message has any attachments, they'll be displayed in the Attachment list

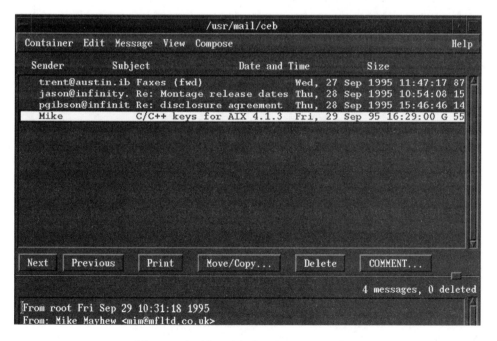

Figure 1–12 Mailer Main Window

area. Select the Reply button to reply to sender, to reply to sender and all
recipients, or to reply to sender or all recipients and include a copy of the
message. (Note that the message area only has the Reply to Sender button—the
other options are available on the Compose pull-down menu.)Whew! Lots of
options.

 Select the Compose function from the menu bar to forward a message, save a
message as text by choosing Save As Text from the Message menu, or find a mail
message in your overcrowded mailbox by choosing Find from the Message
menu. To address, compose, and send a mail message, choose New Message
from the Compose menu, enter the recipient's e-mail address, add a subject and
cc your friends and family (or anyone else who needs to see the mail). Hit Return
and you'll land in the text area. Write your message—edit it using the Compose
Edit menu. You can cut, copy, delete, and most importantly, check your spelling.
If it's an e-mail to your boss, use the Compose Format menu to align paragraphs,
grab templates or add a blind carbon copy to your message (cool function—Add
Bcc: enables you to send a copy of a message to someone without those on the
To: or Cc: line seeing the additional person's address).

The CDE mailer uses mailboxes to organize mail. You create mailboxes by choosing New from the Mailbox menu, entering the mailbox name and location, and
clicking New. The Mailer functionality enables you to file messages in the appropriate mailbox, to drag and drop messages to other mailboxes, and to remove
mailboxes.

Using the Text Editor

The Text Editor is useful for creating and editing short documents and files. To
start the text editor, click on the Text Editor icon. You create and edit a document
in the Text Editor window. You can create a new document or open an existing
document. To open an existing document, select Open from the File menu, select
the name of the document you want to open, and click OK.

To create and enter text, click in the text window and type following the cursor
(I). Use Wrap to Fit to control whether lines are automatically wrapped to fit the
width of the window. Move the cursor in a document by using your up and
down arrows, your left and right arrows, Home to go to the beginning of the current line, End to go to the end of the current line, Control+End to go to the end of
the document, or Control + Home to go to the beginning of the document. To
check your spelling, choose Check Spelling from the Edit menu. The Spell dialog
box lists misspelled or unrecognized words.

You can insert a text file into your document by positioning the cursor where you want to insert the text file, choosing Include from the File menu, selecting the document you want to insert, and clicking OK.

Using Calendar

Use the CDE calendar to schedule appointments and To Do items, set reminders, make and print appointment and To Do lists, browse other calendars, and schedule group appointments. Click on the Calendar icon to bring up the Calendar main window shown in Figure 1–13. You can view the calendar by day, week, month, or year.

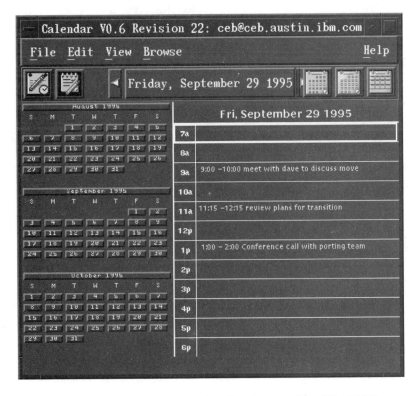

Figure 1–13 My Calendar for September 29, 1995

The Calendar Tool Bar icons include the following:

- The Appointment Editor (enables you to add, delete, or change meetings or appointments)
- The To Do Editor (lets you can create, modify, update, or set reminders)
- The Previous view arrow (displays the previous day, week, month, or year)
- The Today button (brings up the current day, week, month, or year according to your current format)
- The Next View Arrow (displays your schedule for the next day, week, and/or year)

You can view your calendar using Day View (displays your current calendar format with one day's appointments in the window plus a three month mini-calendar); using Week View (shows your week's appointments plus a grid of scheduled times); using Month View (shows your month's appointments); or using Year View (shows a calendar of the year, but NOT all of your appointments).

Using dtterm

The CDE default terminal emulator is dtterm. Click on the Terminal icon from either the Front Panel, Application Manager, File Manager, or Window menu to bring up a dtterm. Use the terminal emulator to enter operating system commands, AIX commands, and to copy and paste text. I've put my Terminal icon on the Front Panel so I can access it quickly (shown in Figure 1–14).

Figure 1–14   dtterm Icon on my Front Panel

Although the desktop provides drag and drop and other user-friendly functionality enabling you to avoid using the command line, those of us who are accustomed to the command line need it around for security reasons (it makes us feel smart when we can remember actual AIX commands).

Getting Help

On-line help is available for each of the standard applications in CDE. Whether you are using File Manager, Calendar, or Mailer, for example, you request and display help topics in the same way. You can also browse help information on your system using the desktop Help Manager (shown in Figure 1–15).

Ways you can request Help include the following:

- Press F1—also known as the "help key"—to get context-sensitive help.
- Choose a topic from an application's Help menu.
- Open Help Manager from the Front Panel to browse help on your system.
- Open the Help subpanel to choose help about the desktop or to choose On Item Help.

Press F1—The Help Key

When you have a question, the quickest and easiest way to get help is to press F1. When you press F1, the application you are using displays a help topic most closely related to the component—a window or button for example—that is high-

Figure 1–15   Help Manager Subpanel

lighted. This type of help is called *context-sensitive* because the application determines which help topic is most appropriate.

Using an Application's Help Menu

Most applications have a Help menu that contains commands for requesting different types of help such as an introduction, application tasks, or reference information.

A typical CDE Help menu includes

- Overview (displays the home topic for the application—the home topic is the first topic of the application's help topic hierarchy)

- Tasks (displays task instructions for most operations performed with the application)

- Reference (displays reference summaries for various components, such as windows and dialog boxes, menus, and application resources)

- On Item (enables you to click an item in any window of an application and view a description of the item)

- Using Help (provides help on using the help windows)

- About *Application* (displays the version and copyright information for the application)

Using Help Manager

Help Manager is a special help volume that lists all the on-line help registered on your system. Clicking the Help Manager control in the Front Panel opens the Help Manager help volume (Figure 1–16).

Click any of the underlined titles to view the corresponding help information. For convenience, you can also find help about the desktop and the Front Panel in the Help subpanel. It also provides On Item help for the Front Panel and its subpanels.

Using Help Windows

The Help System is built into each of the CDE applications (and possibly other applications installed on your system). When you ask for help while using an application, the application displays a help window.

General help windows have a topic tree and a topic display area. The *topic tree* is a list of help topics that you can browse to find help on a subject. When you choose a topic, it is displayed in the lower portion of the help window called the topic display area.

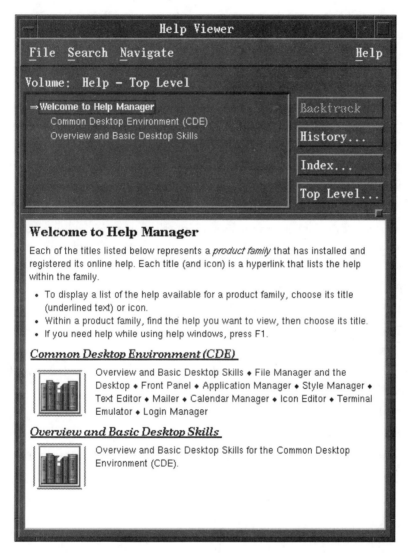

Figure 1–16   Help Manager

Quick help windows are streamlined help windows. A quick help window has just a topic display area and one or more buttons.

Selecting Help Topics

There are two ways to select a help topic. You can choose a topic from the topic tree. Or, within a help topic, you can select a hyperlink.

The topic tree is an outline of a help volume's major topics. Subtopics are indented under main topics. The current topic, whose contents are displayed in the topic display area, is marked with an arrow. You can scroll the topic display area to see all your choices or resize the entire help window.

You can also change the size of the topic panel. To do so, drag the sash control shown in Figure. Then release the mouse button to set the new size.

To select a topic follow these steps:

1.   Move the pointer into the topic tree.

2.   Click mouse button 1 on the topic you want to display.

For example, find out more about the File Manager by clicking on Common Desktop Environment and then selecting File Manager Help.

Browsing Help on Your System

You can browse or search all application help volumes registered on your system without having to start each individual application—just start Help Manager from the Front Panel.

To open Help Manager follow these steps:

1.   Click the Help Manager control in the Front Panel.

     A help window displays a list of help families with on-line help. This is the top level of Help Manager.

2.   Scroll the window to find the product group you are interested in and click its title (underlined).

     This lists the help volumes available for that product.

3.   To open a particular help volume, click its title (underlined text).

4.   To get back to the top of the Help topics, click the Top Level button.

To browse File Manager's on-line help follow these steps:

1.   Click the Help Manager control.

2.   Choose Common Desktop Environment.

3.   Scroll the list of help volumes until you see File Manager Help.

4.   Click File Manager Help.

File Manager's help is displayed. This is the same help information you would see if you opened File Manager and chose Overview from the Help menu.

Displaying a Man Page

1.   Click the Application Manager control in the Front Panel.

2.   Double-click the Desktop_Apps icon.

3. Click the Man Page Viewer icon. A dialog box is displayed, prompting you to enter a man page name.

4. Type the name of the command whose man page you want to see and press Return. The man page is displayed in a quick help window.

5. Click Close to dismiss the man page.

CHAPTER
2

- Commands—Are These Real Words?

- User Configuration—What Environment Am I In?

- Shells

- Fun Commands

- AIX Commands

Using AIX

Commands—Are These Real Words?

The basic AIX commands (and all UNIX system commands) are, for the most part, very short, cryptic, two letter command names. Imagine back years ago, when computers had only very slow teletype keyboards and paper "displays." (Some of us aren't imagining, we're remembering!) Imagine also, people who didn't like typing long commands because there was such a long delay between commands and the computer response. If there were any mistakes, the user had to retype the whole thing (especially aggravating for folks that type with only two fingers!).

Also, some UNIX commands came from university students and researchers who weren't bound by usability standards (no rules, except peer pressure). They could write a very useful, clever command and name it anything—their own initials, for example (awk by Aho, Weinberger, and Kernighan), or an acronym ("yacc," Yet Another Compiler-Compiler). *Get into the spirit of Unix and AIX! These systems have a lot of personality!*

User Configuration—What Environment Am I In?

There are some setup files that create an environment when you log in. These files are executed automatically to give you a customized system. You can use what came in the box, or change it to your special way of working.

The files /etc/profile and /etc/environment are executed for all users of the system and the file ".profile" in your home directory (a hidden file) is executed when you log into the system (except for C shell users).

Usually these files set environment variables such as "PATH" which lists all the directories you want AIX to look into for the command you type in. It can also set your prompt, default editor, and mail message when new mail is received. You can add AIX commands in your .profile that you want executed every time you log in (see `cron` for more information about executing commands automatically at other times of the day or night). My favorite command to put in my .profile file is /usr/games/fortune (this command is in fileset bos.games).

The .dtprofile is used by the common desktop for initial configuration information. The .mh_profile is used by the mail handler, MH, for user customization. The .mwmrc file is used by the motif window manager.

By convention the .kshrc file is executed by the Korn shell when you log in (the line "export ENV=$HOME/.kshrc" must be in your .profile file). Alias definitions are usually stored in the .kshrc file. The .login and .cshrc files in your home directory are executed by the C shell.

A file named /etc/motd (Message Of The Day) is displayed when users log into the system. It doesn't really set anything up but it shows up during your login. You can use this message for daily reminders. If multiple people share the system, it can be used to announce system changes, or more importantly, birthdays!

Shells

UNIX systems offer a shell around the system that allows you to execute commands and write programs with those commands. No compiler is needed. The shell interprets the logic.

Over the years, several shell versions have evolved and AIX provides the ones our customers want. The shells available in AIX systems are the Bourne shell, the C shell, the Korn shell, variations on these shells, the Restricted shell, and the Trusted shell.

The first shell, the Bourne shell (/usr/bin/bsh), was created by Steven Bourne at Bell Labs. The Bourne shell is a popular shell to use when writing "shell scripts", or text files that use shell programming constructs to carry out some task.

The C shell (/usr/bin/csh) was created by Bill Joy at the University of California at Berkeley. It uses a format similar to the C programming language. It lets you recall and employ previously used commands, define and use aliases, and do job control. The phrase "job control" here is not related to empowerment, but rather the ability to suspend currently running programs, resume them, and/or move them to/from the background/foreground.

The Korn shell (/usr/bin/ksh and /usr/bin/sh) was developed by David Korn at AT&T Bell Labs. Although it is based on the Bourne shell, it also draws upon functionality found in the C shell, and thus supports recalled commands, aliases, and job control.

The Restricted shell (/usr/bin/Rsh) is based on the Bourne shell and prevents users from changing directories, changing the PATH and SHELL environment variables, executing programs not specified in the current PATH, modifying or viewing any files not in the current directory, and redirecting output. This may sound pretty restrictive, but to be truly restricted, the system administrator should ensure that the user does not have access to any program such as "vi" in the PATH that could be used to overcome these limitations.

The Trusted shell (/usr/bin/tsh) is based on the Korn shell and gives the user a slightly restricted environment intended to protect from trojan horses (a user modified command that masquerades as a real command), computer viruses, and other undesirables. The Trusted shell does not read in user profile files such as .profile, but rather only reads the /etc/tsh_profile file. It will not support user function and alias definitions or command history, and uses several additional built in commands (logout, shell, and su) to ensure that the intended command is executed. This book does not go into detail about computer security, that's a whole book in itself!

The Bourne shell was the default for AIX Version 3 and the Korn shell is the Version 4 default. That is, on AIX Version 3, /usr/bin/sh and /usr/bin/bsh are the same, and on AIX Version 4, /usr/bin/sh and /usr/bin/ksh are the same. The Korn shell has always been recommended as the default login shell on AIX. It was made the default system shell in AIX Version 4 since the AIX Version is standards compliant (XPG4 and POSIX).

There are several important shell concepts that all users should be familiar with. These include environment variables, aliases, I/O redirection, command history, file globbing, and regular expressions. Each of the shells support programming constructs which allows users to quickly write powerful "shell scripts" which enable automation of nearly anything you can do on the command line. One of the great things about shell programming is that you can edit the shell program and run it without the compiling step; that makes it much faster. However, we will not cover shell programming here. If you are interested in that, or just want to know more about shells you may wish to check out one of the following books:

1. Morris Bolsky and David Korn, *The New Korn Shell Command and Programming Language,* New Jersey: Prentice-Hall, 1995.

2. Daniel Gilly, *Unix in a Nutshell,* Sebastopol, CA: O'Reilly & Associates, 1992.

3. Bill Rosenblatt, *Learning the Korn Shell,* Sebastopol, CA: O'Reilly & Associates, 1994.

4. Stephan Kochan and Patrick Wood, *Unix Shell Programming,* New Jersey: Hayden Books, 1985.

5.   Gary Anderson, *The Unix C Shell Field Guide,* New Jersey: Prentice-Hall, 1986.

6.   Martin Arick, *Unix C Shell Desk Reference,* QED Technical Publishing Group, 1992.

Environment Variables

The environment is the system "sky" all around you when you're using a UNIX system. There are all kinds of things floating around out there (some you see, some you don't) that affect the way the system acts. There are predefined environment variables that contain information you or applications may want to use. You can create variables for your own purposes.

Although each shell supports environment variables, they each tend to have a different method to change them. To set environment variable FOO to AIX, on Bourne shell or Korn shell, type "FOO=AIX; export FOO". When using the C shell, type "setenv FOO AIX". You can change environment variables at the command line, and the change will be effective until you log off. If you want to permanently change your environment then you will have to edit the appropriate configuration file (.profile for the Korn shell and Bourne shell, and .login for the C shell). To view a single environment variable such as FOO, type "echo $FOO". If you want to see all of your environment variables, then type "env" and you will see something like this:

```
MANPATH=/afs/austin/common/usr/man

LANG=En_US

LOGIN=carolynj

NLSPATH=/usr/lib/nls/msg/%L/%N:/usr/lib/nls/msg/%L/%N.cat

VISUAL=vi

PATH=/usr/bin:/etc:/usr/sbin:/usr/ucb:/usr/bin/X11:/sbin:.

HISTFILE=.sh_history

LOGNAME=carolynj

MAIL=/usr/spool/mail/carolynj

LOCPATH=/usr/lib/nls/loc

USER=carolynj

SHELL=/bin/ksh

HOME=/afs/austin/u/carolynj

CMVC_FAMILY=aix

TERM=dtterm

MAILMSG=[YOU HAVE NEW MAIL]
```

```
PWD=/afs/austin/u/carolynj
TZ=CST6CDT
```

Generally environment variables serve to communicate configuration information to either the shell or other system programs. Other environment variables convey information from the shell to the user or other programs. Some of the common environment variables that are supported in all shells include:

- **HOME**   This environment variable refers to your home directory. This is the most frequently used variable.

- **LANG**   This environment variable refers to the current locale. If you set this environment variable to 'C' you will get the best performance. By setting it to other locales, you can make your system support a variety of national languages.

- **MANPATH**   This environment variable specifies a list of paths to search for when looking for man (manual publications) pages with the man command.

- **NLSPATH**   This environment variable specifies where files of translated messages called "message catalogs" can be found.

- **PATH**   This environment variable specifies which directories the shell should check and in what order when looking for a command that you type in.

- **LOCPATH**   This environment variable specifies which directories the system should check when looking for the locale specified by the LANG environment variable.

- **USER**   The shell sets this to your user ID.

- **SHELL**   This environment variable specifies which shell you want to use when executing a shell from another program.

- **TERM**   This variable specifies your terminal type (aixterm, dtterm, xterm, and vt100, are popular values depending on what you use).

- **TZ**   This variable specifies your time zone, along with some interesting information such as whether or not your computer should follow daylight savings time, and so on.

Aliases

Many command line users like to set up aliases for long or complex commands to save typing (or they may have a bad memory). This is especially helpful while a person is learning or if they are used to different commands that map into AIX commands. Frequently typed commands are good candidates.

If you type the "alias" command it will show you all your current aliases:

```
ls='/usr/bin/ls -F'
stop='kill -STOP'
suspend='kill -STOP $$'
myfiles='ls /u/home/trent'
```

To create an alias "ls" that replaces the ls command with a customized option, type "alias ls='ls -F' on the Korn shell. To do the same on the C shell type "alias ls 'ls -F'". (Notice that the C shell does not like the equal sign.) Bourne shell does not support aliases.

I/O Redirection and Piping

Once you get used to redirection and piping, it will be your favorite and frequent sequence of commands. There is no limit to the number of combinations of commands you can put together to get something done. It's easy and quick.

In its simplest form, I/O redirection can be used to prevent output from a command from going to the screen, and instead send it to a file. Likewise, many commands will take input from a file if it is specified with I/O redirection.

For example, you can redirect *output* from the ls command to a file like this:

```
$ ls
Mail a.out hello.c todo
$ ls > output
$ cat output
Mail
a.out
hello.c
output
todo
```

You can also redirect *input* to a command such as cat. (I know this is sort of trivial, since the cat command will take input from a file anyway!)

```
$ cat < hello.c
main()
{
printf("Hello world\n");
}
$
```

More interesting is the ability to "pipe" the output from one UNIX command to another UNIX command. For example, suppose you have a command that generates a lot of output, such as the "ls -al" command on a large directory. You can pipe its output to other commands that process it. For instance you could count the number of lines to get an idea of how many files are in the directory with the "wc -1" command like this:

```
$ ls -al /usr/bin | wc -l
     647
```

Now we know that there are 647 files in the directory /usr/bin.

Piping from one command to another, and maybe another after that, saves you disk space. You don't have to save the output from each command, just the final output. I can't emphasis enough how powerful redirection and piping are!

Command History

Wouldn't you like to reuse the command you typed just a bit ago, instead of re-typing the whole thing? Or would you like to see a list of the commands you just executed to see how you got into a mess? You'll learn how in this section.

Since command history is not supported on the Bourne shell, we will describe how it works on the Korn shell and the C shell. By default the Korn shell keeps track of the last 128 commands. You can see the last 15 of them by simply typing "history". You can then execute a specific command again by typing "r" followed by the number of that command, or you could type "r l" to rerun the last command that started with the letter "l". You can also just use "r" by itself to rerun the last command:

```
$ history
1          ls
2          vi hello.c
3          echo Hi Mom!
4          history
$ r 3
echo Hi Mom!
Hi Mom!
$ r l
ls
a          b          file
```

To use command history with the C shell, you will need to ensure that you are using AIX Version 4.1.4 or later, and that the following two commands are in your .cshrc file:

```
set savehist=100
set history=100
```

Then, similar to the Korn shell, you can list recent commands with the history command, and can rerun commands by using the exclamation point (!) character. To repeat the previous command use "!!":

```
$ history
1          ls
2          vi hello.c
3          echo Hi Mom!
4          history
$ ! 3
Hi Mom!
$ ! 1
a          b          file
$ !!
a          b          file
```

You can recall a recent command, edit it, and then execute the modified command. To do this, you'll have to learn the vi editor (see the chapter on editors) if you don't already know it. You really need to learn vi for many reasons, but I'll give that pep talk later. To set up the ability to edit the recalled commands type:

```
set -o vi
```

Press <Esc> k to recall the last command, then keep pressing the "k" key to get the commands before that until you get to the one you want. Then use the vi editor commands to change the command. Then press "Enter" and execute it.

File Globbing Goes Wild!

File "globbing" is the technical UNIX way to refer to the use of wild cards in file names to specify a group of files. This can also be called "Pattern Matching Notation for Files", but I think that "globbing" sounds more interesting. Most users are familiar with the use of "a*" to refer to all files in the current directory that start with the letter "a". Wherever you can type a file name in a UNIX command, you can generally use file globbing.

This section looks scary because of all the special characters, but don't be intimidated. Read through it and pick out a couple things to try and use. You'll be surprised how useful it will be!

File globbing consists of the use of a number of metacharacters that can be used as a form of shorthand to match other characters and files. There are only three main kinds of file globbing characters. The simplest type of file globbing is the question mark (?) which will match ANY single character. The question mark (?)

will match "a" or "q" or "z" or "w" or any other single character. Typing "ls ?" would list all single character files in the current directory.

The asterisk (*) will match any number of characters including NO characters. Some examples are listed here:

- *   matches all files.

- *a*   matches any file that has an "a" in it somewhere.

- a*   matches any file that starts with an "a".

- *a   matches any file that ends with an "a".

- a*a   matches any file that starts and ends with a different "a", including "abracadabra", and "aa", however it will not match "a", since each "a" in the pattern has to match to a unique "a" in the file name.

The most interesting (and complicated) type of file globbing is the bracket expression. Like the question mark, it only matches a single character. There are three main types of bracket expressions. A simple bracket expression like "[abc]" will match a single "a" or a single "b" or a single "c", but nothing else. Bracket expressions can also contain ranges; "[a–z]" will match any single lower case character in the En_US locale. This form of bracket expression should actually be avoided since the characters in the range from "a" to "z" will depend on the locale and code set being used. Rather, the preferred way to use a bracket expression to match something like "all lower case letters" is to use a "character class expression," such as "[[:lower:]]", which will match any single lowercase character no matter what locale is being used. The following character classes are available for use in bracket expressions in all locales:

- [[:alnum:]]   Match a single alpha-numeric character.
- [[:alpha:]]   Match a single alphabetic character.
- [[:blank:]]   Match a single blank character (space or tab).
- [[:cntrl:]]   Match a single control character.
- [[:digit:]]   Match a single numeric character.
- [[:graph:]]   Match a single graph character (all printable characters minus the space character).
- [[:lower:]]   Match a single lowercase character.
- [[:print:]]   Match a single printable character (including space).
- [[:punct:]]   Match a single punctuation character.
- [[:space:]]   Match a single white space character.

- `[[:upper:]]`   Match a single upper case character.
- `[[:xdigit:]]`   Match a single hexadecimal numeric character.

One nifty feature of bracket expressions is the ability to specify a "nonmatching list" in which the first character in the bracket expression is the exclamation point (!). When this happens the bracket expression will match any character that is NOT inside the brackets. For example "[!abc]" will NOT match "a", "b", or "c", but will match "d", "e", "f", and so on. If the exclamation point is not the first character in the expression then it loses its special meaning. For example "[a!b]" will match "a", "!", or "b". Bracket expressions can also match collating symbols and equivalence classes.

Of course all three of these types of expressions can be combined to form complex and useful patterns. You could use an expression such as "version1.[abc]*.c" to make a list of all files that start with "version1.a" or "version1.b" or "version 1.c" and end in ".c". Or if you want to see a file that is called either "bob" or "Bob" or "8ob", you could use the pattern "?ob". These few constructs allow for a wide variety of file matching possibilities.

Here are a couple of down to earth examples of how I use file globbing:

- `rm *.tmp`   (remove temporary files in directory)
- `cc *.c`   (compile all c programs in directory)
- `cat prog[123]?.c`   (cat certain c programs)
- `ls [adt]*`   (look at all files or directories starting in "a", "d", or "t"

What do you do if you want to actually use one of these special characters in a file name? You can use metacharacters such as *?[] in file names by simply quoting the file name with either single or double quotes. For example, "cat `'*'`" would `cat` a file called '*' rather than `cat` all files in the directory.

Regular Expressions

Regular expressions are related to, but have significant differences from file globbing. There are two types of regular expressions: Basic Regular Expressions (BRE) and Extended Regular Expressions (ERE). For the most part simple BREs will work on programs expecting EREs for input. The type of regular expression a program expects depends on the program. For example, grep expects a BRE as the matching pattern, and egrep expects an ERE as the matching pattern. Although we will cover all major features of regular expressions, we will not detail every nuance. The best source for more information is either IEEE's POSIX or X/Open's XPG4 standards documents. Other useful sources include InfoExplorer, and the O'Reilly book *Sed & awk*.

- BRE Wildcard Metacharacter (.)

In a BRE the period matches any single character. It is similar to the question mark in file globbing.

- BRE Interval Metacharacter (*)

The asterisk matches zero or more occurrences of the previous element. So "a*" will match one or more "a"s. If you wish to make an expression that will match anything, then ".*" is the correct expression rather than "*".

- BRE Beginning of Line Anchor Metacharacter (^)

The circumflex will match the beginning of a line if it occurs as the first character in the pattern. However, it matches itself if it is not the first character in the pattern. (Circumflex has other meanings within bracket expressions.) The command "grep ^a" will match all lines that start with the letter "a", and "grep a^" will match all lines that contain the string "a^". Use of the circumflex to match the beginning of a line is referred to as anchoring, since it anchors the pattern to the beginning of the line.

- BRE End of Line Anchor Metacharacter ($)

The dollar sign will match the end of a line if it occurs as the last character in the pattern. However, it matches itself if it is not the last character in the pattern. The string "grep a$" will match all lines that end with the letter "a", and "grep $a" will match all lines that contain the string "$a". Use of the dollar sign to match the end of a line is referred to as anchoring, since it anchors the pattern to the end of the line.

The $ and ^ metacharacters can be combined to match an entire line. For instance the pattern "^apple$", will only match a line that contains only the string "apple", and "^$" will only match empty lines.

- BRE Subexpressions

Any valid BRE can be enclosed in escaped parenthesis to form a subexpression. For example "\(apple\)" will match the string "apple", as will the pattern "\(app\)\(le\)", as will the pattern "\(a\(ppl\)e\)".

- BRE Backreferences

It is possible to repeat a subexpression with the metacharacter string "\#", where # is a digit between 1 and 9. The string "\1" refers to the first started subexpression, "\2" refers to the second started subexpression, and so on. The pattern "\(apple\)\1" will match the string "appleapple".

- BRE Duplication

Any character, metacharacter, or subexpression can be duplicated a specified number of times. The construct "\{m\}" will match exactly m occurrences of the preceding character, metacharacter, or subexpression, "\{m,\}" will match m or more occurrences, and "\{m,n\}" will match between m and n occurrences inclusive. Examples, "a\{3\}" will match "aaa", "a\{3,\}" will match "aaa", and "aaaaa", but not "aa", "a\{2,3\}" will only match either "aa" or "aaa". Additionally, ".\{3\}" will match any three characters, and "\(apple\)\{2\}" will match "appleapple".

- BRE Bracket Expressions

Similar to file globbing, BREs support bracket expressions that match a single character. Bracket expressions can contain a list of characters to match (for example, "[abc]" still matches either "a" or "b" or "c"), a range expression (for example, "[a–c]" will match "a" or "b" or "c" in the En_US locale), and character class expressions such as "[[:upper:]]" match any single uppercase character. Like file globbing, bracket expressions can also match collating symbols and equivalence classes. Unlike file globbing "nonmatching lists" are specified by using a circumflex as the first character in a bracket expression, rather than the exclamation point. For example "[^abc]" will NOT match "a", "b", or "c", but it will match "d", "e", "f", and so on. If the circumflex is not the first character in the expression, then it loses its special meaning. For example "[a^b]" will match "a", "^", or "b".

- BRE Bracket Expressions

As with file globbing, these expressions and characters can be combined to arbitrary complexity. For example "[abc]\{2,3\}\([[:upper:]]\)\1..foo$" will match a string that has two or three characters from the set "abc", followed by any uppercase character repeated twice, followed by any two characters, followed by the string "foo" that must be at the end of the line.

That pretty much wraps up a simple introduction of Basic Regular Expressions. Extended Regular Expressions provide for several more features than BREs, and in some cases provide for a cleaner pattern, since parenthesis and braces are not escaped as in BREs. I will describe the main differences between BREs and EREs here.

- ERE Subexpressions vs. BRE Subexpressions

With EREs you do not need to precede parenthesis with backslashes. So the BRE "\(abc\)" should be written as "(abc)" as an ERE.

- ERE Brace Range Intervals vs. BRE Brace Range Intervals

As with subexpressions, with EREs you do not need to precede braces with backslashes. So the BRE "a\{5\}" should be written as "a{5}" as an ERE.

- ERE Anchoring with ^ and $ vs. BRE Anchoring with ^ and $

The main difference in anchoring between ERE and BRE is how the meta-characters ^ and $ are treated if they re not at the beginning and end (respectively) of the pattern. With BREs they lost their special meaning and were treated as the characters themselves, however with EREs they are assumed to retain their special anchor meaning. So an ERE like this "a$b" will try to match an "a" at the end of a line, followed by a "b" on the next line. However, most programs that do regular expression matching look at data line by line, and thus this particular line spanning pattern would never match anything.

- New ERE Interval Metacharacter (+)

The new + metacharacter matches one or more occurrences of the previous element. For example the pattern "a+" will match one or more occurrences of the letter "a". The "+" character is equivalent to the ERE expression "{1,}" or the BRE expression "\{1,\}".

- New ERE Interval Metacharacter (?)

The new ? metacharacter matches zero or one occurrences of the previous element. For example, the pattern "a?" will match zero or one occurrences of the letter "a". The "?" character is equivalent to the ERE expression "{0,1}" or the BRE expression "\{0,1\}.

- New ERE Alternation Metacharacter (|).

The new | metacharacter allows the matching of either the element that precedes it or the element that follows it. For example "a | b | c" will match either "a" or "b" or "c". Of course, this particular example is equivalent to the simpler pattern "[abc]". Alternation can also be used on subexpressions or longer patterns, for example, "apple | orange" will match either "apple" or "orange".

- ERE Backreferences

EREs do not support backreferences such as "\(a\)\1" as used in BREs.

File and User Permissions—What's a Root?

The word "root" in AIX (and all UNIX systems), means two things: the root user is the superuser and the root directory is the top of the directory tree.

Root User.   Users have a name in the system. You define your user environment, home directory, and user login name. The system comes with one predefined user, the root. The root user has a password also. The root user can read and write into any directory. (See the file attributes section for more information.) The system is usually protected so that only the root user can change system operating characteristics. To change from your user ID to the root, use the "su" (super-user) command. To go back to your user ID from the root, press <Ctrl> d. If you can't remember which ID you are currently using, type "whoami".

Root Directory.   The top of the file system at "/" is known as the root directory. If you picture a tree upside down, it looks like the file system structure with the "/" as the tree root. Although some system files are at the root, user files should not be stored at the root directory. This tree is a family tree. The directory above your current directory is the "parent" directory. The directories below are child directories. This analogy is also used for process hierarchy. Commands (processes) that invoke another command are "parent" processes with child processes.

User Authorities

There are 3 entities concerning file permission authority:

owner

group

other

Each file has an owner, the creator of the file. Each user belongs to one or more groups that are defined in the system. The system comes with some predefined groups, such as "staff" and "system". The designation of "other" allows anyone the specified access to the files.

Each directory and file has permissions set individually for the file owner, specified group, and other:

read

write

execute

The read permission allows users to look at the contents of a file. Write permission allows modification and deletion of a file, and execution permission allows a program file to execute.

There are additional special bits for advanced users:

set user id

set group id

sticky bit

When a file has the "set user id" attribute, it executes as the owner of the file regardless of who actually typed the command. The "set group id" attribute is similar, but for the group instead of the user. The "sticky bit" attribute changes the way the link permission acts; only the owner of the file can delete it. (Traditionally, the sticky bit was used to request that a program stick around in memory after being accessed.)

To view the permissions on a file go to the Desktop File Manager, click a file, elect "selected," and "change permissions", then you will see something like Figure 2–1.

To view the permissions from the command line, type "ls -l" and you'll see something like this:

```
ls -l

total 33

-rw-r--r--    1 carolynj system    3212 Aug 28 21:15 chapt5

-rw-r--r--    1 carolynj system    1773 Aug 28 21:02 chapt6b

-rw-r--r--    1 carolynj system    5337 Aug 20 15:01 chapt8

-rw-r--r--    1 carolynj system    5337 Aug 28 21:02 chapt8b
```

The files all have read and write "rw" permission for the owner, carolynj. The middle set of three characters "r--" define the read permission of the group "system". The last set of three characters "r--" allow read permission for others.

To change the permissions on a file use the desktop file manager or the "chmod" command. The "umask" sets the default for newly created files. The "chown" command changes ownership of a file (only the root user can do this).

Figure 2–1   CDE File Manager—Permissions Screen

Process Control—Do I have Daemons Running?

Each command is at least one process while it is executing. Some processes run in the background where they are invisible to the user. Others run in the foreground where you can see them running. Some processes run forever; they are called "daemons". OK, UNIX can't spell demon right, but you can get the idea!

Here is a quick list of actions you can perform on processes:

ps	Process Status
kill	Terminate the process
&	Use "&" after a command to execute it in the background
<Ctrl> z	Pause a command (system is waiting on you)
bg	Put the command in the BackGround
fg	Put the command in the ForeGround

To get a list of the processes running in the system, use the "ps" process status command. If you run "ps" without any parameters, you'll get a list of the processes running for just you, in that terminal, for example:

```
> ps
   PID TTY    TIME CMD
 10868 pts/0 0:00 ksh
 11640 pts/0 0:00 ps
```

You can get a very long list of all the processes running in the foreground and background for all users by running "ps -a" (process status for all). The list is too long to show here and will depend on your system setup. The "ps -l" will show the long status:

```
> ps -l
   F S UID PID PPID C PRI NI ADDR SZ WCHAN TTY TIME CMD
200001 A 0 10868 8772 1 60 20 c9e 152      pts/0 0:00 ksh
200001 A 0 11644 10868 9 64 20 857 148      pts/0 0:00 ps
```

There's a lot of information in this read out that you won't usually need, but it's there if you do. I usually use "ps" or "ps -e | pg" to find the process ID, especially the processes that run in the background.

You can kill processes with the "kill" command. You'll need the process identifier (PID). You'll need this command if you have a runaway command you wish you hadn't started. If you execute "kill <pid>", the system will ask the process to die nicely. If it refuses, you'll have to use stronger measures! The "kill -9 <pid>" command kills the process without giving it a chance to clean up before its end. Use "kill -9" as a last resort.

Advanced users can explore the system resource controller (SRC) which provides commands and library calls to start, stop, and get status on processes. AIX uses the SRC to start many of the daemons at boot time. The actions taken by the system when it first starts up is partially defined by the file /etc/rc, other /etc/rc* files, and /etc/inittab.

I'd Rather Call it Sam—Links

You may have a file that belongs in more than one directory. But it is too much trouble (and it would take up more disk space) to copy it over every time you change the file.

Use a symbolic link and the system will give you one file with multiple names or directory paths. Link from the real file to the link, for example:

```
ln -s memo jan.memo

ln -s memo /u/guest/memo
```

Now there will be three names for one file which all appear and act like three different files in different places. But there is only one real file. How can you tell if the file is unique, or a link?

```
$ ls -l

lrwxrwxrwx 1 carolynj system 4 Aug 28 21:35 jan.memo->memo

-rw-r--r--   1 carolynj system 0 Aug 28 21:34 memo
```

The linked file shows up with an arrow pointing to the real file.

Paper Dolls—Cutting and Pasting

Cutting and pasting is a function that is very useful and easy. You can cut text to and from files or onto the command line itself.

Let's say you are looking at a memo your boss sent you and you would like to take part of it and put it into a different memo. There are several methods you could use. It's as easy as 1,2, 3:

1. Bring up your favorite editor for the new memo.

2. Cut: Use the mouse to highlight the parts of your boss's memo that you want (just hold down the left mouse button while moving it across the text).

3. Paste: Move your mouse pointer over to the new memo and click with the middle mouse button (or both mouse buttons, if you have only two).

Now you can quote your boss in your new memo, you can add your own text, save the file, print it, whatever.

If you're not a great typist, cutting commands and long file names will save a lot of aggravation. Here's an example:

```
$pwd
```

```
/afs/austin/projects/framebook/chapt5
```

Now cut the path name using the left mouse button. Type part of the command you want to execute, paste, type the rest:

```
ln -s <paste-it> <type-the-rest>
```

Where Did My Files Go?

Some users get lost and confused by the hierarchical file structure. There are a lot of system files and directories that come with the system, all nested within each other.

Here is a snapshot of many of the AIX directories that come in the system:

`/bin, /usr/bin`	Binary commands
`/lpp, /usr/lpp`	Licensed program product applications
`/etc`	System configuration files
`/home, /u`	User directories (linked directories)
`/dev, /cdrom`	Device system information
`/lib, /usr/lib`	Libraries for program linkage
`/tmp`	Temporary files stored here

If you name your directories in a simple organized manner it helps. Usually boring file names are better than too much creativity. Use a descriptive name for the contents of the file. I wouldn't use "Hawaii" for the file name of my financial report. Mentally keep track of where you are, or change your command prompt to show what directory you are currently in.

If you use the Korn shell you can add this to your `.profile` file:

```
export PS1=' $PWD: '
```

The desktop file manager always shows the directory path of where you are (see the chapter on CDE, the Common Desktop Environment).

If you type in "cd" on the command line with nothing else, you will go to your "HOME" directory. This is the directory where your files are stored by default. The path is usually "/home" followed by your login name. There is a "HOME" environment variable stored in your profile (the .profile file in your home directory) which tells the system the name of your home.

If you lose track of where you put a file, you can search for it in a couple of ways:

- Using the desktop file manager, select "File" then "Find"

- Using a command, type `find <starting point> -name <filename> -print`
  For example: `find /home/sue -name memo -print`
- This command lists all files and directories under the home directory recursively. `ls -R $HOME | more`

Fun Commands

The following commands are all shipped with AIX in the bos.games fileset:

`/usr/games/arithmetic`	Quizzes you on simple arithmetic
`/usr/games/back`	The game of Backgammon
`/usr/games/bj`	Blackjack
`/usr/games/craps`	The game of craps
`/usr/games/fish`	The game of go fish
`/usr/games/fortune`	Displays amusing statements
`/usr/games/hangman`	The game of hangman
`/usr/games/moo`	Guess four digit number
`/usr/games/number`	Displays numbers you type in English
`/usr/games/quiz`	Quizzes you on a variety of subjects
`/usr/games/ttt`	Tic-Tac-Toe
`/usr/games/wump`	Find the Wumpus!!!!

Well, obviously, you didn't purchase your computer to run these programs. But they can lighten up your day for awhile.

AIX Commands

Now we get into the commands that you can use to get work done from the command line. Commands are very flexible and powerful! The list that follows is printed in the book twice so that you can cut out one of the pages and put it next to your computer or in a handy place, as a cheatsheet.

You can get your work done using the desktop functions, but there is a lot more you can do from the command line. If you want to be more of a guru, learn some commands. We grouped similar commands together and capitalized letters in the description that make up the command to help you remember. We also added some of our favorite command combinations that may come in handy!

Commands have two parts: the action and the parameters. UNIX systems care about upper and lowercase. If you type "CP" it's not the same as "cp", theoretically there could be two separate commands. Parameters are usually prefaced by a dash "-" and are one character long. In the example that follows, the parameters are shown in brackets "[ ]". Some commands require file names or other user specified information, such as the "cp" command to copy from the infile to the outfile.

```
cp [-p -r -]... infile [indir] outfile [outdir]
```

Directory Commands

- `mkdir`   MaKe a new DIRectory
- `cd`   Change to new Directory
- `pwd`   Print Working Directory (where am I?)
- `rmdir`   ReMove DIRectory
- `mvdir`   MoVe DIRectory under different directory or rename
- `ls, li`   LiSt, LIst the files in a directory
- `.`   Abbreviation for the current directory
- `..`   Abbreviation for the parent directory
- `df`   Disk Free space status
- `whereis`   Show directories WHERE command IS stored

File Commands

- `cp`   CoPy a file
- `mv`   MoVe a file to a different directory or rename it
- `rm`   ReMove a file
- `ln`   LiNk a filename to another file
- `cat`   Show file contents, conCATenate a file
- `pg`   Show contents of a file, one PaGe at a time
- `more`   Show MORE file contents
- `enq`   ENQueue a file to print
- `chmod`   CHange read/write/execute MODe of file
- `cmp`   CoMPare binary files
- `diff`   Show DIFFerence in text files
- `grep`   Search for text in a file
- `join`   JOIN two files based on first column
- `sort`   SORT contents of a file

Backup Commands

- `compress`   COMPRESS files to take up less backup space
- `uncompress`   UNCOMPRESS the compressed file
- `cpio`   CoPy Input / Output
- `tar`   Tape ARchiver
- `pax`   Portable Archive interchange(X)
- `dd`   Device to Device copy
- `backup`   BACKUP files (use with restore command)
- `restore`   RESTORE files from backup format
- `mksysb`   MAKe SYStem Backup for rootvg volume group

Miscellaneous Commands

- `crontab`   Set commands to run at a specified time/date
                            (CRONological TABle)
- `clear`   CLEAR the screen
- `lpstat`   Check Line Printer STATus
- `date`   Current DATE and time
- `hostname`   Local system HOST NAME
- `whoami`   Current login name
- `su`   Change to another user login (Default Super User)
- `wall message`   Broadcast a message to all logged on users (Warn ALL)
- `banner "text"`   Screen BANNER for text

Help Commands

- `<cmd> -?`   List parameters for command
- `<cmd> -help`   Short help for command
- `man <cmd>`   Online MANual pages for command
- `info`   INFOrmation from the online help
- `learn`   Lessons for a subject or command

Handy Commands

- `ls -1Rs`   Long, recursive sorted file list
                            (sorted by modification date)

- `echo "text" > file`   Create a file with one line in it
- `echo "End" >> file`   Puts a final line on the file
- `ls | more`   List files and pause at each page
- `sed "s/|/ /g" file`   Change all pipe symbols to blanks
- `aixterm -fn Rom22 &`   Use very big font for command line
- `sort file | uniq | more` Show unique sorted list
- `mail user@location < file` Send a file as mail
- `enscript -q -p - -r -f` Print with small font, landscape
  `Courier8`   (to postscript printer)
- `fgrep <string> file | cut` Filter out lines without the string, cut
  `-c1-80 > newfile`   all but columns 1-80, put in "newfile"
- `tee <file> <cmd>`   Write command output to two places,
                            standard out (typically the screen)
                            and a file

- `wc -l file`   Count number of lines in file
- `du | sort -rn | pg`   Disk usage sorted for largest first
- `sdiff file1|file2`   Compare two files side by side
- `for i in *.txt; do lpn` Print all files in current directory that
  `$i; done`   end in ".txt".
- `find . -print |xargs grep` Find all files that contain pattern in the
  `pattern`   current directory hierarchy.

Directory Commands

- `mkdir`   MaKe a new DIRectory
- `cd`   Change to new Directory
- `pwd`   Print Working Directory (where am I?)
- `rmdir`   Remove Directory
- `mvdir`   MoVe DIRectory under different directory or rename
- `ls, li`   LIst, LiSt the files in a directory
- `.`   Abbreviation for the current directory
- `..`   Abbreviation for the parent directory
- `df`   Disk Free space status
- `whereis`   Show directories WHERE command IS stored

File Commands

- `cp`   CoPy a file
- `mv`   MoVe a file to a different directory or rename it
- `rm`   ReMove a file
- `ln`   LiNk a filename to another file
- `cat`   Show file contents, conCATenate a file
- `pg`   Show contents of a file, one PaGe at a time
- `more`   Show MORE file contents
- `enq`   ENQueue a file to print
- `chmod`   CHange read/write/execute MODe of file
- `cmp`   CoMPare binary files
- `diff`   Show DIFFerence in text files
- `grep`   Search for text in a file
- `join`   JOIN two files based on first column
- `sort`   SORT contents of a file

Backup Commands

- `compress`   COMPRESS files to take up less backup space
- `uncompress`   UNCOMPRESS the compressed file
- `cpio`   CoPy Input / Output
- `tar`   Tape ARchiver
- `pax`   Portable Archive interchange(X)
- `dd`   Device to Device copy
- `backup`   BACKUP files (use with restore command)
- `restore`   RESTORE files from backup format
- `mksysb`   MAKe SYStem Backup for rootvg volume group

Miscellaneous Commands

- `crontab` — Set commands to run at a specified time/date (CRONological TABle)
- `clear` — CLEAR the screen
- `lpstat` — Check Line Printer STATus
- `date` — Current DATE and time
- `hostname` — Local system HOST NAME
- `whoami` — Current login name
- `su` — Change to another user login (Default Super User)
- `wall message` — Broadcast a message to all logged on users (Warn ALL)
- `banner "text"` — Screen BANNER for text

Help Commands

- `<cmd> -?` — List parameters for command
- `<cmd> -help` — Short help for command
- `man <cmd>` — Online MANual pages for command
- `info` — INFOrmation from the online help
- `learn` — Lessons for a subject or command

Handy Commands

- `ls -lRs` — Long, recursive sorted file list (sorted by modification date)

  `echo "text" > file` — Create a file with one line in it
- `echo "End" >> file` — Puts a final line on the file
- `ls | more` — List files and pause at each page
- `sed "s/|/ /g" file` — Change all pipe symbols to blanks
- `aixterm -fn Rom22 &` — Use very big font for command line
- `sort file | uniq | more` — Show unique sorted list
- `mail user@location < file` — Send a file as mail
- `enscript -q -p - -r -f Courier8 <file>` — Print with small font, landscape (to a postscript printer)
- `fgrep <string> file | cut -c1-80 > newfile` — Filter out lines without the string, cut all but columns 1-80, put in "new file"
- `tee <file> <cmd>` — Write command output to two places, standard out (typically the screen) and a file

- `wc -l file` — Count number of lines in file
- `du | sort -rn | pg` — Disk usage sorted for largest first
- `sdiff file1|file2` — Compare two files side by side
- `for i in *.txt; do lpr $i; done` — Print all files in current directory that end in ".txt".
- `find . -print |xargs grep pattern` — Find all files that contain pattern in the current directory hierarchy.

AIX Command Details

You'll need details on some of the AIX commands. We've included some of the commonly used commands, but not all the commands, because there are so many. See the appendix for more details. There are whole reference books for all the commands and libraries that you can get if you're a real guru, guru wanna-be, or writing your own programs.

This list of reference books will get you started:

RISC System/6000 Technology

Elements of AIX Security

Printing for Fun and Profit Under AIX

AIX Performance Monitoring and Tuning Guide

AIXtra Magazine

AIXpert Magazine

Life with Unix, Ressler Libes

The Design of the Unix Operating System, Back, Prentice-Hall

Unix in a Nutshell, Billy, O'Reilly & Associates

Unix Power Tools, Peek, Loukides, O'Reilly

POSIX Programmer's Guide, Lewine

Practical C Programming, Oualline

Using C on the UNIX System, Curry

UNIX for FORTRAN Programmers, Loukides

Software Portability with imake, DuBois

AIX Operating System Technical Reference

CHAPTER
3

- OK, Give Me Some Hints

- Hey, DOS Windows and AIX Windows Are Easy!

- Crib Notes: DOS to AIX

- File Names

- Wildcards

- File Attributes

- Directories

- DOS Functions in AIX

- SoftWindows Runs Microsoft Windows and App's

- AIX Connections Brings Them All Together

I Know Windows/DOS, What's AIX?

OK, Give Me Some Hints

The windows user interfaces of AIX and DOS have many similarities. You'll be able to use AIX windows (CDE) very easily. The crib notes for DOS to AIX commands will help you get productive in quick order. You will also need to use the Appendix to see which parameters to use. This section includes info on other DOS functions available in AIX to use DOS diskettes, windows applications, and share remote files between DOS and AIX systems.

Hey, DOS Windows and AIX Windows Are Easy!

If you are used to Windows on DOS systems, you won't have any trouble with the AIX Common Desktop Environment (CDE)! The borders on each of the two windows are quite similar and they act a lot alike. The following is a list of similarities and differences:

- Both windows have an icon on the top left to act on the whole window. It includes these commands:

  Restore

  Move

  Size

  Minimize

  Maximize

  Close

- DOS Windows 3.11 (before Windows 95) has a "Switch-To" option, where CDE has an "Occupy Work Space" option, and Windows 95 has a task bar which can be hidden (auto hide).

- Both have a title on the window top which you can select with the mouse (hold down the left button) and move the whole window around.

- Both allow you to resize the window using the mouse (put the mouse cursor on the window border edge, press and hold down the left button, and resize away!).

- Both have an icon on the top right corner to Maximize the window (make the window fill the whole screen). They each have a different button indicator—DOS Windows 3 .11 has a down arrow where AIX CDE has a box. When the CDE icon is "pressed in" the window is maximized. Windows 95 has an icon representing a single sheet of paper for Maximize and it changes to several tiled sheets of paper when the window is not maximized.

- Next to the Maximize icon is the Minimize icon. This will hide the window and present only a small icon in its place. AIX and Windows 3.11 have you double click on the small icon to bring it back to its previous form and Windows 95 requires a single click in the taskbar.

- You can have lots of windows open at the same time on the screen. Both let you click on the window title to bring it to the front. All the applications in all those windows can run at the same time with AIX.

Crib Notes: DOS to AIX

A quick reference may be your best friend while you are learning AIX. The following table is a list of the basic commands that you will use all the time. We put the crib sheet in this book twice so that you can cut one out and put it next to your computer for easy access. Highlight it and write all your notes on it!

BASICS		
DOS	**AIX**	**Description**
COPY <from> <to>	cp <from> <to>	File copy
DIR	ls	Directory listing
MD and MKDIR	mkdir	Make a new directory
MOVE <from> <to>	mv <from> <to>	File move
DELETE and ERASE	rm, del	Delete/Remove
TYPE <file> | more	pg <file> or cat <file> | more	Show file contents
|	|	Pipe output to another command
>	>	Redirect output
<	<	Redirect input
PRINT <file>	enq <file> or lpr<file>	Print/Enqueue file
/ <flag>	- <flag>	Command flags
CD \ and CHDIR	cd /	Change directory (note the difference in the slash)
RENAME <from><to>	mv <from> <to>	Rename a file
CLS	clear	Clear screen
CONFIG.SYS, AUTOEXEC.BAT	/etc/rc, /etc/inittab, .profile (in user directories)	System and user configuration scripts

MORE COMMANDS

DOS	AIX	Description
MSBACKUP COPY and XCOPY RESTORE DISKCOPY REPLACE	backup tar cp cpio	File backups
FDISK	smit	Modify disk partitioning
ATTRIB	chmod	Change file read/write access
FC /B <file1> <file2>	cmp <file1> <file2>	Compare binary files
FC /L <file1> <file2>	diff <file1> <file2>	Compare text files
PKZIP/PKUNZIP	compress, uncompress zcat	Compress files
VER	oslevel	Show system version
DELTREE	rm -r	Erase entire directory and subdirectories
FIND	grep, fgrep	Find character string in files
FORMAT	format	Format a disk
DOSHELP HELP F1 function key <cmd> /?	man <cmd> <cmd> -? <cmd> -help	Help information

BASICS

DOS	AIX	Description
COPY \<from> \<to>	cp \<from> \<to>	File copy
DIR	ls	Directory listing
MD and MKDIR	mkdir	Make a new directory
MOVE \<from> \<to>	mv \<from> \<to>	File move
DELETE and ERASE	rm, del	Delete/Remove
TYPE \<file> | more	pg \<file> or cat \<file> | more	Show file contents
|	|	Pipe output to another command
>	>	Redirect output
<	<	Redirect input
PRINT \<file>	enq \<file> or lpr\<file>	Print/Enqueue file
/ \<flag>	- \<flag>	Command flags
CD \ and CHDIR	cd /	Change directory (note the difference in the slash)
RENAME \<from>\<to>	mv \<from> \<to>	Rename a file
CLS	clear	Clear screen
CONFIG.SYS, AUTOEXEC.BAT	/etc/rc, /etc/inittab, .profile (in user directories)	System and user configuration scripts

MORE COMMANDS

DOS	AIX	Description
MSBACKUP COPY and XCOPY RESTORE DISKCOPY REPLACE	backup tar cp cpio	File backups
FDISK	smit	Modify disk partitioning
ATTRIB	chmod	Change file read/write access
FC /B \<file1> \<file2>	cmp \<file1> \<file2>	Compare binary files
FC /L \<file1> \<file2>	diff \<file1> \<file2>	Compare text files
PKZIP/PKUNZIP	compress, uncompress zcat	Compress files
VER	oslevel	Show system version
DELTREE	rm -r	Erase entire directory and subdirectories
FIND	grep, fgrep	Find character string in files
FORMAT	format	Format a disk
DOSHELP HELP F1 function key \<cmd> /?	man \<cmd> \<cmd> -? \<cmd> -help	Help information

File Names

DOS file names are restricted to one to eight characters but AIX file names can have up to 256 characters! DOS file names ignore upper and lowercase; AIX uses upper, lower, and mixed case as different file names. DOS displays everything as uppercase on the command line; AIX displays mixed case as it is used.

DOS file names allow characters, numbers, and special characters except the following:

```
* ? = + | { } ; / < > , "
```

AIX file names allow ALL characters, numbers, and special characters except the slash. However certain characters such as the following should be quoted or escaped:

```
* ? | { } ; / < > , " ! ( ) # &
```

So, think of the possibilities with AIX ! You could have a file named "Great_Proposal_1.1_with_Illustrations". But don't get too crazy, you'll have to type this long file name a lot and your fingers will get tired! Also, your coworkers will gripe at you for long, mixed case, and special character file names. But if you use graphical point and click interfaces and don't usually type file names, use whatever file names are the most useful.

Wildcards

DOS uses wildcards for each part (name and extension) of a file name. For example "dir a*.*" will list

```
abc.bat
```

```
arrival.exe
```

You have to tell DOS about both parts of a file name. AIX looks at the file name as a series of characters. For example " ls a* " will list all files starting with "a". You have a lot of flexibility to list just what you are looking for. For example " ls aug*9*95 " will list

```
august_090795
```

```
august_090895
```

```
august_090995
```

```
aug.9.9.95
```

AIX will also list files at the current directory and subdirectories: " ls -R " will list all the files at the current directory and all the files below it. The DOS command DIR /S accomplishes the same result in DOS.

DOS allows you to copy all the files in the current directory by typing

```
COPY *.* <directory>
```

DOS copies subdirectories with the XCOPY command. In AIX, you can copy the current files, subdirectory structures, and subdirectory files by typing

```
cp -r <from-directory> <to-directory> (-r is for recursive)
```

In DOS, "DELETE *.*" doesn't erase all subdirectories, but the "DELTREE" will (including the hidden files). In AIX, type " rm -r " to delete all subdirectories and files.

Be careful! If you get confused about where you are in your directory structure, you could do a lot of damage!

In DOS, if you use the "DELETE *.*" command, DOS will ask, "Are you sure?" In AIX (typical for UNIX systems), it won't warn you! Power users would get irritated with a bunch of warnings! You can, however, use the "del" command and it will ask first before deleting.

File Attributes

Files have certain characteristics that you can change, such as being writable or not. You can change the default characteristics that come with the creation of a file. AIX will check the current permissions (attributes) on the file to see if you are allowed to change it.

DOS files have the following attributes:

- read only
- read write
- archived
- not archived
- hidden
- system

AIX files have these attributes for the file owner, group, and other categories:

- read
- write
- execute
- sticky

Additional attributes of an AIX file are the owner and group(s) that read/write/execute permissions apply to. To change these, use the "chown" and "chgrp" commands (see the section on users, groups, and root for more information).

To list hidden files you need to use additional parameters:

```
In DOS type: "DIR /A:H" (attributes hidden)
In AIX type: "ls -a" (a is for all).
```

Hidden DOS files are not copied, moved, or erased with wildcards (DELETE *.*) until you take off the hidden attribute. In AIX, a file is hidden when the first character is a period (.) . Even if you accidently name a file ".sam" it will be a hidden file! If you want to change it to be visible, just change the file name. AIX is similar to DOS in its treatment of hidden files with copy, move, or remove operations as they aren't copied, moved, or removed with wildcards. If you type the file name in AIX, all operations work as if the files were not hidden. In DOS, the hidden attribute must be removed before anything can be done with the file.

Other attributes of files are the date and time of its last modification. The operating systems take care of this information for you but you can change it yourself by entering the AIX command "touch <file>" and it will now have the current day and time.

The DOS copy will preserve the original date and time on the newly copied file. AIX will put the date and time that the copy operation was performed on the new file, unless you use the -p option to preserve the original date and time.

Directories

Both DOS and AIX have hierarchical directory systems. The thing you'll notice the most is that DOS and AIX (all UNIX systems) use different symbols for the directory separators. DOS uses " \ " and AIX uses " / ". DOS uses " / " for command parameters where AIX uses " - ". AIX puts commands in standard directories: /bin, /usr/bin, /etc . DOS allows the user to install the DOS commands in any directory.

DOS Functions in AIX

AIX allows you to put a diskette with DOS files into an AIX drive to read and write the files into and out of AIX. Use these commands to exchange files between DOS and AIX:

- dosdir
- dosread
- doswrite
- dosformat

The AIX "dosdir" command lists DOS files from AIX. The "dosread" command reads a DOS file in and makes a copy into an AIX file system format. The "doswrite" command copies an AIX file onto a DOS formatted disk in DOS file format. The "dosformat" command formats a floppy disk for use as a DOS diskette.

If you intend to take an AIX file to a DOS system with a command like "doswrite", you may need to replace the tabs with the appropriate number of spaces with the "untab" command.

DOS text files use a two character line termination sequence (^M^J) which is <linefeed, carriage-return>, or in C terminology "\015\012". AIX uses only "\012" to terminate a line. This means that text files may need to be cleaned up a little after transfer unless you use the -a option. These DOS compatibility functions must be selected during install, they are not on the system by default.

SoftWindows Runs Microsoft Windows and Spreadsheets!

There's a separate product you can install to run Windows 3.11 and Windows applications from your AIX system called "Soft Windows." This will come in handy if you have some favorites. It could also save you some money if you have invested in a bunch of applications!

Soft Windows is separately ordered and installed. Since the system will be running two operating systems at the same time, it might need more memory, be sure to check. Bring up an AIX window from the Common Desktop Environment (CDE) or use the AIX command line and type "swin" to run SoftWindows (see Figure 3–1). You can use your Windows and MS-DOS applications as well as customize it to come up the way you want. You can run your spreadsheets, word processors, databases, graphics packages or, ugh, do your taxes!

SoftWindows is compatible with most Windows and MS-DOS applications which makes it easy to use. These programs can be run as-is with SoftWindows. All Microsoft Windows functions including control panels, the program manager, help, the file manager, and the print manager are available.

You can cut and paste between windows and between them and AIX windows. DOS commands may be used. Object linking and embedding (OLE) and dynamic data exchange (DDE) are supported between Windows applications, which gives leading edge app's more power.

SoftWindows works with Novell NetWare, LAN Server, LAN Manager, Windows NT, and Banyan VINES. It has full TCP/IP networking support and support for LAN WorkPlace for MS-DOS too. Now you're connected! There is also

Figure 3–1   SoftWindows AIX Running MS-Windows 3.11

an on-line user's guide and administrator's guide from the help system within SoftWindows.

AIX Connections Brings Them All Together

Read the Connectivity chapter and the AIX Connections section to find out more about how to get your different PC's hooked together to share files and printers.

The beauty of AIX Connections is that you can connect a DOS system up to an AIX system and use the AIX system to store the DOS user files. Both systems can access the files, the DOS system uses DOS or Windows to see the files and the AIX system uses AIX and CDE to access the same files.

CHAPTER 4

Editors

In this chapter we will explain how to use vi, Emacs, CDE text editor, and INed; the most popular editors available on AIX. When you have finished reading this chapter, you will know the fundamental differences between each editor and you will have acquired survival skills in each. All of these programs are text editors, which means that they create and modify text files. That is all that they do. Unlike modern word processors and desktop publishing programs, text editors do not allow you to do things like change fonts, incorporate graphics, bold or italic characters, and so on. Text editors are, however, very useful tools for editing system files, programs, and simple data files. In fact, since they are all screen-based editors, they are considerably easier to use than their predecessors, line-based editors.

You might want to try each editor if you haven't settled into a favorite. Bring it up and see how it looks and acts. Each editor has its forte. The CDE editor is very easy to use; it has pulldown menus and help. The INed editor uses the PF keys and has excellent block operations. The vi editor is very fast—you can get in, change what you want, and save the file in seconds. The Emacs editor is very powerful and integrates a variety of functions.

VI

If you only want to learn one editor, and want to be able to edit on any UNIX platform out there, vi is for you. The vi editor (rhymes with "bye" or pronounced by spelling it out (V-I)), is the most widely available UNIX editor. (It is even available in public domain form on other platforms such as DOS.) The name vi comes from the first two characters in the word "visual". As the name implies, vi was written to be a visual screen editor, as opposed to a line-based editor.

You may have to talk yourself into learning vi because it is a little intimidating with the key combinations. It's really not that hard—you've learned a lot more complex things than this! You need to be able to use vi because it is available on all UNIX systems. When you become a vi user, you will be an official UNIX user and you will be respected by the techies. One other reason to learn vi is for the shell command line editing; you'll use vi key combinations to edit retrieved commands. If you are a command user, this is a must. Give it a whirl!

A concept that would be good to keep in mind is that for the most part the text you are editing with vi is in "volatile" memory until saved. This means that if you make a mistake and want to revert to the previous saved version of a document you are editing, you can do so by quitting without saving your changes. On the other hand, it also means that if the power goes out during an editing session you may lose your changes. However, see the FAQ section at the end of this chapter for a nifty way around this.

Installing and Invoking VI

Vi is installed on every AIX machine by default. You do not have to do anything special to get vi.

An important thing to keep in mind when using vi is that it has two main modes; a command mode in which you can enter commands and move the cursor around the screen and document, and an input mode in which you can type new text.

To start editing a new document, simply type

```
vi
```

You will see a blank screen (well, not quite blank, vi will show a bunch of lines that each contain a single tilde (~) to indicate the end of the document).

Adding Lines

When you first start vi, it is in the command mode. The easiest command is probably "i", which switches you into the input mode. Enter the following text, using the "i" command:

```
i        <do not press return>
```

Notice nothing appears to have changed on the screen. However, vi is now in the insert mode, and characters that you type will be added to the document at the cursor position. Try typing the following (remember to press the return key after each line):

```
The quick brown fox
jumps over the
lazy dog.
```

Now lets switch back to the command mode by simple pressing the escape key:

```
<esc>
```

Saving a File

Saving a file in vi is pretty simple. To save a file called "testfile", type the following (from the command mode):

```
:w testfile
```

If testfile already exists and needs to be replaced, then you may need to type this:

```
:w! testfile
```

When you do this, you should see a status line on the bottom of the screen that tells you the name of the file you wrote, along with the number of lines and characters in this file.

Loading a File

To load a file from vi, type the following in the command mode:

```
:e testfile
```

Quitting vi

There are a couple of ways to exit vi. All of them require you to be in the command mode, so if you're not sure which mode you are in, pressing escape a couple of times should ensure that you are in the command mode. The recommended method to exit vi is to simply type "ZZ". The advantage of this command is that it will automatically save the file for you. If you need to exit without saving your changes then enter

```
:q!
```

Invoking vi and Editing an Old File

Let's try editing the message of the day file that is displayed each time a user logs on. If you are root you can actually change this file, otherwise you will only be able to get practice using vi. Type the following:

```
vi /etc/motd
```

You should now see the message of the day file displayed on your screen, with a status line at the bottom that tells you the name of the file, as well as the number of lines and characters that are in this file. This status line will change when you type other commands.

Moving the Cursor

The ability to move the cursor is fairly critical, so spend some time experimenting with the following basic cursor movement commands:

j   Moves the cursor one line down

k   Moves the cursor one line up

h   Moves the cursor one character left

l   Moves the cursor one character right

^F   (Control-F) Jump forward one page

^B   (Control-B) Jump backward one page

Hint: These commands must be done from the command mode, so press the escape key if you have to. Notice that the j, k, h, and l keys are right next to each other on the keyboard and are in a natural position. That will make it easier to remember which keys do what.

Editing Text

Here are the basic editing commands that you will need to know. To edit, ensure that you are in the command mode. Use the cursor movement commands above, and place the cursor where you want to change text. Then use one of the following basic editing commands:

i   Insert text starting at the cursor. This puts vi into the input mode.

          Press escape when done.

x   Delete the character the cursor is on.

dd   Delete the line the cursor is on.

Additional vi Tricks

You can precede commands with a number to cause that command to occur that number of times. For example 57j will move down exactly 57 lines. Likewise, you can delete 10 characters at the cursor by typing "10x."

If you would like to know for sure when you are in the input mode you can type ":set showmode" from the command mode. This will display the text "INPUT

MODE" on the status line whenever you are in the input mode. If you type ":set noshowmode" vi will not show the mode you are in.

If you would like to see line numbers displayed for the document you are editing, type ":set number" from the command mode. To hide line numbers type ":set nonumber".

If you do programming and want to verify that parenthesis, braces, or brackets balance, or if you would like to see which character they match, then place the cursor on one of these characters and press the percent key (%). Then vi will jump to the matching symbol if one exists.

To jump to the first line in the file, type ":1" from the command mode. To jump to the last line in the file, type ":$" from the command mode. To jump to the fifty-seventh line in the file, type ":57" from the command mode.

Emacs

Although Emacs can be called a text editor, it is an incredibly powerful editing environment, from which you can do literally anything you can think of. In addition to editing normal text files, it has special commands and macros to facilitate editing a variety of types of text files ranging from different programming languages, to nroff files, to outlines, to ASCII art, and so on. It also has built-in modes to compile programs, read and send mail, manipulate files, read net news, and execute shells and other programs. If this isn't enough, Emacs is expandable, since you can write and incorporate lisp functions into your Emacs environment.

Although there are several flavors of Emacs, we will describe GNU Emacs, which we will only briefly introduce since there are several fine books dedicated to the subject.

Installing Emacs

Use anonymous FTP to get the file /u2/emacs/GETTING.GNU.SOFTWARE from prep.ai.mit.edu. (See the chapter on Internet for more information on using anonymous FTP.) Once you get this file, follow the instructions in it to obtain the software. After you have acquired it, unless you are able to find a binary executable for the AIX operating system, you may need to compile it before you can use it.

Using Emacs

Emacs supports a large number of buffers, each of which can be used for a different task, such as editing various documents, reading e-mail, and so on. It is possible to switch between buffers, as well as define multiple text windows in a single screen. This ability to break a single window or screen into several smaller ones, made Emacs a very attractive editing environment in the days before X-Windows and graphical window based computing environments. Currently, many potential Emacs users find Emacs's complexity somewhat daunting.

In this section, text such as "C-x" means press Control-X. Something like "M-x" (Meta-x) means press the escape key, then press the x key.

Although text you enter appears directly in the main window, commands and their arguments are generally displayed in the "echo area" at the bottom of the screen. If you should need to abort a command sequence before it is done, type C-g (Control-G).

Invoking Emacs

Emacs can be invoked by typing in the name "emacs", optionally followed by a file name to edit:

```
emacs
```

or

```
emacs filename
```

Adding Lines

After invoking emacs, you are automatically in a text editing buffer that you can use to enter text. You could go right ahead and type the following text (press return at the end of each line):

```
The quick brown fox
jumps over the
lazy dog.
```

Saving a File

To save a file, type

```
C-x C-s <filename>
```

Where "C-x" means Control-X and "C-s" means Control-s. You may be prompted to enter a file name if this is a new file, otherwise Emacs will automatically supply it.

Quitting Emacs

To quit Emacs, type the following and you will be asked if you wish to save your file (if it hasn't already been saved):

```
C-x C-c
```

To merely suspend Emacs, so that you can return to it later without having to restart the entire program, type:

```
C-z
```

Invoking Emacs and Editing an Existing File

To invoke Emacs to edit an existing file just type:

```
emacs filename
```

For instance, the following command will load in the message of the day file:

```
emacs /etc/motd
```

Loading an Existing File From Emacs

To load a file into an Emacs buffer, type:

```
C-x C-f filename
```

You can load in the message of the day file by typing:

```
C-x C-f /etc/motd
```

Moving the Cursor

The following keys are the fundamental cursor movement keys:

C-f	Move Forward one character.
C-b	Move Backward one character.
C-p	Move up one line to the Previous line.
C-n	Move down one line to the Next line.
C-v	Move forward by one page.
M-v	Move back by one page.

Editing Text

After placing the cursor where you wish to insert text, all you have to do is type. The characters you type will be inserted at the cursor. You can delete text by using the DEL key to delete the character before the cursor.

Additional Emacs Tricks

Since a large portion of the power of Emacs is involved with creating and changing buffers and windows, this section would not be complete without a brief description of some of the commands that can be used to accomplish this.

Since each time you load a file, you are creating a new buffer, it would be nice to find a way to manage these buffers. You can list all current buffers by typing:

```
C-x C-b
```

You can switch the current window to another buffer by typing:

```
C-x b <buffername>
```

Hint: You will be prompted to enter the name of the buffer you wish to switch to.

You can remove a buffer by typing:

```
C-x k <buffername>
```

Hint: You will be prompted to enter the name of the buffer you wish to switch delete. This will not affect an actual file.

To split your current window in two vertically, type:

```
C-x 2
```

To split your current window in two horizontally, type:

```
C-x 5
```

To move to another window, type:

```
C-x o
```

Hint: This is a small oh.

To delete the current window, type:

```
C-x 0
```

Hint: This is a zero.

Common Desktop Environment (CDE)—Text Editor

The Common Desktop Environment (CDE) is the result of combined efforts of IBM, HP, SUN, and Novell to create a common user interface that would have the same look and feel on any UNIX system.

Since CDE provides all of the necessary tools to do a wide range of work, it is only natural that one of these tools should include a text editor. The CDE text editor is a fairly easy to use, fairly powerful text editor, that is available on platforms that support CDE. The Common Desktop Environment (CDE) comes standard with all AIX 4.1 or later systems in fileset X11.Dt.rte, so there is no need to install anything special in order to use the CDE text editor.

Using the CDE Text Editor

The CDE text editor is a Graphical User Interface (GUI) based application that can use either the mouse or the keyboard in an intuitive fashion. There are no particular modes to worry about; all operations are menu driven. Although all commands can be typed with a keyboard, the mouse can be used as well.

Invoking the CDE Text Editor

There are several methods to invoke the CDE text editor. Perhaps the easiest is to press the Note Pad icon on the lower left of the CDE Front Panel. It is also possible to run the CDE text editor under any X-Windows or CDE session by typing "/usr/dt/bin/dtpad".

Adding Lines

As with Emacs, adding text is a matter of simply typing. After invoking the text editor, you can start typing text right away. Using the return key between lines, try typing the following:

```
The quick brown fox
jumps over the
lazy dog.
```

Saving a File

You can either use the keyboard or the mouse to save a file:

Mouse:	Keyboard:
Click <File>	ALT-F
Click <Save as...>	A
type the filename	type the filename
Click <OK>	press <return>

Hint: When the "Save As" screen shows up, you may wish to change the path or folder name.

Hint: If you save an existing document, you don't have to use "Save As", you can use "Save", which will not prompt you for file names or paths or anything. It will just save the file.

Quitting the CDE Text Editor

Note the two methods of quitting the CDE text editor:

Mouse:	Keyboard:
Click <File>	ALT-F4
Click <Close>	

Invoking the CDE Text Editor and Editing an Old File

To start editing a file in an existing CDE text editor session, do the following:

Mouse:	**Keyboard:**
Click <File>	ALT-F
Click <Open...>	O
Type path and filename in the appropriate spots	Type path and filename in the appropriate spots
Click <OK>	Press <return>

You can also specify the filename as an argument when starting the CDE text editor from the command line, for example:

```
/usr/dt/bin/dtpad /etc/motd
```

Moving the Cursor

Cursor movement is a snap with the CDE text editor. If you like keyboards, you can use the arrow keys, along with the page up and page down keys to move the cursor.

If you like the mouse, you can use the scroll bar to move through the document. You can also point the mouse where you want the cursor to be and then press the mouse button.

Editing Text

Editing text with CDE text editor is a breeze, to add text, just point the mouse, click where you want to add text, and start typing. If you want to delete, you can either point and click and start pressing the backspace key a number of times, or you can highlight the text you want to delete (click and drag) and just press the backspace key once. In other words, this is the sort of intuitive, easy to use functionality we have come to expect from PC-based word processors. In fact as you explore and experiment with this editor, you will find many of the features one has come to expect from word processors, including mouse-based cut and paste, spell checker, on-line help, formatting, and so on.

INed

Similar to the other editors in this chapter, INed is a screen-based text processing system. INed has a lot of on-line help and documentation available. INed is installed on AIX 4.1 by installing the bos.ined fileset. See the chapter on installation for more information.

Using INed

Since the many key strokes used to control INed change drastically depending on your terminal type, I would recommend using another text editor such as the CDE text editor. If you get an error message, press CANCEL to continue. CANCEL is Scroll Lock on aixterm, and F4 on dtterm.

Invoking INed

INed can be invoked by typing in the name "e", optionally followed by a file name to edit, or a directory:

```
e
```

or

```
e filename
```

When you do not specify a file name, INed will start the file manager. You can use the file manager to select a file to edit. Place the cursor on the file (using the arrow keys) and press ZOOM-IN (or F-11).

To create a new text file, type:

```
e filename
```

Then, select "Create a text file (without history)", with the up/down arrow keys. Then press EXECUTE (CTRL/ACT on aixterm, and Control-a enter on dtterm).

To edit an existing file use the same syntax as for creating a file.

```
e filename
```

Adding Lines

Adding lines to a file can be done by simply typing text. For example, you can type the following, pressing the return key between lines:

```
The quick brown fox
jumps over the
lazy dog.
```

Saving a File and Quitting INed

Saving a file is accomplished by typing ALT-s on an aixterm, or Control-a s on a dtterm.

You can quit INed by typing Control-\ on either terminal.

Moving the Cursor and Editing Text

Cursor movement is done with the arrow keys. You move to the next page by using page up and page down on aixterm, and Control-a plus either page up or page down on dtterm.

The default mode is insert, so adding text can be accomplished by placing the cursor at the desired position, and simply typing. Pressing the insert key on either terminal will toggle the mode between insert and overwrite, so you can change a word by switching into overwrite mode and typing over it.

INed documentation makes continual references to nonexistant keys or "editor functions" that often have very little to do with your actual keyboard. The following Tables 4–1 and 4–2 map INed virtual keys (editor functions) to actual key sequences used for aixterm, dtterm, and the LFT. For example, the documentation may talk about ZOOM-IN, but if you look at these tables, you will see they actually mean F11.

Editor FAQs

Subtitled: Give Me a Couple Wizardries to Impress My Friends!

This section answers commonly asked questions, and includes tidbits that will help you use these editors productively in short time.

I lost power before I got a chance to save a fifty page report I just typed in. What can I do?

vi

> "vi -r" should list files. Then use "vi -r filename" to reload the backup version of your document.

Emacs

> Since Emacs makes a point of saving backups fairly often, you can just edit the last backup. Backups have a tilde (~) appended to the file name.

CDE

> The CDE text editor creates a recovery file if it can that has a pound sign added before and after your file name. For example, if your file name is foo, then the recovery file will be called "#foo#". To use the recovery file, simply load it in as you would a normal file.

INed

> INed creates *.bak files as backups. So, if your file was foo, then try reading foo.bak. In addition, after abnormal program termination, INed will attempt to recover lost data if invoked without any arguments, i.e., just type "e".

How do I spell check my document?

vi

> I simply use the spell command to test spelling of documents created with vi. Then I go back into vi to fix up the spelling.

Table 4–1   INed Functions and Key Sequences for aixterm and LFT

Editor Function	Key Sequence	Editor Function	Key Sequence
BACKSPACE	Backspace	PAGE UP	Alt-Page Up
BACKTAB	Shift Tab	PICK COPY	F9
BEGIN LINE	Alt-Left arrow	PICK UP	F7
BOX MARK	Alt-b	PREVIOUS	Alt-F11
BREAK	Ctrl-c	PRINT	Alt-Print Screen
CANCEL	Scroll Lock	PUT COPY	F10
CENTER	Alt-c	PUT DOWN	F8
CURSOR RIGHT	Right arrow	QUIT	Ctrl-\
CURSOR UP	Up arrow	QUOTE	Alt-q
DELETE CHAR	Delete	REFRESH	Alt-z
DELETE LINE	Alt-Delete	REPLACE	Alt-End
DO	Alt-x	RESTORE	Alt-Insert
END LINE	Alt-Right arrow	RETURN	Enter
ENTER	Ctrl/Act	RIGHT	Alt-r
EXECUTE	Ctrl/Act	SAVE	Alt-s
EXIT	Alt-d	SEARCH DOWN	Alt-Down arrow
FONT	Alt-f	SEARCH UP	Alt-Up arrow
FORMAT	F5	SET TAB	Alt-v
GO TO	End	TAB	Tab
HELP	F1	TEXT MARK	Alt-t
HOME	Home	(1)	Alt-F1
INSERT LINE	F6	(2)	Alt-F2
INSERT MODE	Insert	(3)	Alt-F3
LAST ARG	Alt-a	(4)	Alt-F4
LEFT	Alt-l	(5)	Alt-F5
LINE DOWN	Page Down	(6)	Alt-F6
LINE UP	Page Up	(7)	Alt-F7
MARGIN	Alt-m	(8)	Alt-F8
MENU	F3	USE	Alt-u
NEXT	Alt-F12	WINDOW	Alt-w
NEXT WINDOW	Alt-n	ZOOM IN	F11
PAGE DOWN	Alt Page Down	ZOOM OUT	F12

Table 4–2   INed Editor Functions and Key Sequences for dtterm

Editor Function	Key Sequence	Editor Function	Key Sequence
(1)	CTRL-a F1	LOCAL-MENU	F3
(2)	CTRL-a F2	MARGIN	CTRL-a m
(3)	CTRL-a F3	MENU	F2
(4)	CTRL-a F4	NEXT	F12
(5)	CTRL-a F5	NEXT-WINDOW	CTRL-a n
(6)	CTRL-a F6	PAGE DOWN	CTRL-a Page Down
(7)	CTRL-a F7	PAGE UP	CTRL-a Page Up
(8)	CTRL-a F8	PICK-COPY	F9
BACKSPACE	BACKSPACE	PICK-UP	F7
BEGIN-LINE	CTRL-a Left arrow	PREVIOUS	CTRL-a F11
BOX-MARK	CTRL-a b	PRINT	CTRL-a p
BREAK	CTRL-c	PUT-COPY	F10
CANCEL	F4	PUT-DOWN	F8
CENTER	CTRL-a c	QUIT	CTRL-\
DELETE-CHARACTER	Delete	QUOTE	CTRL-a q
DELETE-LINE	CTRL-a Delete	REFRESH	CTRL-a z
DO	CTRL-a x	REPLACE	CTRL-a =
DOWN-ARROW	Down arrow	RESTORE	CTRL-a i
END-LINE	CTRL-a Right arrow	RETURN	Enter
ENTER	CTRL-a Enter	RIGHT	CTRL-a r
EXECUTE	CTRL-a Enter	RIGHT-ARROW	Right arrow
EXIT	CTRL-a d	SAVE	CTRL-a s
FONT	CTRL-a f	SEARCH DOWN	CTRL-a Down arrow
FORMAT	F5		
GO-TO	CTRL-a g	SEARCH UP	CTRL-a Up arrow
HELP	F1	SET-TAB	CTRL-a v
HOME	CTRL-a h	TAB	Tab
INSERT-LINE	F6	-TAB	CTRL-t
INSERT-MODE	Insert	TEXT-MARK	CTRL-a t
LAST-ARG	CTRL-a a	UP-ARROW	Up arrow
LEFT	CTRL-a l	USE	CTRL-a u
LEFT-ARROW	Left arrow	WINDOW	CTRL-a w
LINEFEED	LINEFEED	ZOOM-IN	F11
LINES DOWN	Page Down	ZOOM-OUT	F12
LINES UP	Page Up		

Emacs

Type "M-x spell-buffer".

CDE

With the mouse click <Edit>, then click <Check Spelling...>. Or with a keyboard type ALT-E, then press k.

INed

Like vi, INed does not have a built in spell checker.

You said there are public domain versions of vi. How can I get a copy for my DOS machine? Can I get Emacs for DOS?

vi

Try using anonymous ftp to get the contents of /usenet/comp.sources.unix/volume15/stevie on ftp.wustl.edu. (See the chapter on Internet for more information on anonymous ftp. You may also want to use archie to look for other or newer sites.)

Emacs

See the section on installing Emacs.

How do I search for text?

vi

From the command mode type "/string<return>" to search for a string "string".

Emacs

Type "C-s <ESC> string <RET>".

CDE

With the mouse click <Edit>, then click <Find/Change...>, then you can type the text to search for, and click <Find>. Or with a keyboard, you can just type Control-F, and then type the text to look for and press <return>.

INed

Press ENTER string +SEARCH, or on aixterm, type Ctrl/act string Alt-Down arrow, and on dtterm type Control-a Enter string Control-a Down arrow.

I made a mistake, how do I undo my last entry?

vi

Type "u" from the command mode. Vi can only remember one change, so the second time you press "u" in a row, the undo is undone.

Emacs

Type "C-x u." The nice thing about undo in Emacs is that you can continue to type "C-x u" and it will continue to undo your changes (unlike vi which will only undo a single change).

CDE

With the mouse, click <Edit>, then click <Undo>. Or with a keyboard, just type Control-Z.

INed

Well, you could go back to a prior saved version of your document...

How do I replace every occurrence of "evrone" with "everyone"?

vi

Type "1,$s/evrone/everyone/g".

Emacs

Type "M-x replace-string <RET> evrone <RET> everyone <RET>".

CDE

With the mouse, click <Edit>, then click <Find/Change...>, then specify the text to search for ("evrone") and the text to replace it with ("everyone"), and then click <Change all>. With a keyboard type Control-F, then type in the text to search for, press tab, then type in the text to replace it with ("everyone"), and press <return>.

INed

First, go to the beginning of the document, then type

```
ENTER 99991 "evrone" "everyone" DO
```

On aixterm

```
Ctrl/Act 99991 "evrone" "everyone" Alt-x
```

On dtterm

```
Control-a Enter 99991 "evrone" "everyone" Control-a x
```

What kind of on-line help or tutorials are available?

vi

Well, you can use InfoExplorer to look up the man pages for vi.

Emacs

Try "C-h t" to invoke the Emacs tutorial, or just typing "C-h" will give you some on-line help.

CDE

With the mouse, click the Help button in the upper right hand corner of the screen. With a keyboard, type ALT-H.

INed

Press F1 on either terminal, then using arrow keys select an entry, press ENTER (aixterm: Ctrl/Act, dtterm: Control-a Enter), and follow the on screen directions.

The following reference charts (Tables 4–3 to 4–13) give you a quick way to lookup how to perform common operating with each of the editors discussed in this chapter.

Reference Charts

Invoking

Table 4–3   Invoking Editors with Optional File Name

vi	Emacs	CDE	INed
vi [file]	emacs [file]	dtpad [file]	e [file]

Exiting

Table 4–4   Exiting an Editor

Description	vi	Emacs	CDE	INed
quit and save	<ESC>ZZ	C-x C-c	ALT-F4	EXIT
quit no save	<ESC>:q!<RET>	C-x C-c	ALT-F4	ENTER q EXIT

Cursor Movement

Table 4–5   Moving the Cursor

Description	vi	Emacs	CDE	INed
Previous char	h	C-b	left arrow	LEFT-ARROW
Next Char	l	C-f	right arrow	RIGHT-ARROW
Previous Line	k	C-p	up arrow	UP-ARROW
Next Line	j	C-n	down arrow	DOWN-ARROW
Previous Screen	C-b	M-v	page up	PAGE UP
Next screen	C-f	C-v	page down	PAGE DOWN
Beginning of Line	0	C-a	home	BEGIN-LINE
End of Line	$	C-e	end	END-LINE
Beginning of File	:0<RET>	M-<	Control-Home	GOTO
End of File	:$<RET>	M->	Control-End	ENTER GOTO
goto line x	:x<RET>	C-x goto-line <RET>x<RET>	Control-G, new # <ret> (if needed, ALT-o s shows status)	ENTER x GOTO

Searching

Table 4–6   Searching for Text

Description	vi	Emacs	CDE	INed
Forward search	/text<RET>	C-s text	Control-F text <RET>	ENTER text SEARCH DOWN
Backward search	?text<RET>	C-r text	—	ENTER text SEARCH UP

File Manipulation

Table 4–7   File Manipulation Commands

Description	vi	Emacs	CDE	INed
Save current file	<ESC>:w!<RET>	C-x C-s	ALT-F s	SAVE
Save As	<ESC>:w! file <RET>	C-x C-w file	ALT-F A file <RET>	ENTER file SAVE
Load File	<ESC>:e file <RET>	C-x C-f file	ALT-F O file <RET>	ENTER file USE

Insertion (vi Only)

Table 4–8   Inserting Text with vi

Description	vi	All Other Editors
Insert at cursor	i	Just position cursor and type!
Insert at end of line	A	Just position cursor and type!
Start new line below cursor	o	Just position cursor and type!

Deletion

Table 4–9   Deleting Text

Description	vi	Emacs	CDE	INed
Delete character	x	C-d	backspace and delete	DELETE-CHARACTER
Delete entire line	dd	C-a C-k	home control-delete	DELETE-LINE

Miscellaneous

Table 4–10   Miscellaneous Editor Commands and Information

Description	vi	Emacs	CDE	INed
Meta-	—	<ESC>	—	—
Cancel Command	<ESC>	C-g	<ESC>	CANCEL
Undo	u	C-x u	Control-z	—
Refresh Screen	<ESC> C-l	C-l	automatic	REFRESH
Spell Check	—	M-x spell-buffer<RET>	ALT-e k	—
Shell Command	:! <cmd> <RET>	M-! <cmd> <RET>	—	ENTER <cmd> MENU

Help

Table 4–11   On-line Help

Description	vi	Emacs	CDE	INed
Help	—	C-h	Control-Z	HELP
Tutorial	—	C-H t	—	—
Documentation	InfoExplorer	C-h i	—	Infoexplorer

Buffer (Emacs Only)

Table 4–12   Buffer Management Commands (Emacs only)

Description	Emacs
List Buffers	C-x C-v
Switch to buffer	C-x b buffername <RET>
Kill buffer	C-x k buffername <RET>

Windows (Emacs Only)

Table 4–13   Windows Management Commands (Emacs only)

Description	Emacs
Split horizontal	C-x 2
Split vertical	C-x 5
Return to one window	C-x 1
Move to other window	C-x o (letter oh)
Close current window	C-x 0 (zero)

References

1.   Cameron, Debra and Roseblatt, Bill, *Learning GNU Emacs*, Sebastopul, CA: O'Reilly & Associates, 1991.

2.   Lamb, Linda, *Learning the vi Editor*, Sebastopul, CA: O'Reilly & Associates, 1986.

3.   Stallman, Richard, *GNU Emacs Manual*, Cambridge, MA: Free Software Foundation, 1987.

4.   IBM, *AIX V4.1: The INed User's Guide*, Form number SC23-2524-00.

5.   CDE Documentation Group, *Common Desktop Environment 1.0 User's Guide*, Reading, MA: Addison-Wesley, 1995 (see chapter 10).

CHAPTER
5

- How to Get AIX Up and Running

- How is AIX Packaged?

- All Right! Installation Assistance!

- Network Installation Manager

Installing AIX

T he nitty-gritty of AIX installation is thoroughly covered in the *AIX Version 4.1 Installation Guide* (SC23-2550). In this chapter, we're going to tell you how AIX installation just got easier and how network installation is now a possibility. We'll touch on the AIX installation highlights, and then we're going to dig into the GUI tools that make installation entertaining—the Install Assistant, the Install and Update Software Manager, and the Maintain Installed Software Manager. We'll show you how to do a network install—undertaking a network install is extremely useful when you're ready to knock 'em dead. So, sit back, tighten your AIX headgear, and get ready to take off!

How to Get AIX Up and Running

Unlike those wimpy shrink-wrapped operating systems you can just buy off the shelf, AIX offers you significant installation functionality (Figure 5–1). You can install AIX on stand-alone systems (a system that starts up by itself); you can manage the installation and configuration of diskless, dataless, or stand-alone systems from a network installation server; or you can get AIX preinstalled at the factory. Refer to the *AIX Version 4.1 Installation Guide* if you're installing a stand-alone machine; see the *AIX Version 4.1 Network Installation Management Guide and Reference* if you're tackling a network install; and refer to your *Start-up Instructions for Preinstalled Systems* if you took the easy way out and had your system preinstalled.

If you're installing AIX from a CDROM or tape, load the tape or CD into the appropriate drive and get going—you can accept default settings and begin installation immediately. Or, you can verify or change system settings before beginning the installation. You also have the option of customizing the BOS Install

Figure 5–1   AIX Installation Options

program. (BOS is an acronym for *base operating system* and is used inter-changeably with AIX by seasoned AIX system administrators.) AIX system administrators can modify the bosinst.data file enabling installation without the set of menus usually displayed—this might speed up installation but be careful that you don't get misdirected in the process.

You can also install optional software and service updates—service updates are "fixes" that the AIX development team makes available for bugs discovered between major releases. AIX installation also includes a migration path that allows you to move from AIX Version 3.2.x to the most recent version, while keeping customized configuration information and installed optional software. Any configuration files that cannot be migrated will be saved in a specific directory.

AIX Version 4.1 introduces a software license management system that allows an application to operate in compliance with the terms and conditions of its license agreement. For example, when you load your AIX CSet++ compiler, you will be asked for your license or "key" to the code. You obtain this code through your point of sale.

How is AIX Packaged?

Software products include those shipped with AIX and those purchased separately. For example, the AIX client package includes Motif and AIXwindows; however, if you wanted the AIX multimedia product, Ultimedia, you would purchase that software package separately from the AIX base operating system.

AIX is organized into small, installable filesets. You can install only what you need! AIX 4.1 has approximately 2,200 filesets. Each fileset can be serviced separately—fixes are delivered in fileset packages and are cumulative.

A function previously installed automatically with **bos.obj** (hardware diagnostics, extended RAS) for example, is packaged separately and installed only if you select it. To simplify installation (by helping you determine which filesets to install), filesets are now grouped into bundles; sets of filesets (of a certain type) that are apt to be installed by most users.

Packaging Definitions

The following terms are packaging definitions:

*   **Fileset**   Filesets provide a specific function. For example, **bos.net.tcp.nfs** is a fileset in the **bos.net** package. A fileset is the smallest individually installable unit.

*   **Package**   A group of filesets with common function.

*   **Bundle**   A collection of filesets and fileset updates that provide specific functions. Predefined bundles contain a specific set of filesets. Now this is a cool idea—you can create your own bundle by using the SMIT Custom Install path or the Install and Update Software Manager graphical application. Bundle definitions are stored in the **/usr/sys/Inst.dat/sys_bundles** directory.

*   **Product Offering**   Selected sets of packages are grouped together to meet the needs of specific customers. Product offerings contain all of the filesets that go on the media, while a bundle defines some subset of these filesets to actually install on a system. For example, AIX 4.1 for Clients is a product offering.

*   **Licensed Program Products (LPPs)**   Complete software product including all packages and filesets associated with the LPP. For example, the Base Operating System (BOS) is an LPP.

Example of Packaging Term Usage

Licensed Program Product
bos

Package
```
bos.diag
```
Fileset
```
bos.diag.rte
```

Product Offerings

Filesets are grouped together into different sets to meet the needs of different customers. AIX product offerings include the following:

- AIX 4.2 for Advanced Servers

- AIX 4.2 for Workgroup Groups

- AIX 4.2 for Clients

- AIX 4.2 for Entry Clients

- AIX 4.1 for Clients

- AIX 4.1 for Servers

- Licensed Program Products

- DES (Data Encryption Standard)

- InfoExplorer Hypertext

- Diagnostics

- OpenGL and GL32

- PEX and graPHIGS

AIX bundles include these offerings:

- Client Bundle

- Personal Productivity Bundle

- Server Bundle

- Hardware Diagnostics Bundle

- Application Development Bundle

Understanding AIX Version Control

AIX release numbering indicates the Version Release Modification Fix level (VRMF); for example, the AIX 4.1.1 bos.rte.up fileset had a VRMF of 4.1.1.0, indicating Version 4, Release 1, Modification Level 1, Fix Level 0.

Version numbers are incremented to indicate a new product. Major functional enhancements occur every one to two years. Release numbers are incremented to show a product enhancement and generally fall one year apart.

The modification level is incremented for two reasons: accumulation of maintenance and support of new processors or devices that DO NOT change the behavior of the product on existing systems. This occurs generally three to six months apart.

The fix level field is incremented when a fix is added to a fileset. Fixes for AIX 4 are produced on customer demand. Note that maintenance and fix levels for AIX 4 do not change application interfaces; applications that are written to documented interfaces should function identically on different maintenance and fix levels.

After installing the AIX base operating system, AIX will run with default settings: one user (root); the date and time set for where the system was manufactured; and other general settings. To change some or all of these settings and to provide system and network information for communication with other systems, use the Installation Assistant.

All Right! Installation Assistance!

Installation Assistant supports software installation and the initial configuration of RISC System/6000s. The task of supporting installations is divided into three applications: Installation Assistant, Install and Update Software Manager, and Maintain Installed Software Manager.

Installation Assistant

Installation Assistant is displayed when you first start-up your system; Installation Assistant walks you through the tasks needed to install options (the software you want to install) and configure the system for use. You can also bring up the Installation Assistant by entering "install_assist" on the command line.

Use the Installation Assistant for the following purposes:

- Set date and time
- Set root password
- Set installation device
- Configure network communications
- Manage system storage and paging space
- Manage language environment
- Create users
- Define printers
- Import existing volume groups

- Install license passwords and software applications

- Backup the system

The Installation Assistant start-up screen is shown in Figure 5–2. The Installation Assistant task list provides the following for each task:

- Task title

- Numbered steps on how to perform each task

- Suggested reading

- Hypertext link to proceed to the next task

- Hypertext link to return to the initial menu

How Do I Get Started?   To make changes to the system configuration during installation, you can choose one of two paths. Clicking on the *i* icon (shown in Figure 5–3) before each task walks you through the information path, explains why each task should be executed, and then provides step-by-step instructions. For example, if you click on the iconified *i* next to the **Set Date and Time** task, you would see the informational screen shown in Figure 5–4.

Clicking on the airplane (shown in Figure 5–5) leads you directly to the action listed on the screen. Using this path, the application related to the selected topic can be started and displayed beside the Installation Assistant. Completing tasks by clicking on the airplane enables you to simultaneously read and execute instructions step-by-step.

If you'd like more information on how the Installation Assistant works before beginning your system configuration, click on Using Installation Assistant (it's underlined indicating that it's a hypertext link). Selecting Using Installation Assistant invokes the screen shown in Figure 5–6.

Easy Install and Install and Update Software Manager

Easy Install enables you to install a software bundle already created to meet specific needs—installing through Easy Install requires minimal decision making. First, you select how the software bundle is to be installed (either from tape, directory, or CD). Then select which software bundle is to be installed (for example, the client or server bundle). If all the functionality you want from AIX is in a particular bundle, use this application. This application only installs the software for which you have a license or that does not require a license. The software is committed at the same time it is installed without saving the previous version of the software. (Note that once you have *committed* software, there is no turning back to the previous level.) Bring up Easy Install by entering

```
xinstallm -ez
```

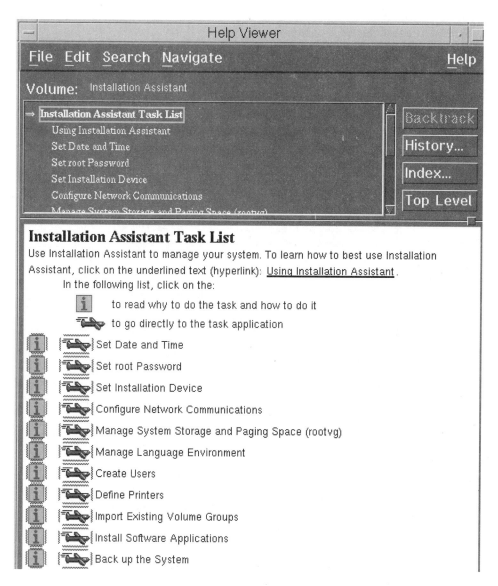

Figure 5–2   Installation Assistant Startup Screen

Figure 5–3   Information Path Icon

Set Date and Time

 Why Do This Task

Before you begin, determine the geographic time zone and if Daylight Savings Time is in effect.

⚠ *Caution:* Complete all the steps before selecting OK. Selecting OK closes the Set Date and Time application. The system time is set to what is displayed in the time fields. Since the time fields are static, reset the time just before selecting OK.

Instructions

1.

   Click the picture and wait for the Set Date and Time graphical dialog to open.

2. At the top of the window, locate the Current System Time field. If the date is not correct, locate the Date area and set the correct date using the Year, Month, and Day fields provided.

3. Add new step.

4. At the right of the Selected Time field, locate the Time Notation option menu. Make sure the displayed notation is correct.

   For example, if it is set to 24-hour and your network uses the 12-hour clock, specify AM or PM depending on your current 12-hour clock.

5. In the lower right side of the window, locate the Time Zone field. Make sure the displayed geographical time zone and standard time indicator are correct. (If daylight savings time is in effect, the DST indicator should be displayed.)

   To change the standard time indicator or the time zone, click List.

   a. To change the daylight savings time indicator, click the Daylight Savings Time check box.

Figure 5–4   Set Date and Time Information Screen

You can also bring up Easy Install by clicking on the Easy Install icon in the Application Manager System_Admin directory. The Easy Install interface is shown in Figure 5–7.

The Install and Update Software Manager enables users to understand the relationships between licensed products, installable filesets, maintenance levels, enhancements, and fixes.

Figure 5–5   Task Execution Icon

Using Installation Assistant

Installation Assistant simplifies customizing your system by guiding you through post-installation tasks and, in some cases, automatically installing software packages for you. In addition, the Installation Assistant introduces you to various interfaces, providing only the help you need, when you need it. If you are unfamiliar with using a mouse or with terms like "click" and "drag and drop," select the following hyperlink: Using a Mouse.

How to Use the Installation Assistant Task List
You can follow the learning path or the fast path.

[i]   Learning Path – Click the "i" for information on why you would want to do a task, what the prerequisites are, and how to complete a task. Click the "i" for the first task "Set Date and Time," then select the" To Continue" button at the end of each task to step through the tasks in the suggested order.

✈   Fast Path – If you are familiar with the tasks and know how to use SMIT and graphical interfaces, then click the airplane to skip the instructions and go directly to the task application.

How to Use the Task Instructions
Each task contains the following sections:

Title	Identifies the task. Some tasks lead into subtasks.
? Why Do This Task	The reasons for performing the task, and its advantages. Click the ?.
Prerequisites	Prerequisites or suggestions to consider.
Instructions	A picture (graphic hyperlink) to start the task application and instructions to complete the task. Read through the instructions once, click the picture, adjust the windows so you can read the instructions as you complete the task. To learn how to manage your windows, select the following hyperlink: Moving and Resizing Windows
To Continue:	The suggested order for completing the tasks. For instance, you should make all the changes to the system before you make a backup copy of it. If you choose not to follow the suggested order, select tasks from the Installation Assistant Task List or the topic tree in the upper pane of this window.

Figure 5–6   Using Installation Assistant Startup Screen

You can use the Install Update Software Manager for the following tasks:

- Install or update software packages
- Set default install settings
- Preview size/options required for install packages (prerequisites)
- Copy install images for use in future installs
- Create new install bundles

Figure 5-7   Easy Install Startup Screen

The Install and Update Software Manager provides users with a Visual System Manager application to execute the installp command. Bring up the Install and Update Software Manager by clicking on the **Install Software Applications** task on the Installation Assistant start-up screen. Clicking on the **Install Software Applications** task brings up the Software Installation & Maintenance SMIT screen. You can also bring up the Install and Update Software Manager by entering

xinstallm

From the Installation & Maintenance SMIT screen, select **Install Selectable Software (Custom Install)** to bring up the Install and Update Software Manger. You can also bring up the Install and Update Software Manager by clicking on the Install Manager icon in the Application Manager System_Admin directory. The Install and Update Software Manager startup screen is shown in Figure 5-8.

The Install and Update Software Manager helps users select the correct install device (for example, tape, CDROM, or diskette) and bundle (for example, client, server, or personal productivity) for installation. See the information on AIX packaging for more information on AIX software bundles.

After you select the installation device you want to use, the installation device is read and the list of software available on the media is displayed in the work area.

When a user selects a bundle, the Install and Update Software Manager selects all of the software titles in the bundle that are also on the install media enabling you to quickly select the software you want to install.

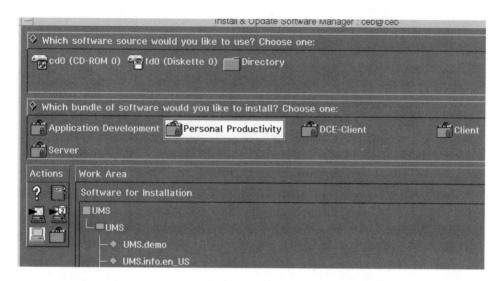

Figure 5–8   Install and Update Software Manager
Startup Screen

Using the Install and Update Manager, you can select or deselect additional software titles, or specify any of the following actions for the selected titles:

- Install the selected software
- Schedule the installation to occur later
- Preview the selected software for size
- Save the selected objects as a new bundle (create your own bundle)

The relationship between the filesets, files, and fixes is presented in a tree view.
You can also specify any of the following actions for the installation task:

- Show the following install settings

  Apply and commit

  Install requisite software

  Extend the filesystem if needed

  Include language packages
- Show or change the scheduled activities
- Delete the bundle or object

Maintain Installed Software Manager

The Maintain Installed Software Manager manages software that has already been installed. Users can select objects from the product list and specify any of the following actions:

- Commit the selected software
- Reject the selected software
- Cleanup installed software
- Verify that the selected software is complete

You can also find specific objects by name and delete software (de-install). Bring up the Maintain Installed Software Manager by clicking on the Application Manager located on the CDE Front Panel. Double-click on the System_Admin icon, then the Maintain Software icon. Or, you can enter

```
xmaintm
```

Clicking on the Maintain Software icon brings up the Maintain Installed Software Manager start-up screen as shown in Figure 5–9.

Network Installation Manager

You can install AIX using tape or CDROM or by using the Network Installation Manager (NIM). NIM is not only an excellent tool for installing multiple ma-

Figure 5–9   Maintain Software Manager Start-up Screen

chines over a network, it can also be used for software maintenance and machine customizations. Using NIM, you can set up an installation once for machines with identical requirements or customize the specific needs of given machines. The number of machines you install simultaneously depends on the throughput of your network, the disk access throughput of the installation severs, and the platform type of your servers. System administrators can perform tasks for multiple machines from NIM including running diagnostics and installing fixes. Note that the Network Installation Manager utility is thoroughly discussed in the *AIX Version 4.1 Network Installation Management Guide and Reference.*

Advantages of network installation include the ability to share installation images. Since the installation images are on the network, it is easier to share them between machines. Installation can be initiated by either the NIM master or a NIM client. If the master initiates it, it is called a push install. If the client initiates it, it is called a pull install.

With push capability, an administrator can update machines for people. If some new software comes in, the administrator can push the files onto his client machines. The machine users do not have to get involved. With pull capability, the clients can customize their own machines. A NIM resource server can be used as a software library. Since it is on the network, the installer does not have to hunt down the media.

What do you gain by using NIM? If your organization has strong central network administration, NIM is extremely useful for updating machines. NIM is also great for environments where many machines are installed/updated simultaneously because machines can share the installation media on the network. Using NIM also reduces installation time—network communication is faster than tape and CDROM input/output. How big can your NIM environment be? You can define the size; the NIM environment is easily expandable from your development lab to your multiple corporate sites to your international offices (Figure 5–10).

NIM Environment

The NIM environment is composed of two basic machine roles: *master* and *client*. The NIM master manages the installation of the rest of the machines in the NIM environment. The master is the only machine that can remotely execute NIM commands on the clients. All the other machines participating in the NIM environment are clients to the master, including machines that may also serve resources. A smallscale NIM environment is shown in Figure 5–11.

The types of machines you can install are *stand-alone*, *diskless*, and *dataless*. A stand-alone machine is one that can boot (start up) by itself. Diskless and dataless systems cannot boot by themselves. They must use remote resources to boot.

Figure 5–10   Expandable NIM Environment

Figure 5–11   Small-scale NIM Environment

Diskless systems have no disk drive. Dataless systems have a local disk drive but they cannot boot from it. This book provides concepts and procedures for setting up the NIM environment and initiating the installation of stand-alone machines and the initialization of resources for diskless and dataless machines.

Most installation tasks in the NIM environment are performed from one server, called the *master*. A set of installation tasks can also be performed from NIM clients. Once the administrator completes the network installation setup, users of stand-alone clients can, from the client, install software that is available on NIM servers.

The machines you want to manage in the NIM environment, their resources, and the networks through which the machines communicate are all represented as *objects* within a central database that resides on the master. Each of these objects has *attributes* that give it a unique identity, such as the network address of a machine or the location of a file or directory. With this information, you can install the base operating system and optional software on multiple machines, managed from a central location.

NIM Master.   There is only one NIM master per NIM environment. The master is fundamental for all operations in the NIM environment. This machine must be set up and functional before you can perform any NIM operations. The master must be a stand-alone machine, running AIX Version 4.1, with the NIM master fileset installed. The master manages the NIM configuration database and provides the central point of administration for the NIM environment.

The rsh command is used to remotely execute commands on clients. To use the rsh command, the .rhosts file on the client is configured automatically by NIM so that the master has the permissions required to execute commands on the client. Once a NIM client is running, a user with root authority on a client can disable the master's permissions to push commands onto the client. A user with root authority on a client can also enable the master's push permissions for the client.

NIM Clients.   NIM clients can have the following configurations:

- Stand-alone
- Diskless
- Dataless

Stand-alone clients have all the required file systems on a local disk after installation. Diskless clients access all their resources from servers in the network. Dataless clients have a combination of local and remote resources.

The installation processing that occurs on diskless and dataless clients involves populating the root directory for the client with files from a resource known as a Shared Product Object Tree (SPOT) that is located on a NIM server. A SPOT is a /usr file system or an equivalent file system that is exported by servers in the NIM environment for remote client use.

While the master can push installation resources onto NIM clients, a running stand-alone NIM client can also initiate the installation by *pulling* resources from another NIM machine.

Diskless and dataless clients cannot initiate installations because these resources are not stored on the client.

NIM Objects

NIM stores information about the physical environment as objects in the NIM database. There are three *classes* of objects:

- Networks
- Machines
- Resources, which are files and directories required to perform NIM operations

Network Objects

Network objects represent information about each local area network (LAN) that is part of the NIM environment. These objects and their attributes reflect the physical characteristics of the network environment. This information does not affect the running of a physical network but is used internally by NIM for configuration information.

There are three types of network objects. These objects represent the following types of networks that are supported in the NIM environment:

- Token-Ring
- Ethernet
- Fiber Distributed Data Interface (FDDI)

Each network object contains the following information:

- The network interface type: Token-Ring, Ethernet, or FDDI
- The Internet Protocol (IP) address of the network
- The subnet mask of the network
- The NIM routing information for the network, if required.

Clients use resources that are usually provided by other machines in the NIM environment. The NIM routing information is required to define which gateways should be used when establishing communication with clients on different networks.

On Network objects you can perform the following management operations:

1. **Define:** Creates a new object.

2. **Change:** Adds new attributes or changes the existing attributes of the object.

3. **Remove:** Removes the network object from the database.

Machine Objects

There are three types of machine objects. These objects represent the following machine configurations that are supported in the NIM environment:

*   Stand-alone

*   Diskless

*   Dataless

Each machine object in the NIM database has associated attributes representing information about each client that participates in the NIM environment. This information includes the following:

*   The type of machine: diskless, dataless, or stand-alone

*   The hardware address of the client's network interface

*   The TCP/IP host name for the client

*   The name of the network object that represents the network to which the client is connected

*   The ring speed of the Token-Ring network or the cable type for the Ethernet network connection.

A client can have multiple network interfaces. The first interface that is defined is called the *primary interface*. This attribute of the machine object specifies the interface that a client must use to access NIM resources.

There are two types of operations that can be performed on machine objects: *management* and *control* operations. The management operations manipulate the object instances in the NIM database. The control operations initiate an action to be performed on the client.

Resource Objects

Resource objects represent the available resources in the NIM environment. All operations on clients in the NIM environment require one or more resources. NIM resource objects represent files and directories that are used to support some type of NIM operation. Because NIM resources are ordinary file system objects in the AIX operating system, most of them are provided to clients with standard Network File System (NFS) software. This means that many resources must reside locally on the servers providing these resources, because NFS can only export file system objects that are stored on local media in the machines from which they are exported.

Shared Product Object Tree

The Shared Product Object Tree (SPOT) is a fundamental resource in the NIM environment. It is required to install or initialize all machine configuration types. A SPOT provides a /usr file system for diskless and dataless clients, as well as the network boot support for all clients.

Everything that a machine requires in a /usr file system, such as the AIX kernel, executable commands, libraries, and applications, is included in the SPOT. Machine-unique information or user data is usually stored in the other file systems. A SPOT can be located on any stand-alone machine within the NIM environment, including the master. The SPOT is created, controlled, and maintained from the master, even though the SPOT can be located on another system.

There are two ways to create a SPOT. You can convert the /usr file system (/usr SPOT) or you can locate the SPOT elsewhere within the file system (non-/usr SPOT) on the server.

A SPOT is also used to create and maintain the network boot images and the support for network boot processing. The network boot images are created using the files that reside in the SPOT and reside in the /tftpboot directory on the SPOT server. Network boot images are limited in size and cannot include all the code necessary to boot a system. A SPOT provides these files for the client boot process by exporting the resources with NFS.

The Network Boot Process

The AIX boot process brings a machine to a specific execution state. Every machine requires a *boot image* that can be loaded after the machine is turned on or reset. A boot image contains the AIX kernel and a RAM file system containing libraries and programs necessary to reach a specific state. Stand-alone machines use a boot image stored on the local disk. Network-dependent systems, such as diskless or dataless systems, retrieve a boot image from a server on the network every time the system is turned on. The boot image is called a *network boot image*.

To obtain a network boot image, NIM clients use the BOOTP and TFTP protocol. The BOOTP protocol consists of a client sending a request to a server for a boot image, which enables the client to achieve a specific state.

In the NIM environment, a network boot image is also required to install stand-alone machines over the network. After installation, the stand-alone machines boot using the boot image that resides on the local disk.

Initial Program Load (IPL) Read Only Memory (ROM) Emulation

The Initial Program Load (IPL) Read Only Memory (ROM) is a piece of firmware in each machine that is responsible for locating and loading an AIX boot image. After the boot image is located and loaded, the IPL ROM's role is complete. It is the loaded boot image that brings the machine to a specific state.

All versions of IPL ROM can search local devices for an AIX boot image. However, only some versions, known as BOOTP-enabled IPL ROM, can use a network communications adapter to search for a remote boot image. The BOOTP-enabled versions use the boot protocol (BOOTP) to find a network boot image and retrieve it using Trivial File Transfer Protocol (TFTP).

Some machines do not have a BOOTP-enabled IPL ROM. These machines must use the IPL ROM emulation program, which enables the machine to search for a remote boot image. The IPL ROM emulation program can be stored on a diskette (or a tape). The program is created on the NIM master.

The client machine will boot from the media to provide the same function as the BOOTP-enabled IPL ROM. The IPL ROM emulation media should be left in the drive of the target machine so the machine can be rebooted remotely from the master.

CHAPTER
6

- Using SMIT to Install Devices

- Printers

Setting up Peripherals

I n this chapter we will explain how to use smit to set up devices such as CD-ROMs, generic devices, and most importantly, printers. Since printers are so crucial to everyday work, we will go into detail on how to set up, administer, use, and troubleshoot your printer under AIX.

Using SMIT to Install Devices

The Software Management Interface Tool (SMIT) is a useful graphical interface for nearly all system management tasks. After you have physically plugged in any new devices (be sure the power is off first!), log into your computer as root and run SMIT with the command "smit devices" (you can also select "devices" from the main SMIT menu). If you run SMIT from a graphical environment such as the CDE desktop, or from an X-Windows session, you will see the screen in Figure 6–1, otherwise you will see a text-based version with the same prompts and labels.

Adding, removing, and configuring peripherals is easily done by selecting the type of device you wish to work with from the menu above. Although each device has its own unique installation quirks, there are several concepts that apply to all devices that you should be familiar with. Devices can be defined, supported, and available. Nearly all device menus have options to display supported and defined devices. A supported device is one that AIX knows how to use. An unsupported device can also be used on AIX if additional software or configuration data is loaded. A defined device is one that has actually been configured to work on your system; your system knows about that particular device. To "define" a device on your system you must select one of the "add xyz device"

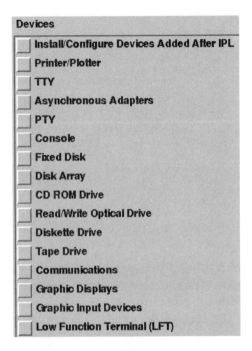

Figure 6–1   SMIT Devices Screen

options. An available device is one that is supported, defined, and on-line. It is available for immediate use.

Let's take a look at some examples. You can see all supported devices (all devices that your system is preprogrammed to deal with), by selecting "List Devices" from the "Devices" menu in SMIT (Figure 6–2). Now select "List All Supported Devices" (Figure 6–3).

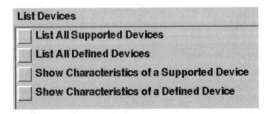

Figure 6–2   List Devices SMIT Screen

Output:

```
adapter    colorgda   mca    Color Graphics Display Adapter
adapter    fda        sio    Standard I/O Diskette Adapter
adapter    fda_2      sio    Standard I/O Diskette Adapter
adapter    fda_iod    sio    Standard I/O Diskette Adapter
adapter    hscsi      mca    SCSI I/O Controller
adapter    hscsi      sio    Standard SCSI I/O Controller
adapter    keyboard   sio    Keyboard/Tablet Adapter
adapter    keyboard_2 sio    Keyboard Adapter
adapter    mouse      sio    Mouse Adapter
```

Figure 6–3   All Supported Devices SMIT Screen

You can also take a look at all defined devices (the ones that your system is explicitly aware of) by selecting "List Devices" from the "Devices" menu, and then selecting "List all Defined Devices" (Figure 6–4).

You will notice that with this list, some devices have the status "available" where as others simply have the status "defined." This is because available devices are also by definition "defined." This list can be used to answer such questions as, "exactly how much disk space or memory is installed on my system?"

Using SMIT to Install a CD-ROM

Since the concepts behind installing a CD-ROM are applicable to almost all other devices, we will use this as a detailed example. After physically plugging in the CD-ROM, and typing in "smit devices" as the root user, you should select "CD ROM Drive" (Figure 6–5).

The first step is to add the CD-ROM, so that it will be "defined," then you can configure the CD-ROM, and it will become "available." As illustrated by Figures

Output:

```
lvdd    Available          LVM Device Driver
mem0    Available 00-0A    16 MB Memory Card
mem1    Available 00-0B    8 MB Memory Card
mem2    Available 00-0C    16 MB Memory Card
mem3    Available 00-0E    16 MB Memory Card
mem4    Available 00-0F    8 MB Memory Card
mem5    Available 00-0G    16 MB Memory Card
mouse0  Available 00-00-0M-00 3 button mouse
```

Figure 6–4   All Defined Devices SMIT Screen

CD ROM Drive

- [ ] List All Defined CD ROM Drives
- [ ] List All Supported CD ROM Drives
- [ ] Add a CD ROM Drive
- [ ] Change / Show Characteristics of CD ROM Drive
- [ ] Remove a CD ROM Drive
- [ ] Configure a Defined CD ROM Drive
- [ ] Generate an Error Report
- [ ] Trace a CD ROM Drive

Figure 6–5   CD ROM Drive SMIT Screen

6–6 through 6–10, installing a CD-ROM is a simple matter of clicking on buttons and answering appropriate questions. This example is for a SCSI device. (Hint: you may need to look at the setting of switches on the back of any SCSI device for the SCSI address. The manual that comes with your device will have useful information. Read it!)

First click on "Add a CD ROM Drive" (Figure 6–6) then select the type of CD-ROM devices you wish to add.

Figure 6–6   Select CD ROM Drive Type SMIT Screen

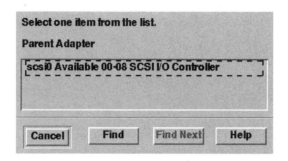

Figure 6–7   Select Parent Adapter SMIT Screen

Selecting the Parent Adapter on the next screen is a "no-brainer" (Figure 6–7). After answering the following questions on the screen shown in Figure 6–8 click "OK". Press "List" or "Help" if you are not sure of something.

Now that you have added, and thus "defined" your CD-ROM drive, you will need to configure it, in order to make it "available." From the "smit cdrom" menu select "Configure a Defined CD ROM," and select the device you have just defined (Figure 6–9).

After you have defined a device, you can change its characteristics by selecting "Change/Show Characteristics of CD ROM Drive." First you will need to select

CD ROM Drive type	cdrom1			
CD ROM Drive interface	scsi			
Description	CD-ROM Drive			
Parent adapter	scsi0			
* CONNECTION address			List	
RESERVE device on open	no		List	▲ ▼
PREVENT ejection of media when open	no		List	▲ ▼

| OK | Command | Reset | Cancel | ? | Help |

Figure 6–8   Describe CD-ROM SMIT Screen

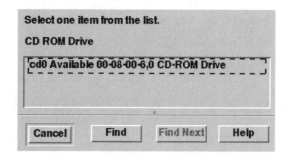

Figure 6–9   Select CD-ROM Drive Screen

the CD-ROM drive you wish to change or show. You can then view and modify
the attributes shown in Figure 6–10.

Printers

Installing and Configuring a Local Printer

Although there are a variety of techniques that could be used, we will introduce
the most straightforward method which will allow you to define the printer and
create new queues in the same step. The technique we describe here is new in
AIX Version 4. In AIX 3.2 it was necessary to define and configure the printer,
then create and start a queue. This required a number of seemingly unrelated

CD ROM Drive	cd0		
CD ROM Drive type	cdrom1		
CD ROM Drive interface	scsi		
Description	CD-ROM Drive		
Status	Available		
Location	00-08-00-6,0		
Parent adapter	scsi0		
Connection address	6,0		
RESERVE device on open	no	List	▲ ▼
PREVENT ejection of media when open	no	List	▲ ▼

Figure 6–10   View/Modify CD-ROM Attributes SMIT
Screen

Select one item from the list.

Add an Additional Printer to an Existing Print Queue

# ATTACHMENT TYPE	DESCRIPTION
local	Printer Attached to Local Host
xstation	Printer Attached to Xstation
ascii	Printer Attached to ASCII Terminal
hpJetDirect	Network Printer (HP JetDirect)
file	File (in /dev directory)
other	User Defined Backend

Figure 6–11   Select Attachment Type SMIT Screen

steps to be executed in precision by the user. I think you will agree that the new path is a snap to use!

From the command line type "smit mkpq," and you will see the screen shown in Figure 6–11.

Although it is possible to add a variety of different printer types, for this example, we will add a local printer. After clicking "local" you will see a menu of selections that looks something like those in Figure 6–12 (the exact printer names may be different on your system).

In our example, we selected "IBM". The next screen is a long list of possible printer types. In this example, we will truncate the list to the last five items, and select the generic printer at the end (Figure 6–13).

The following screen attempts to identify the exact printer being installed. In this case, the answer is simple since there is only a single option (Figure 6–14).

After selecting "Generic Printer", we are given a selection that may look like that shown in Figure 6–15. This screen will show all currently defined queues. If you wish to add the printer to an existing queue, for instance "lp0", then click that queue name. Otherwise if you wish to add a new queue then select, "+ Add NEW Printer." For this example we will add a new printer.

Next, select the interface to use. In this example, we will use a parallel interface (Figure 6–16). Then select the adapter type (Figure 6–17).

Select one item from the list.

Printer Type

Bull
Canon
Dataproducts
Hewlett–Packard
IBM
OKI
Printronix
QMS
Texas Instruments
Other (Select this if your printer type is not listed above)

Figure 6–12   Select Printer Type SMIT Screen

ibm6186   IBM 6186 Color Plotter
ibm6252   IBM 6252 Impactwriter
ibm6262   IBM 6262 Printer
ibm7372   IBM 7372 Color Plotter
Other (Select this if your printer type is not listed above)

Figure 6–13   Select Printer Model SMIT Screen

Select one item from the list.

Printer Type

generic Generic Printer

| Cancel | Find | Find Next | Help |

Figure 6–14   Select Printer SMIT Screen

Description	Generic Printer
Names of NEW print queues to add	
ASCII	asc_queue
GL Emulation	
PCL Emulation	
PostScript	ps_queue
Printer connection characteristics	
* PORT number	p
Type of PARALLEL INTERFACE	standard
Printer TIME OUT period (seconds)	60
STATE to be configured at boot time	available

Figure 6–15   Select Printer Queue SMIT Screen

You will now see the screen shown in Figure 6–18. In general the default values are usually OK to use. The "List" option is very useful when selecting other values. In this case we added two queues for this printer; an ASCII queue called "asc_queue" and a postscript queue called "ps_queue." (Generally queue names are much shorter, for instance "lp1" or "ps1" and so on.) After you are satisfied, select the OK button, and printer configuration and its queues will be added (Figure 6–18).

Select one item from the list.

Printer Interface

parallel
rs232
rs422

| Cancel | Find | Find Next | Help |

Figure 6–16   Select Printer Interface SMIT Screen

Select one item from the list.

Parent Adapter

ppa0 Available 00–00–0P Standard I/O Parallel Port Adapter

Figure 6–17   Select Printer Parent Adapter SMIT Screen

We have now added a printer and its queues. Before you use it, you may wish to try the "smit chpq" command, and see if there are any details that you wish to configure. You may now use your printer with any of the printer commands supplied with AIX.

Creating a Remote Printer Queue

If your computer is connected to a local area network, then you may have access to printers connected to other computers on your network. For example, many

Description	Generic Printer	
Names of NEW print queues to add		
ASCII	asc_queue	
GL Emulation		
PCL Emulation		
PostScript	ps_queue	
Printer connection characteristics		
* PORT number	p	List
Type of PARALLEL INTERFACE	standard	List
Printer TIME OUT period (seconds)	60	List
STATE to be configured at boot time	available	List

Figure 6–18   Printer Configuration SMIT Screen

Figure 6–19 Add Remote Printer Queue SMIT Screen

companies and schools have a central printer server with a number of printers connected to it that all users in an organization can share. In order to use a remote printer you must ask the administrator of the printer server to give you access to the printer queue. The administrator should tell you the host name of the printer server as well as the name of the printer queue on that machine. Once you have done this, you should run SMIT as before (type in "smit mkpq" from the command line). First select "remote," next select "Standard Processing." You will see the screen in Figure 6–19.

At this point you should type in the name you wish to use for your local queue (Name of QUEUE to add), the name of the machine that is acting as the printer server (HOSTNAME of remote server), and the name of QUEUE on remote server. You may optionally specify a one line description of this queue; for example, "Jim's color postscript holograph generator."

Common Questions about Common Printer Commands

How do I see the print jobs on the queue?

Use either the qchk or the lpq command:

```
$ lpq
Queue Dev   Status Job Files      User      PP % Blks      Cp Rnk
---- ---   ----- -- ------- ---- ---- - ----- --- ---
pr    @prin READY
pr    b906p READY
```

How do I remove a print job from the queue?

Use either the qcan or lprm commands:

```
$ lprm 1
Message from qdaemon:
Job number 1 has been deleted from the queue.<EOT>
```

What commands can I use to print with?

Use either the qprt, enscript, lp, or lpr commands. Commands lp and lpr are fairly simple commands that are good for printing text files without adornment. These commands are also the commands to use when printing postscript files. Commands qprt and enscript are slightly more powerful commands for printing. I like to use the "enscript -Gr2f Courier6" command to print program listings since it prints sideways in two columns with a small font. You can also use the enscript command to generate postscript files by specifying the "-p ps.file" option.

How can I print graphics files?

I recommend using a utility such as xv (available via anonymous ftp from ftp.cis.upenn.edu in directory /pub/xv) to save the file as a postscript file. You can then print the postscript file with lpr.

Trouble-shooting

First make sure that the printer itself is OK. Double check that it is properly connected to your computer, plugged in to the power outlet, and turned on. Next, be sure that the printer has enough paper, is not jammed, or is not low on toner (or needs a new ribbon). The manual that comes with your printer should offer other suggestions. You may wish to run any self-tests that come with the printer to be sure that it is working properly.

In some cases, the printer will notify the spooling system when certain errors occur (such as running out of paper or jamming). When this happens, a diagnostic error message is usually displayed on the console, and the print queue "goes down." You can bring the queue back up by typing the following command as root (be sure to substitute <queuename> with the name of the queue you are using!):

```
qadm -U <queuename>
```

You can generally send files directly to your printer by copying text straight to the printer file. Default printer files are /dev/lp, /dev/lp0, /dev/lp1, and so on. For example, this command would print the message of the day file directly:

```
cat /etc/motd >> /dev/lp0
```

If this does not work then there is something wrong with the printer itself, the physical connection to the printer, or the printer is not configured. If this does work, but normal print spool commands do not work, then the problem is in the spooler configuration.

In some cases you may get the error, "cannot awaken qdaemon." If you notice that the "qdaemon" process is not running when you do a "ps -ef | grep qdaemon" command, then you may wish to try running "startsrc -s qdaemon".

I recommend reading the book *AIX Version 4.1 Guide to Printers and Printing* available from IBM (order number SC23-2783-00) to guide you in troubleshooting.

CHAPTER
7

- AIX Web Browsers & Servers: AIX WebExplorer, Netscape, Mosaic

- AIX Welcome Center

- AIX 4.2 Bonus Pack: Java, Adobe Acrobat, Ultimedia, etc.

- AIX Connections Bring Them All Together

- File Transfer, Remote Login

- E-Mail

- Distributed File Systems

Communicating with the World

I n the global environment we now live in, it's more and more important to be able to connect to other systems. AIX provides many methods to connect to all kinds of computer systems, whether they are IBM systems or not. AIX 4.2 includes a great deal of internet software not available in prior releases. There is so much new code that AIX 4.2 is shipped on multiple CD's instead of just one!

AIX Web Browsers & Servers: AIX WebExplorer, Netscape, Mosaic

Of the currently available web browsers, we will briefly describe how to obtain and use the three main ones for AIX. These are the AIX WebExplorer, Netscape, and Mosaic. Browsers give you an easy way to access information that is on the Internet. Menus, help text, and lots of colorful pictures are all accessible at the click of a mouse!

Selecting the right browser and client/server setup is very important. Sometimes you might want to connect to a web site that is literally on the other side of the world. This means that it could take a very long time to get the connections through and get large files (graphic images) sent over just to view the home page. If your system is a client, then the files are sent to your server first to be stored and then displayed on your client.

AIX WebExplorer

The AIX WebExplorer is shipped with the standard install media for AIX Version 4.1.4 and 4.1.5. To use it, you need to ensure that the X11.internet fileset is installed. You can check this by typing in "lslpp -L all | grep internet" on the command line. If it is not installed, then follow these directions:

- Insert your install media (CD-ROM, tape, or so on) in the appropriate device.

- As the root user, type "smit install_latest", and select the input device/directory (Hint: use the LIST button).

- On the next screen specify "X11.internet" as the package to install. You can use the LIST button here to keep things easy.

After installing the software, take a look at any readme files in /usr/lpp/explorer regarding configuration or other important issues. When you are ready to try out WebExplorer, just type "explorer" at the command line. One of the nice things about the AIX WebExplorer is that it displays pictures and text as they are being loaded. It also contains a clickable map of where you have been (see Figure 7–1).

Figure 7–1   AIX WebExplorer Map Screen

AIX 4.2 includes a Web Server as well as the browser. The server code allows your system to act as an Internet server, that can be shared by many users and other systems.

Netscape

The Netscape browser and server applications are part of the AIX 4.2 and later packages. Just use the CD with Netscape on it and install it normally (see the install chapter) with SMIT.

Prior to AIX Version 4.2, obtain the Netscape web browser for AIX by calling 1-415-528-2555 (USA) between 7:00 A.M. and 5:00 P.M. PST to order an official package. If you already have a web browser running, you can take a look at http://www.netscape.com/. Alternatively, you can download a copy via ftp. To use ftp, first read about how to use it later on in this chapter, then using your new found knowledge, do an anonymous ftp to ftp10.netscape.com. First get and read file /netscape/unix/README for late breaking information. After typing "bin" in ftp to ensure that the binary download works, download the AIX version of Netscape. At the time of writing, the latest full version was /netscape/unix/ netscape-v112-export.rs6000-ibm-aix3.2.tar.Z After downloading this file, type "zcat netscape-v112-export.rs6000-ibm-aix3.2.tar.Z | tar -vxf -" to uncompress and untar the files. After reading the README file, you can try Netscape by simply typing "netscape" at the command line.

When you get Netscape up and running, you can expect to see a Netscape Home Page (see Figure 7–2).

Mosaic

To obtain the Mosaic web browser for AIX, first read about how to use ftp later on in this chapter, then using your new found knowledge, do an anonymous ftp to ftp.ncsa.uiuc.edu, and take a look at directory /Mosaic/Unix/binaries. Currently the available versions are 2.6 and 2.7b. Next, I would recommend obtaining the README file in the directory you are interested in. If you wanted to get Version 2.6, then you can get file /Mosaic/Unix/binaries/2.6/Mosaic-ibm-2.6.Z. Be sure to type "bin" in ftp to make sure that the binary file is unaltered on download. After downloading the file to your system, uncompress the file by typing "uncompress Mosaic-ibm-2.6", and then make the file executable by typing "chmod a+x Mosaic-ibm-2.6". You can run the program by typing "Mosaic-ibm-2.6". You can obtain documentation and further information in one of two ways. If you have a web browser of some kind working, you can connect to the NCSA Mosaic Home Page (http://www.ncsa.uiuc.edu/SDG/Software/Mosaic/MCSAMosaicHome.html), as shown in Figure 7–3, or you can ftp documentation from directory /Web/Mosaic/Unix/Documents on ftp.ncsa.uiuc.edu.

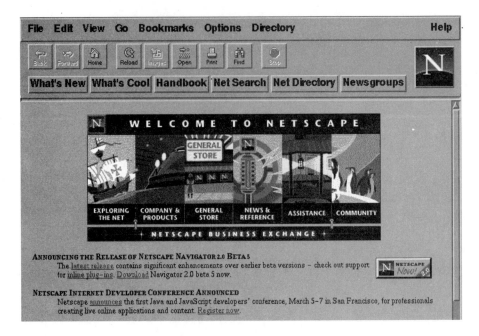

Figure 7-2   Netscape Home Page

AIX Welcome Center

New with AIX 4.2 is an Internet application that navigates you through a wealth of information available on your local system and on the web. It's a set of home pages set up to welcome you to AIX!

The Welcome Center has a fun and interesting way of taking you around the system with graphics artwork and images, with audio clips that will surprise you, with service information, pointers to WWW sites dedicated to AIX, and everything else you wanted to know about IBM and AIX but were afraid to ask . . .

You need to order the Welcome Center when you order AIX and ask for feature code 0598. You can also see it by pointing your web browser at http://www.r56000.ibm.com/support/welcome

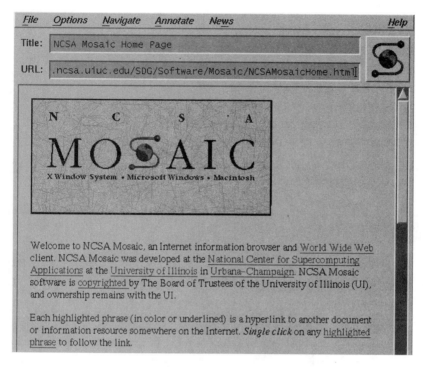

Figure 7–3 Mosaic Home Page

AIX 4.2 Bonus Pack: Java, Adobe Acrobat, Ultimedia, etc.

AIX 4.2 includes additional applications on several different CD "Bonus Packs".

The Bonus Pack CD's fall into two main categories, just as the AIX operating system does. Those categories are Client and Server. Some of the neat stuff found on the client CD includes:

- The Adobe Acrobat reader.

- The Java development kit, runtime environment, and samples.

- The AIX Ultimedia services package.

Some of the neat stuff found on the server CD includes:

- The Adobe Acrobat reader.

- The Java development kit, runtime environment, and samples.

Figure 7–4   The AIX Welcome Center

- The AIX Ultimedia services package.
- The IBM internet Connection Server.

Yes, you can use the server Bonus Pack CD to set up your very own web server!

Bonus Pack Software Installation

Installing any of these packages is fairly straight-forward and simple. However, you may wish to review the chapter on installation if this sounds confusing.

1.   Insert the CD-ROM into your CD-ROM drive, and start SMIT as root.

2.   Select "Software Installation and Maintenance."

3.   Select "Install and Update Software."

4.   Select "Install and Update Software from all Available Software."

5.   Select the input media. (hint: use the "List" button.)

6. Press the "List" button next to after software to install and select which packages you want to install.

7. Click "OK" when you are ready.

What's on the CD?

Let's briefly describe a couple of the packages included.

JAVA

If you haven't heard of Java, then you probably also haven't heard about the OJ trial. In a nutshell, the developers of Java describe it as a "simple, object-oriented, distributed, interpreted, robust, secure, architecture neutral, portable, high-performance, multithreaded, and dynamic language. (I've seen some claims that it is also buzz-word compliant.) What does this mean? It's a neat new programming language whose objects will run on all major platforms, and is ideal for development of applets which can be loaded and run in a Java compliant browser such as the latest version of netscape. You can find more information by checking out http://java.sun.com/.

After you have installed the Java distribution package, take a look at the readme file in /usr/lpp/Java/README, and then try running the demo applets. (First you need to add /usr/lpp/Java/bin to your path. You can either do this in your .profile file, or type (in ksh):

```
export PATH=$PATH:/usr/lpp/Java/bin
```

Then change to the /usr/lpp/Java/demo directory and take a look at the files. You will see a number of subdirectories including: BouncingHeads and TicTac-Toe. To run my favorite, the bouncing heads demo do this: (Remember to set your path to include /usr/lpp/Java/bin!)

```
cd /usr/lpp/Java/Demo/BouncingHeads
appletviewer example1.html
```

Since the source code to each of these demos (*.java files) is included along with a Java interpreter, you can try your hand at creating your own Java applets!

Adobe Acrobat Reader

Another neat application is Adobe's Acrobat Reader. It is a program that displays audio, video, and multimedia images from scripted file type. The power of Adobe Acrobat is that any Adobe Portable Document Format (*.pdf) file can be viewed on any major platform, including Macintosh, Windows, DOS, and Unix.

For more information about Adobe Acrobat you may wish to take a look at their homepage on the internet: http://www.adobe.com/

To use Acrobat, after installing it from the bonus pack CD, type the following:

1.   cd /usr/Adobe/acrobat.

2.   Read any readme or information files such as AIX.CDE.README and INSTGUID.TXT

3.   type INSTALL and follow the directions.

Run the program by typing: /usr/lpp/AcroRead/bin/acroread.

AIX Ultimedia Services (UMS)

The AIX Ultimedia services include software and demonstrations that show off speech recognition, text to speech generation, and of course the usual multimedia presentation that we have all gotten used to.

After installing UMS, you can play with the different multimedia samples included. You can either use the CDE file manager to go into /usr/lpp/UMS/samples and start clicking on interesting files, or you can use the command line and type the following:

```
cd /usr/lpp/UMS/samples
/usr/lpp/UMS/bin/run_ums dtmedia_player
```

Now use the GUI interface to select and display interesting looking files.

If you have a sound card you can also play with the text to speach program. For example:

```
echo "Shall we play a game?" | /usr/lpp/UMS/Demos/tts/bin
```

AIX Connections Bring Them All Together

The AIX Desktop Connectivity Server (ADCS for short) gives you the ability to get more from your PCs by hooking them up to an AIX system. Have you noticed how many different kinds of computers there are in the offices these days?

Wouldn't it be nice to get them connected better and take advantage of AIX's power? ADCS will let you connect to many different kinds of PC operating systems and network software, such as the following:

- DOS
- OS/2
- NT
- Windows
- Macintosh AppleShare
- Novell NetWare
- SPX Clients
- SMB Compatible Servers

ADCS allows these remote systems to store their files on the AIX system server. Both systems may access the files with their own operating system commands. ADCS also allows multiple different systems to share printers and terminals.

You can customize the AIX Desktop Connectivity Server with the SMIT application so that makes it easy to set up. There's plenty of help from the InfoExplorer on-line publications system, and PostScript files. It comes with AIX 4.1.4 and later only if you select it with your order.

LSserver

The LSserver allows an AIX computer to provide file, print, terminal emulation, and other network services to client PCs running DOS, OS/2, NT, or Windows. It uses the ServerMessage Block (SMB) protocol and is compatible with IBM's LAN Server and Microsoft LAN Manager specifications for LAN servers. Other servers may participate on the same network using SMB-compatible software; for example, an IBM LAN Server.

MACserver

MACserver runs on AIX allowing it to act as a Macintosh AppleShare server host, providing file and print services to Macintosh client computers on an Ethernet network. It also manages network connections and user accounts.

NWserver

NWserver running on AIX allows it to provide file, print, and terminal emulation services to NetWare-compatible PCs. It also includes an SPX protocol stack to support SPX clients.

TNclient

TNclient provides access from AIX to NetWare-compatible and SMB-compatible servers for file and print services. TNclient allows AIX workstations to participate in LANs as well as behave as clients. PC file attributes are preserved when accessed by AIX users. TNclient also provides the capability to mount Netware volumes, LAN Manager shared resources, and LAN Server shared resources.

Additional References

AIX Desktop Connectivity Server LSserver User's Guide, SC23-1759

AIX Desktop Connectivity Server MACserver User's Guide, SC23-1760

AIX Desktop Connectivity Server NWserver User's Guide, SC23-1761

AIX Desktop Connectivity Server TNclient User's Guide, SC23-1762

NetBIOS for AIX: Administration Guide, SC23-2685

NetBIOS API Reference, SC23-2758

File Transfer, Remote Login

FTP and telnet are popular commands that are a part of TCP/IP. These are very commonly used on the Internet, so it's a good idea to learn them. This chapter is marked with a hot pepper because you'll be hot stuff when you've mastered it, but its almost a basic on the Internet.

FTP

The "ftp" and "tftp" commands (file transfer protocol) allow you to get and put files from your system to and from another system across the wire. This isn't like e-mail that adds a header for the To, From, Subject, and so on. This is like a file copy. With FTP you won't have to use "Sneaker-Net"! That's when you copy a file to a diskette, run it over to someone else's computer, and copy it in.

When you use the ftp command on a machine that you don't have a login or password to, often times it is set up for "anonymous ftp". You login with the name "anonymous" and use your full electronic mail address as the password.

Anonomous FTP is used commonly on the Internet to allow users to grab public files.

The ftp command puts you into a mode where you have limited commands into the remote file system. The following passage is an example of logging in, asking for help, getting the directory name, listing the files, and getting a file.*

---

*   The **bold** statements are book commentary and the other statements are from ftp.

First, start the file transfer program with remotehost:

```
$ ftp remotehost

Connected to remotehost.

220 remotehost FTP server (Version 4.1 Thu Jun 15 12:28:17 CDT
1995) read

Name (remotehost:carolynj):
```

If this is your login name, press enter, otherwise type in your login ID.

```
331 Password required for carolynj.

Password:
```

The password is invisible.

```
230 User carolynj logged in.
```

Now, get some help on available commands.

```
ftp> ?
```

Commands may be abbreviated. Commands are:

!	help	recv
$	image	reinitialize
account	lcd	remotehelp
append	local	rename
ascii	ls	reset
bell	macdef	restart
binary	mdelete	rhelp
block	mdir	rmdir
bye	mget	rstatus
carriage-control	mkdir	runique
case	mls	send
cd	mode	sendport
cdup	modtime	site
close	mount	size
copylocal	mput	status
cr	nmap	stream
delete	nlist	struct
debug	non-print	sunique
dir	ntrans	system
disconnect	open	telnet
ebcdic	prompt	tenex

exp_cmd	proxy	trace
file	put	type
form	pwd	user
get	quit	verbose
glob	quote	
hash	record	

Print working directory:

```
ftp> pwd
257 "/home/carolynj" is current directory.
```

List the files:

```
ftp> ls
200 PORT command successful.
150 Opening data connection for ..
.profile
.sh_history
fminit
.dt
.dtprofile
book
.Xauthority
226 Transfer complete.
```

Change the working directory to "book":

```
ftp> cd book
250 CWD command successful.
```

Now the important part, get the file "chapt5" from remotehost and it will be copied onto the working directory of localhost:

```
ftp> get chapt5
200 PORT command successful.
150 Opening data connection for chapt5 (7330 bytes).
226 Transfer complete.

ftp> quit
221 Goodbye.
$
```

In the session shown, we logged into the system called "remotehost". Then we asked for help by typing "?" at the ftp command line and it listed all the commands available in the FTP mode. We printed the working directory (pwd), listed the files there (ls), changed directories to the "book" directory, and then finally got the file named "chapt5". The file was sent across the wire to the local system and copied into the current directory. Then we quit the ftp session which logged us out.

That wasn't hard! The difficulty for some people is keeping a clear head about the local and remote hosts. The key is remembering the host you start from. We did a "get" from the remote host during the ftp session because we wanted to get it and copy it to the local host.

TFTP

The tftp command is more like other commands with parameters expected versus the ftp command which puts you into a logged in mode in the remote system. The default for the system is for the tftp command to be turned off for security reasons. To turn it back on, you or the system administrator should edit the /etc/inetd.conf file and take the comment (#) off the line that starts the tftp program as the root user. Then refresh the program with the command

```
refresh -s inetd
```

If we do the same function we just finished with ftp, but use tftp instead, it would look like the following to get help and then get the file:

```
        tftp -?
        usage: tftp {-r|-g|-o|-w|-p} <local file> <host> <for-
eign file> [netascii|image]
          tftp -g chapt5 remotehost /home/book/chapt5
```

Ping

The ping command refers to the sound a sonar makes. AIX will send a *ping* over to another system across the wires and wait for a response. That's how you can find out if the other system is up. Let's see if the system "austin.ibm.com" is up and running with tcp:

```
ping austin.ibm.com

PING austin.ibm.com: (129.35.208.96): 56 data bytes

64 bytes from 129.35.208.96: icmp_seq=0 ttl=255 time=0 ms

64 bytes from 129.35.208.96: icmp_seq=1 ttl=255 time=0 ms
```

(Enter Ctrl c to stop the pinging, or it will continue forever!)

```
- - - - austin.ibm.com PING Statistics - - - -
2 packets transmitted, 2 packets received, 0% packet loss
```

This shows that two "pings" were sent and two "responses" were sent back. The system is up and running.

Remote Login and Execution

There are three similiar commands to login to someone else's system:

- tn
- telnet
- rlogin

These commands are easy to use. Just type the command and the system name and you will be prompted for your user login name and password. Then you are on the remote system and can do most of the normal stuff. You will be using the environment set up on the remote system and it could be different than the one you are used to; you may also have limited directory access.

What if Casey has a really clever program set up on her system that you'd like to try out? You could install it on your system, but why not just use hers (if it's OK with her)? You will need a login and password on her machine and the exact name of her system.

Here comes a tricky part. If the program uses graphics or other fancy output, you'll need to set a couple things up. Let's use the remote host name "casey" in our example, and the local hostname of "me":

```
xhost +casey
tn casey
(login and password)
export DISPLAY=me:0.0
```

(Now invoke that clever program!)

The xhost command gives permission to allow casey to put stuff on this display (after all, we don't just allow anyone displaying who-knows-what on our display). Then we telnet'd into the casey remote system (and entered the remote login and password). The export DISPLAY command tells the remote system to display all output on the "me" system instead of on the "casey" system.

The application will execute on the "casey" system using Casey's files and memory. Your system will show the application on your display using some of your memory and resources.

You can execute totally on the remote system by telnetting in without the export DISPLAY command, but you will be limited to commands and applications that are not graphical in nature.

Other TCP/IP Commands

There are many useful TCP/IP commands. Read the appendix if you want more details on the following commands:

- rexec—remote execution of commands

   You can enter the command on your local system and have it totally run on the remote system, including the output.

- rsh—remote execution shell

   Similar to the rexec command but you get more of the shell with it.

- rcp—remote copy

   You can copy files to someone else's file system from your system.

- on—unauthenticated remote execution

   Uses NFS (network file system) to run commands on a remote system with the current environment passed on over.

- finger, f, rusers—query remote users

   This command displays information about people logged into remote systems.

- talk—carry on a conversation from the keyboard and screen

   Two people invoke this command and can have a computerized conversation back and forth.

- rwall—remote broadcast message

   Sends messages to all users on the remote system (remote worn all).

E-Mail

I Can Send Mail My-Way !

The AIX system offers several electronic mail (e-mail) programs that users may choose from. Like editors mail programs are a personal choice. Different strokes for different folks! The e-mail choices include the following:

MH (Mail Handler)

Berkeley Mail

Desktop Mail

There are additional mailer programs that are available in the public domain (not shipped in AIX), such as "elm," "pine," and "emacs," etc.

Some mailer programs have different (incompatible) mail storage systems. If you choose one, you can't always switch between one and the other and expect your mail to be converted.

There is a program that runs in the background, invisible to you, that waits for mail to come in. It's called "sendmail". When a mail message is received, sendmail appends the message to a long file, called the spool, in the directory /usr/spool/mail. There is one spool file for each user. When you invoke the mailer of your choice, it breaks up that long spool file into messages and allows you to act on each message separately.

Each mailer gives at least the basic operations on mail:

Create a new message and send it

View a message

Remove a message

Reply to the sender of a message

Forward a message to another user

List your messages

New users will probably like the desktop mail program the best. It's easy to learn and shows you all the prompts from menus. It has help screens and shows you the list of mail (your inbox) on the screen at all times. To invoke the desktop mailer, select the mail icon at the bottom of the desktop. (See the section on the Common Desktop Environment for more information.)

The MH mail handler concepts are used in the desktop mail program but it's a set of commands rather than menu screens. The common desktop mail application cannot be used interchangeably with MH shell commands. Advanced users like MH because it is so flexible and can be used with shell functions. Each action in MH is a shell command.

The Berkeley mail system is also pretty easy to use. There is one main command and several subcommands with help.

E-Mail Etiquette

Some general tips about e-mail will keep you from being unpopular. When you get a message and you're one of a long list on the "To" or "Cc" list, don't reply to the whole group unless you're sure that they all want to hear it, just reply to the sender. Pay attention to the folks on the mailing list.

If you are sending a message to a very long list of e-mail addresses, send to them as a "blind copy" or "Bcc:". It's not that you don't want them to know who's getting the message, the issue here is that the people receiving the message will tire of reading through all the e-mail names and addresses before getting to the meat of the message. It's a waste of time. You can let folks know who you're sending the message to by using "X-to:<comment>" such as

```
X-to: Screen-Team
```

Don't get into mail wars! That's when you pop off some terse snippy reply without cooling off first and then they reply back, and on and on. It's better to cool off, keep it professional, and just pick up the phone or drop by to talk about the problem. This is also known as a "flame".

Here's another tip. DON'T SHOUT. If you use all uppercase characters, it reads like you are shouting!

What's the Address?

When you send electronic mail you need to pay attention to the address. The Internet follows a convention for addresses across the world. Reading left to right, the address starts specific and becomes more general, kind of like name, street, town, state. Typically used addresses have "com" for commercial companies, "gov" for government, "edu" for educational institutes, and so on.

The address of bozo@austin.ibm.com goes to a commercial company "com", IBM, in Austin, to the user bozo. Mail will be delivered to "bozo" "at" Austin IBM.

There are other address forms that aren't as common that use a different format. The safest way to get mail there is to get the exact address you are sending to or to reply to a message from them!

Another address type, a Universal Resource Locator (URL), is used for an Internet browser to bring up World Wide Web home pages. These addresses use the location part of the e-mail address with the directory name and a protocol type attached; for example

```
http://www.ibm.net/inter.html
```

The http stands for hypertext transfer protocol. "www.ibm.net" is the address of a computer, and then a sometimes optional directory name and/or file name follows. In this case, "inter.html" is the file name.

Berkeley Mail

Bring up the Berkeley mail program with the command "mail". You'll then be inside the mail program and have its sub-commands to use until you "quit" and go back to the AIX command line. The mail prompt is a question mark (?). The AIX commands may be used while you're inside the mail program if you precede the AIX command with an exclamation point (!).

The mail is received into a mail spool file, one for each user in /usr/spool/ mail/<user> . The Berkeley mail program leaves the mail in the spool and acts on it there.

This is what the Berkeley mail program looks like with two messages queued:

```
> mail
Mail [5.2 UCB] [AIX 4.1] Type ? for help.
"/var/spool/mail/carolynj": 2 message
> 1 carolynj Sat Sep 16 16:11 32/806 "hello, it's me"
> 2 carolynj Sat Sep 16 16:11 34/808 "2nd message"
```

Ask for a list of the mail commands by entering a "?" or "help" and you'll get the following displayed:

- Control Commands:

q	Quit—apply mailbox commands entered this session
x	Quit—restore mailbox to original state
! <cmd>	Start a shell, run <cmd>, and return to mailbox
cd [<dir>]	Change directory to <dir> or $HOME

- Display Commands:

t [<msg_list>]	Display messages in <msg_list> or current message
n	Display next message
f [<msg_list>]	Display headings of messages
h [<num>]	Display headings of group containing message <num>

- Message Handling:

e [<num>]	Edit message <num> (default editor is ex)
d [<msg_list>]	Delete messages in <msg_list> or current message

`u [<msg_list>]`	Recall deleted messages
`s [<msg_list>] <file>`	Append messages (with headings) to <file>
`w [<msg_list>] <file>`	Append messages (text only) to <file>
`pre [<msg_list>]`	Keep messages in system mailbox

- Creating New Mail:

`m <addrlist>`	Create/send new message to addresses in <addrlist>
`r [<msg_list>]`	Send reply to senders and recipients of messages
`R [<msg_list>]`	Send reply only to senders of messages
`a`	Display list of aliases and their addresses

MH (Mail Handler)

The Mail Handler (MH) is a set of commands you use from the command line. For experienced command line users, the MH commands can be very powerful when combined with other AIX commands.

MH Startup.   The first thing to do is an "inc" to incorporate the mail messages from the spool in /usr/spool/mail/<user> (where <user> is your login name) to your local mail directories. The directory "Mail" in your home directory will contain an "inbox" directory where each new mail message will be kept as a separate file.

You may "refile" messages into as many different folders (directories) as you want. If this is the first time, it will ask you whether you want to set MH up now; answer "yes". It will copy a hidden profile (.mh_profile) and create the directories needed into your home directory. It will show you a list of mail message headers: the message number, the date, sender, and subject:

```
inc
Create folder "/home/carolynj/Mail/inbox" <yes/no>? y
Incorporating new mail into inbox...
   1+ 09/16 carolynj@austin 1st message << Hello, It's me !
   2+ 09/23 carolynj@austin Meeting Notice <<Project Status
```

Message Identifiers.   The message identification number is used extensively with the MH commands. One of the messages is kept as the "current" one which is the default. The message number is used as the file name when the messages

are stored. Message number ranges may be used to perform one action on multiple messages. That's handy for junk mail! For example, you can refile messages
in the range 3 to 11 in the mail folder named "followup". You can also remove
messages 45 through 53 with one command.

```
refile 3-11 +followup
rmm 45-53
```

Folders.   You can set up folders for each topic you get mail on and want to keep
for your records. Then you can scan a specific folder and get a list of messages in
that folder, refile into it, forward from it, remove mail or any of the regular actions. You designate the folder name with a plus "+":

```
scan +action
30 09/29 ceb@AUSVM6.AUSTIN ART files needed <<FROM THE DE
31 09/28 trent@austin.ibm.co Re: prototype ready (forw)
```

```
refile 31 +followup
folder +fyi
fyi+ has 201 messages (4269-5496); cur=5316; (others).
```

This scans the folder named "action" and displays a list of stored messages, then
files message number 31 from the "action" folder to the "followup" folder. Then
we changed folders to the "fyi" folder. The "fyi" folder has 201 messages wait-
ing, from message number 4269 to number 5496 with the current message being
number 5316. Looks like there's a lot of mail stacking up!

MH Commands.   These MH commands are the most frequently used:

inc	Incorporate from the spool into the local mail
scan	Scan the mail messages and show a list of them
show	Show a message contents
forw	Forward a message on to another
rmm	Remove mail message
next	Show the next message
prev	Show the previous message
refile	Refile message from the inbox into a different folder

comp   Compose a new message to send

folder   Show a summary status of the current folder; can also change folders with this command

folders   Show a list of mail folders

You can use these commands on the inbox, or on one of the mail folders. This lets you get a list of new or old messages and show, forward, or remove, the messages there.

The "comp" command allows you to compose a new message. It prompts for the mailing address with "To:", carbon copy (no real carbons with electronic mail these days !) with "Cc:", file copy with "Fcc:", the message subject with "Subject:", and then you can type in your message body. Whether all these prompts are displayed is determined by each user's customization. When you are finished, type <Ctrl> <d> (hold down the <Ctrl> key and then press the "&" key). It will ask, "What now?" If you need help, type "?" and you'll get the following:

```
What now? ?
Options are:
display [<switches>]
edit [<editor> <switches>]
list [<switches>]
push [<switches>]
quit [-delete]
refile [<switches>] +folder
send [<switches>]
whom [<switches>]
```

You can get help with each of the commands by adding "-help" to the command. It will show you the options available for that command.

Advanced MH Commands. There are over thirty more commands for the advanced user. You can pack the messages into a single file. You can set up digests and bulletin boards. You can also write shell scripts and use AIX commands on these mail messages with MH commands. This is due to the MH design where messages are stored as separate files and each of the MH actions are separate commands. This is especially useful for people that get huge amounts of mail.

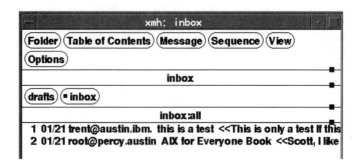

Figure 7–5   Sample XMH Screen

Here are some ideas for MH users with gobs of mail:

```
scan | fgrep -i meeting        Look for all meetings
scan | sort +2                 Sort messages by sender
```

 Removed messages aren't really erased; they are renamed to the same file name but preceded with a comma ",". New messages you send are kept in a file named "draft" or in a folder (if you create it) named "drafts".

XMH.   XMH is a sample program that is an X-Windows user interface to the MH mail system (see Figure 7–5). It has the same terminology and functionality but instead of AIX commands, it uses menus with point and click. It looks a lot like the Common Desktop Mail application. Menu selections are shown as buttons at the top of the screen. The body of the window shows the folders as buttons and then the list of mail messages.

Common Desktop Mail

The Common Desktop Mail Manager uses the same terminology as MH and is integrated into the Common Desktop Environment (see Figure 7–6). Invoke it by selecting the Mail icon from the control panel. Some of the underlying directory structure is different. It uses the "mbox" directory and a different profile file. The menu selections are available as buttons. The body of the window contains a list of mail messages and then the contents of the current message. See the CDE. chapter for more information.

Distributed File Systems

Copying files using ftp and tftp is really nice, but it sure would be nice if the operating system would take care of that for you! That's what distributed file

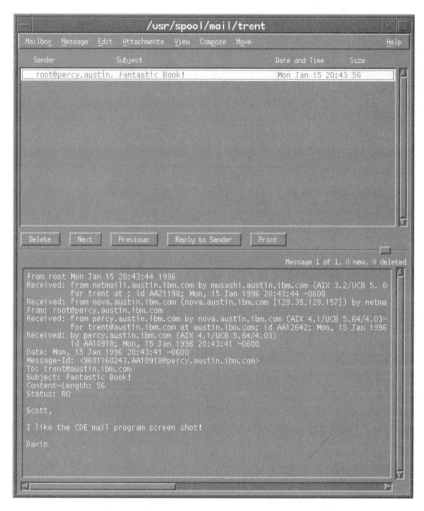

Figure 7-6 CDE Mail Manager Sample Screen

systems do. You tell the operating system that the files are really across the network, but they look like they are on the computer in your office! Not just you, but all your coworkers can share files this way.

So if you get organized, you can set up one computer system with a lot of hard file storage; that's your "server," sometimes also called a "host." Everyone in the office can use the files on the servers from their local systems, the "clients" (sometimes also called a "slave"). There are a couple different types of distributed file systems available in the industry and on AIX. RS/6000 systems with AIX make great servers and clients!

Network File System (NFS)

Originally developed by Sun Microsystems, NFS has become a defacto networking standard. NFS is independent of hardware, operating systems, and network architectures. So you can share files with coworkers that have computers from many different companies using various network wiring. This independence was achieved through the use of two sets of protocols:

- Remote procedure call (RPC) protocols
- Data standardizing External Data Representation (XDR) protocols

In addition to the RPC and XDR, NFS uses the TCP/IP protocol to implement data transmission. NFS requires TCP/IP to be installed, configured, and operational. The NFS facility can be started upon request or simply configured to start up when the operating system is booted.

NFS has Daemons!   NFS functions are controlled by a set of daemons. The master daemon associated with NFS is called inetd. inetd is not just for NFS but is also the master for other daemons on the system. It essentially triggers the startup of the following daemons when/if needed:

- portmapd
- mountd
- nfsd
- pcnfsd
- biod

The biod daemon is required to run on all of the machines that are serving as NFS clients. The pcnfsd daemon is needed on the server machine only if a PC's files are mounted. The rest of the daemons run on the server machine.

File Permissions.   NFS also supports access control lists (ACL). ACLs are used with the read/write/execute permission structures that are part of the UNIX operating systems. That's because there are so many systems, there could be users named "carolyn" on more than one. I don't want her looking at my files just because we share the same name!

Mapped Files.   Mapped files are also supported under NFS running AIX. This feature allows programs on clients to be accessed as if they were in real memory instead of on disk storage. That makes them much faster to access! You have to write a program to use the shmat system call, and that maps areas of a file into memory address space.

Secure NFS.   Secure NFS is also implemented under AIX in addition to the standard UNIX authentication. NFS uses the Data Encryption Standard (DES) and public key cryptography to authenticate users and machines in networks. A DES key is generated from two components: a public key published for general availability and a private key used to encrypt and decrypt data.

Locking Keeps Things Straight.   The NFS-compatible Network Lock Manager supports file and record locking over the network (records are rows of the file). The network lock manager contains both the client and server functions. The status monitor performs *health-check* duties and keeps a record of relevant failures at the client and the server end. This is a list of frequently used NFS commands:

Command	Description
exportfs	Exports and unexports directories to NFS clients
mount	Makes a file system available for use
nfsstat	Displays statistics pertaining to the ability of client/ server to receive calls
on	Executes commands on remote systems
rusers	Displays a list of users currently logged in on remote machines
rup	Displays status of a remote host
rpcinfo	Reports the status of RPC servers
rpcgen	Generates C code to implement an RPC protocol
rwall	Sends message to all users on the network
showmount	Displays a list of all clients that have remotely mounted a file system spray; sends a specific number of packets to a host to report performance statistics.

High Availability for Network File System (HANFS)—It's Done with Mirrors

Let's face it, hardware wears out sometimes and systems have occasional problems. HANFS makes sure that your data will be safe in spite of Murphy's Law.

HANFS is an extension to NFS that supports higher availability of data than that provided by a standard NFS configuration. The main feature of HANFS is improved availability of servers through disk impersonation. Data availability is optimized through an option to mirror disks. It can survive planned outages and failures of the operating system, system planar, adapters, and internal and external disks.

In addition to the NFS daemons, HANFS requires three additional daemons to facilitate configuration and reconfiguration of the system and of Object Data Manager (ODM) databases. The additional daemons are hanfsd, hacfgd, and hapngd.

It takes some extra hardware to use mirrors! Hardware required by HANFS includes a backup server with multiple shared volume groups with external disks that are individually connected to a disk adapter of the server on one end and to the backup machine on the other. HANFS requires that both the server and its backup must be POWERstation or POWERserver computers. There is a redundant set of network adapters, also. The server and backup use four network adapters: one each for normal operations, the third to impersonate the server by the backup in case of server failure, and the fourth to impersonate the backup by the server in case of backup failure. Whew! That should cover a really unlucky day!

Network Information Service (NIS)—The Old Yellow Pages

NIS is a centralized database service that offers centralized control of networked machines. NIS was formerly known as "Yellow Pages" (YP). Rather than having to manage each host's files (for example /etc/hosts, /etc/passwd, and /etc/group), system administrators maintain one database for each file on one central server. Machines that are using NIS retrieve information as needed from these databases.

NIS consists of clients and servers, logically grouped together in domains using maps (databases) that provide information such as host names or passwords. An NIS slave is a client that uses the maps to share information.

NIS reduces the effort of maintaining repetitive databases of information. It also helps users by making their password, directories, and files available on other systems. Network administration becomes easier and less time consuming.

Typical information stored in an NIS database includes password files and host files whose contents are essentially the same for different nodes on a single network.

The following is a list of frequently used NIS commands:

Commands	Description
domainname	Lists the name of the current NIS domain system for a NIS host
makedbm	Creates the NIS database maps
ypbind	Enables a client process to connect to a server
ypcat	Lists the contents of NIS maps
ypinit	Builds and installs NIS maps on an NIS server
ypmatch	Displays the values of one or more keys within an NIS map
yppasswd	Allows users to change NIS passwords from any NIS host
yppoll	Identifies the version of a NIS map on the NIS server
yppush	Forces propagation of updated NIS maps from the master server to slave servers
ypserv	Looks up information in the local NIS databases
ypset	Points the ypbind process to a specific server
ypwhich	Identifies which machine is the NIS server of an NIS client
ypxfr	Transfers an NIS map from an NIS server to a local host

Andrew File System

The distributed Andrew file system (AFS) machines allows users to access information stored anywhere on a network. The AFS file system uses a client/server model—file server machines store data and transfer it to client machines.

AFS uses a hierarchical file structure—a tree with */afs* as the root. The next level of directories consist of *cells*. Cells are subtrees of the AFS file space and consist of related directories and files. The cell controlling a specific user workstation is termed a local cell; other cells in the AFS file space are termed foreign cells. The directories and files under */afs* make up the AFS *file space*.

AFS client machines use a Cache Manager to access information stored in the AFS file space. When a user accesses a file, the Cache Manager stores the file as a copy on the client workstation's local disk. This enables the client to use the local copy of the cached file rather than continuously sending network requests to the file server machines for data. When the file closes, the Cache Manager sends the changed file back to the appropriate file server, and the changed version replaces the file stored on the server.

Because AFS is a distributed file system, several security techniques are used to protect the many users: passwords, mutual authentication, and access control lists (ACLs). ACLs allow individual users to restrict access to their own directories. Each ACL entry has two parts: a user or group name and the access control rights. Access control rights include:

r   read

l   lookup

i   insert

d   delete

w   write

k   lock

a   administer

For example,

```
fs setacl . jenny rl
```

would give Jenny read and lookup permission only on the current directory.

Frequently used AFS commands follow:

Command	Description
fs listacl	Lists a directory's ACL
fs setacl	Sets one directory's ACL
fs setacl -dir	Sets multiple directories' ACLs
fs copyacl	Copies a directory's ACL to one or more other directories
kpasswd	Changes AFS password
fs whereis	Lists the file server housing a file or directory
fs checkservers	Checks the status of file servers
klog	Authenticates with Server to obtain tokens
tokens	Displays all tokens
pts	Sets up and lists group membership

You can get help for each of the commands by typing the command and then "help". This will give you a list of all the parameters for that command with a description. You can get help on the syntax for the command and parameter by entering the command, the parameter, and then "-help"; for example,

```
$ fs sa -help
```

```
Usage: fs sa -dir <directory>+ -acl <access list entries>+
[-clear ] [-negative ] [-id ] [-if ] [-help ]
```

CHAPTER
8

- System Management Interface Tool (SMIT)

- Distributed System Management (or Why Just Worry About One Machine When You Can Multitask?!)

- Visual System Manager

- Backup—and Make Restore an Option!

SMIT Happens! Administering AIX

N o, it's not a misspelling! AIX Version 4.1 system administration has a suite of system management tools, including the System Management Interface Tool (SMIT), a menu-driven system management tool. DSMIT, Distributed SMIT, is available for distributed environments. AIX also includes Visual System Management (VSM), an object-oriented, drag-and-drop graphical interface for managing devices, printers, storage, users, and lots of other system management tasks. We'll review some system backup and restore commands you can use at the command line to impress your friends and boss—we don't want this to look too easy!

Read through this chapter to find out about these topics:

- System Management Interface Tool (SMIT)

- Distributed System Management Interface Tool (DSMIT)

- Visual System Manager (VSM)

- Backup and restore

To get started, boot the operating system. (*Boot*?! Computer terminology for *turn the system on*.) During the boot process, the system tests the hardware, loads and executes the operating system, and configures devices. The system finds all information necessary to the boot process on its disk drive.

When the system is first installed, the bosboot command creates a boot image from a RAM (random access memory) disk file system image and the operating system kernel. The boot image is transferred to a particular media such as the hard disk. When the machine is rebooted, the boot image is loaded from the media into memory.

To shut down your system, type "shutdown" and press the Enter key. The system shuts down; the system waits one minute before stopping the user processes and the init process. There are several reasons for shutting down the system:

- After installing new software or changing the configuration for existing software

- When a hardware problem exists

- When the system is hung

- When system performance is degraded (slow)

- When the file system is possibly corrupt

System Management Interface Tool (SMIT)

SMIT is a tool for managing the system that presents a natural-language, task-oriented interface, enabling you to quickly perform tasks that might otherwise require MANY typed commands.

SMIT steps you through adding a user or mounting a file system (only two of many tasks) with the use of menus, selectors, and dialogs. What does this mean to you? You don't have to remember the details of complex command syntax, valid parameter values, and system command spelling. Because you might need help remembering how you added a user yesterday, SMIT creates log files that you can use to duplicate work you did yesterday or to learn how to use specific commands. SMIT help is available on each menu and field label. "Using SMIT" on the main menu discusses how to use the interface and some of the features.

Note that for most system management SMIT tasks, you must have root authority. Use SMIT for the following reasons:

- Reduce need for memorization and need for documentation

- Make system administration easy to learn

- Structure your decision-making process

- Shorten training for novice system administrators:

  Use the F6 function key and command output window to see the commands you built while completing a SMIT task

  Use the F8 function key to capture SMIT screens in your smit.log

- Reduce keystrokes (and typing errors!)

- Review the smit.log file in your home directory and identify:

  Menu paths taken to complete SMIT tasks

  Fast paths

  Command output needed to complete a SMIT task from the command line

- Access Help!

But Why Should I Care About SMIT?

You should care about SMIT, because SMIT enables you to configure and administer AIX like a pro. Consider the following options:

- Software Installation & Maintenance

  Use this option to install products fixes, list installed software, and verify your software installation.

- Devices

  Use this option to add, move, change, remove, configure, and trace devices (for example, printers, CD-ROM drives, and tape drives).

- Physical & Logical Storage

  Use this option to mount and unmount file systems as well as to backup and restore file systems; add and/or activate paging space; and manage your physical and logical volumes.

- Security & Users

  Use this option to add, remove, list, and change users and groups and to assign passwords to users.

- Communications Applications and Services

  Use this option to configure TCP/IP and NFS.

- Spooler (Print Jobs)

  Use this option to start, cancel, and prioritize print jobs; to manage print queues; and to manage local and remote printer subsystems.

- Problem Determination

  Use this option to generate error reports, manage dump devices, run hardware diagnostics, and validate software.

- Performance & Resource Scheduling

  Use this option to set system run level, report system activity, and to list and schedule jobs.

- System Environments

    Use this option to stop the system, set the date and time, broadcast messages, and to change the language environment.

- Processes & Subsystems

    Use this option to show or remove processes and to query, start, stop, and trace subsystems and subservers.

- Using SMIT (information only)

    Use this option for help on the SMIT windows and features.

How to Get SMIT Up and Running

To start up GUI SMIT, enter "smit" on the command line. Your output will look like the screen shown in Figure 8–1.

To start up ASCII SMIT, enter "smitty" or "smit -C" on the command line. Your output will look like the screen shown in Figure 8–2.

When you are using the ASCII version of SMIT, the valid functions are displayed at the bottom of the screen. Only those functions that are valid for the specific menu, selector, or dialog are displayed. Table 8–1 describes all functions in SMIT. If you use a key sequence (Esc+*Number*), press and release the Esc key, then immediately press the number key.

Use SMIT to Add a Tape Drive

You can use SMIT to add a tape drive. We're going to add the tape drive using ASCII SMIT. Begin by logging in as root, enter "smitty," then click on Devices. Your output will look like the screen in Figure 8–3.

Scroll down to Tape Drive on the Devices menu. Select Tape Drive. The Tape Drive menu pops up (Figure 8–4).

We want to add a tape drive, so scroll down to Add a Tape Drive and select the highlighted function. When you select Add a Tape Drive, you'll see the menu shown in Figure 8–5.

This menu shows the tape drive configured with your system. Which of these tape drives do you have attached to your system? I have physically attached (and powered on) a 5GB tape drive, so I'll select that option. Once I've selected that option, SMIT asks me to give it some more information (indicated by the + to the right of some of the fields). Once you've done this, hit Enter.

```
 ──     System Management Interface Tool

 Exit  Edit  Show

 Return To:




 System Management

  │ │ Software Installation & Maintenance
  │ │ Devices
  │ │ Physical & Logical Storage
  │ │ Security & Users
  │ │ Diskless Workstation Management & Installation
  │ │ Communications Applications and Services
  │ │ Spooler (Print Jobs)
  │ │ Problem Determination
  │ │ Performance & Resource Scheduling
  │ │ System Environments
  │ │ Processes & Subsystems
  │ │ Applications
  │ │ Using SMIT (information only)
```

Figure 8–1   GUI SMIT Startup Screen

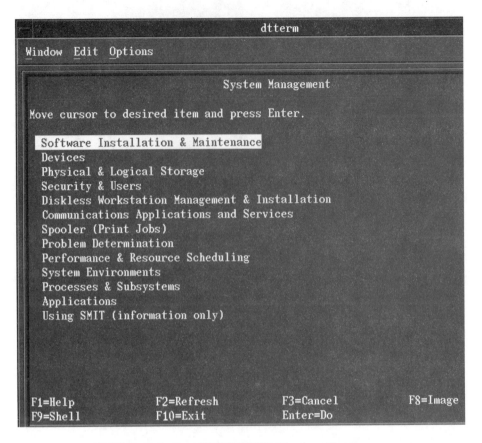

Figure 8–2   ASCII SMIT Startup Screen

The OK following "Command" indicates that you have successfully added the tape drive. Congratulations! You have completed your first of many SMIT tasks.

What are All of Those Weird Symbols on the Screen?

Oh right, I forgot to tell you about those. Table 8–2 will help you figure them out.

What Do I Do If I Need More SMIT Help?

For a general overview of how to use SMIT, select the Using SMIT option (in either ASCII or GUI) to access the following information:

- Overview

- Understanding the Menu Window

- Understanding the Dialog Window

- Understanding the Path Window

- Understanding the Command Output Panel

Table 8–1   Functions in SMIT

Function Key	Command	Description
F1 or Esc+1	Help	Gives more information on the topic to which the cursor points.
F2 or Esc+2	Refresh	Redraws the screen. Use if console messages over-write the screen.
F3 or Esc+3	Cancel	Returns to the previous screen. F3 in the main menu exits SMIT.
F4 or Esc+4	List	Presents a list of choices for the highlighted entry field. A pop-up selector screen displays a scrollable list of choices.
F5 or Esc+5	Reset	Resets the entry field to the original setting.
F6 or Esc+6	Command	Displays the command that SMIT is building.
F7 or Esc+7	Edit	Presents the highlighted text-entry field in a wide, pop-up selector screen for editing.
	Also: Select	Makes individual selections on multiselect lists.
F8 or Esc+8	Image	Displays the *FastPath* parameter for the current menu or dialog screen. Also saves a screen image in the smit.log file so that you can print it later.
F9 or Esc+9	Shell	Escapes to a shell. A confirmation pop-up menu or message is displayed.
F10 or Esc+0	Exit	Exits SMIT.
Enter	Do	Executes the command built by SMIT or commits list entries to a dialog.

- Making Selections from a List of Choices
- Using SMIT Functions
- Using SMIT Fastpath
- Related Information in InfoExplorer

Distributed System Management (or Why Just Worry About One Machine When You Can Multitask?!)

The Distributed System Management Interface Tool (DSMIT) adds functionality to SMIT by enabling the SMIT interface to build commands for system manage-ment and distribute them to other clients on a network. DSMIT has most of the functionality of the SMIT program, such as fast paths, log files, and flags.

DSMIT works in a Client/Server model. One RS/6000 running AIX 4.1 must be defined as a DSMIT Server machine. This machine will be the single point to per-

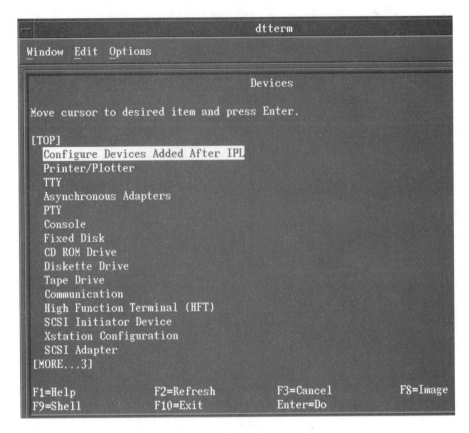

Figure 8–3   Select Devices Screen

form all the systems management tasks, sending commands over the network to DSMIT Client machines. These client machines could be RS/6000, Sun, or Hewlett-Packard workstations. A heterogeneous DSMIT environment would look like that shown in Figure 8–6.

DSMIT runs in both concurrent and sequential modes. Concurrent mode means that the DSMIT server builds a command and routes it to the clients simultaneously. Sequential mode means that the DSMIT server builds a command and routes it to the clients one machine at a time. After you build a command on the server and press the Enter key, a menu appears asking in which mode you wish to run DSMIT.

Start DSMIT by entering the dsmit command for the ASCII interface or mdsmit for the GUI interface at the command line. When you start the DSMIT program, you must define the working collective of clients. DSMIT provides a simple

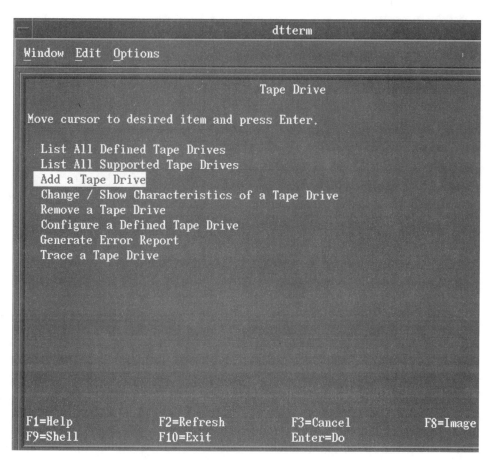

Figure 8–4 SMIT Tape Drive Menu

mechanism for exiting. The function keys enable you to exit a particular screen or to stop DSMIT when you complete a task.

DSMIT allows you to change a domain. You can add a new client to the domain, delete a client from the domain, or redefine the domain's member list entirely. Use the chdsmitd command or the interface to change a domain. When you use the interface, you can view the domain and any changes you are making to them. The Manage Domains of Machines menu provides options to assist in altering domains.

Defining clients for the Distributed System Management Interface Tool (DSMIT) program enables clients to run commands built by the DSMIT server. To define a

```
 ─                          dtterm

Window  Edit  Options

                          Tape Drive

Move cursor to desired item and press Enter.
lqqqqqqqqqqqqqqqqqqqqqqqqqqqqqqqqqqqqqqqqqqqqqqqqqqqqqqqqqq
 x                     Tape Drive Type
 x
 x Move cursor to desired item and press Enter.
 x
 x     1200mb-c scsi 1.2 GB 1/4-Inch Tape Drive
 x     150mb    scsi 150 MB 1/4-Inch Tape Drive
 x     3490e    scsi 3490E Autoloading Tape Drive
 .x    4mm2gb   scsi 2.0 GB 4mm Tape Drive
 x     4mm4gb   scsi 4.0 GB 4mm Tape Drive
 x     525mb    scsi 525 MB 1/4-Inch Tape Drive
 x     8mm      scsi 2.3 GB 8mm Tape Drive
 x     8mm5gb   scsi 5.0 GB 8mm Tape Drive
 x     8mm7gb   scsi 7.0 GB 8mm Tape Drive
 x     9trk     scsi 1/2-inch 9-Track Tape Drive
 x     ost      scsi Other SCSI Tape Drive
 x
 x F1=Help            F2=Refresh            F3=Cancel
 x F8=Image           F10=Exit              Enter=Do
F1x /=Find            n=Find Next
```

Figure 8–5   SMIT Tape Drive Information Menu

client, you must add it to the /usr/share/DSMIT/hosts file by editing the file directly or with the DSMIT interface.

The working collective specifies the current list of clients that receive commands built by the Distributed System Management Interface Tool (DSMIT) program. The working collective is a temporary list of clients and must be respecified with each new DSMIT session. By default, the server is the only machine in the working collective when you start DSMIT. For more information on DSMIT, see *Distributed SMIT 2.2 for AIX: Guide and Reference*, SC23-2667.

Visual System Manager

Visual System Manager (VSM) is a graphical interface that enables you to perform system management tasks through direct manipulation of icons. Most of the tasks performed in VSM consist of drag-and-drop actions.

Table 8–2   Symbols

Symbol	Symbol Name	Meaning
*	Asterisk	An entry is required. Appears to the left of the field name or prompt.
#	Number sign	Enter a number.
X	The letter X	Enter a hexadecimal number.
/	Slash	Enter a file name.
+	List of options or Option ring	Displays a list of current, available choices generated by the system. To view list, press the List key (F4 or Esc+4). An option ring offers a fixed set of options, such as Yes or No. Press the Tab key to display ring options individually in the entry field.
[ ]	Brackets	Beginning and end of an editable field.
<	Less than sign	More text to the left of the visible field.
>	Greater than sign	More text to the right of the visible field.

Figure 8–6   DSMIT Environment

Figure 8–7   Creating a User

For example, to add a user, click on the Users and Groups Manager found in the Application Manager. Drag the New User icon onto the Users Work Area. You will be asked for the User Name, as shown in Figure 8–7.

After selecting OK, casey will be added to the list of users and is now enabled for login. To add casey to a user group, drag the casey user icon to the Groups Work Area and drop the icon on the appropriate group. Even better, when you want to delete one of your back-stabbing cohorts, just drag their user icon into the Trash Can—feel better?

You can access VSM through the Application Manager (on the right hand side of the desktop—the icon with the pens and calculator). Double-click on Application Manager, click on System_Admin, then select one of the following:

- Users and Groups Manager
- Storage Manager
- Device Manager
- Print Manager
- Applications to support software installation and maintenance

How Does VSM Help Me Manage My System?

VSM enables you to perform installation and system management tasks through direct manipulation of objects (icons). With VSM you no longer need to remember complex command syntax, or search through SMIT menus to complete a task. For instance, deleting a user is as simple as dragging and dropping the User object onto the Trash Can.

This easy-to-use interface openly displays system objects and actions (tasks). In addition to basic tasks, you can create new objects from system or user-defined templates, sort, filter, and find objects, and display the objects in a variety of views.

VSM applications include the following:

- Device Manager

  Use to define and change devices attached to the system.

- Print Manager

  Use to define and change the print queues and printers on your system and manipulate the jobs in those queues.

- Storage Manager

  Use to define and manipulate the volume groups, physical volumes, logical volumes, and file systems.

- Users and Groups Manager

  Use to define and change the users of the system.

- Install and Update Software Manager

  Use this installation GUI to support easy and custom installations.

- Maintain Installed Software Manager

  Use to manage software that has already been installed.

VSM Application Common Interface Design

The VSM application user interfaces are similar in design. Each application has a template area, actions area, work area, and information area. The illustration in Figure 8–8 defines the roles of each area and how they interact with each other.

How Do I Start VSM?

Use the following options to start VSM applications:

- From the Command Line

  Device Manager `xdevicem`

  Print Manager `xprintm`

  Storage Manager `xlvm`

  Users & Groups Manager `xuserm`

  Easy Install `xinstallm -ez`

  Install/Update Software Manager `xinstallm`

  Install Assistant `install_assist`

  Maintain Installed Software `xmaintm`

Template Area
Contains type buttons and templates for creating new objects. Design your own templates or use the defaults.

Action Area
Contains objects representing the commands necessary to complete a task.

Work Area
Contains system objects, view and display controls, and a trash can.

Information Area
Displays context-sensitive help based on the cursor position.

Buttons
Perform various application window functions.

Figure 8–8 VSM Common Interface Design (Copied with Permission from IBM)

- From AIXwindows Desktop

  From the Front Panel, select the Application Manager. Within Application Manager, select the System_Admin directory. Within System_Admin, select the desired application icon.

More Details on VSM Applications

Device Manager.   Device Manager provides an easy way to manage the many devices supported by AIX. The Device Manager enables you to access the Object Data Manager (ODM) database, define new devices, configure and unconfigure devices, show/change characteristics of devices, and delete a device. The Device Manager interface looks like the screen in Figure 8–9.

Print Manager.   Print Manager enables you to access the print queues; add new printers and queues; show/change characteristics of printers and queues; en-

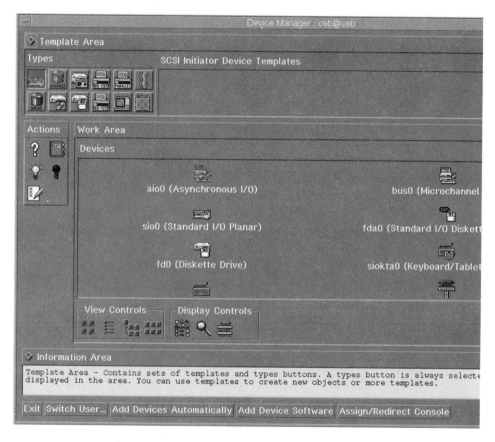

Figure 8–9   Device Manager User Interface

able/disable printers and queues; set printer policy for a queue, delete printers, queues or print job (Figure 8–10).

Storage Manager.   Storage Manager enables you (among others tasks) to create new file systems, logical volumes, and volume groups; to show/change characteristics of file systems, logical volumes, and volume groups; enable or disable objects for use; backup and restore file systems or the entire system; synchronize a file system; and delete a file system, logical volume, or volume group. The Storage Manager user interface is depicted in Figure 8–11.

Users and Groups Manager.   The Users and Groups Manager lets you create users and groups; show/change characteristics of users and groups; enable and

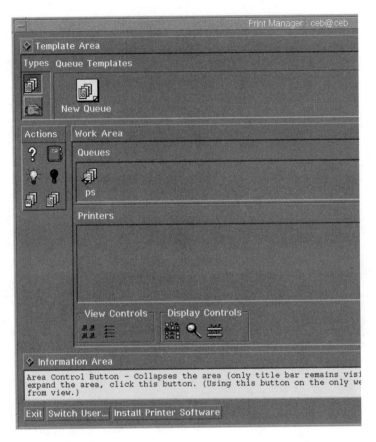

Figure 8–10   Print Manager User Interface

disable users for login; change the password for a user; and delete users and groups. Figure 8–12 depicts the Users and Groups user interface.

Install and Update Software Manager.   The Install and Update Software Manager enables users to understand the relationship between licensed products, installable filesets, maintenance levels, enhancements, and fixes. Use the Install Update Software Manager to install or update software packages; set default install settings; preview size/options required for install packages (prerequisites); copy install images for use in future installs; and create new installation bundles. Figure 8–13 shows the Install and Update Software Manager user interface.

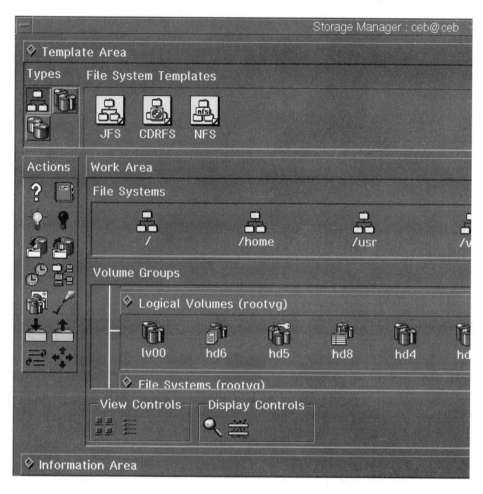

Figure 8-11   Storage Manager User Interface

Maintain Installed Software Manager.   The Maintain Installed Software Manager allows users to manage software that has already been installed. Users can select objects from the Products list and commit the selected software, reject the selected software, cleanup installed software, and verify that the selected software is complete. The Maintain Installed Software Manager user interface is shown in Figure 8–14.

How Do I Get Help in VSM?

To access help in the interface, use the Information Area, VSM Online Help System, Item Help Action, and/or the Help Buttons in the dialog and message windows (see Figures 8–15 and 8–16).

Figure 8–12   Users and Groups Manager User Interface

Selecting the Help button in the lower left corner of the User's and Groups Manager opens the application's Online Help System at the home topic (start of the topic hierarchy). (Note that the Help button is located in the same place for all of the Visual System Manager applications.) The home topic provides link paths to all of the help for the application, explaining the various areas and objects, as well as how to complete a dialog, or use the mouse.

Dropping the Item Help (?) action on a target opens an Online Help System window, which takes you directly to the help for that target (Figure 8–17).

The ? button in a dialog opens a help window that provides context-sensitive help on dialog fields and the buttons at the bottom of the dialog window. The displayed help information is based on the cursor position. The Help button opens the Online Help System window displaying the help topic for dialog windows. The Help button in a message window provides more information about the message.

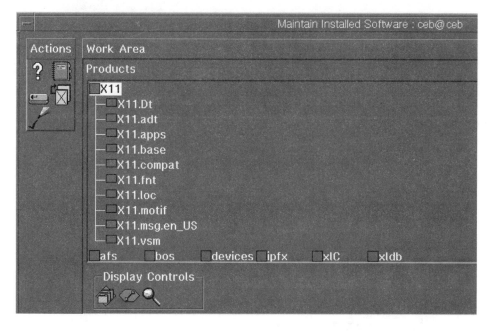

Figure 8–13 Install and Update Software Manager User
Interface

Figure 8–14 Maintain Installed Software Manager User
Interface

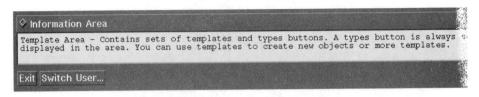

Figure 8–15   VSM Information Area

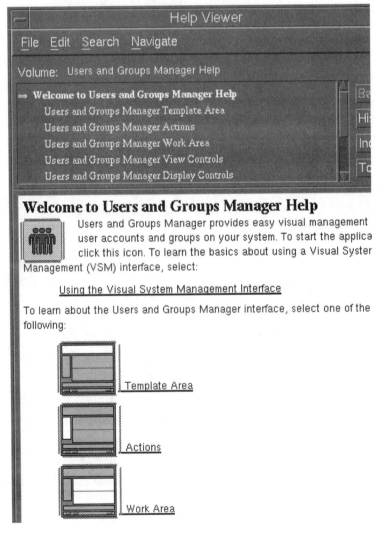

Figure 8–16   VSM On-line Help System

Figure 8–17 On-item Help Action

Backup—and Make Restore an Option!

Congratulations! You are up and running—but just in case you delete a file (or files) or work with any unhappy employees possibly interested in destroying your data, keep a spare copy of your data on hand (well, on a tape, CD-ROM, or another hard disk). This spare copy of your information is called a *backup*. Tape drives are commonly used for backup due to their speed and large data capacity. You can also use a CD-ROM attached to your system to download system files.

AIX Version 4 provides multiple ways of backing up your systems. You can use SMIT or the command line. Backup commands available include cpio, tar, pax, dd, backup, restore, and mksysb. SMIT also provides a menu-driven method of backing up and restoring AIX files or the entire rootvg volume group. After restoring your files using SMIT, you can use the fsck command to check the integrity of the file system.

backup Command

The backup command creates copies of your files on a backup medium, such as a magnetic tape or diskette, in one of two backup formats:

1. Specific files backed up by name using the -i flag. The backup command reads standard input for the names of the files to be backed up. You can generate file names with the find command, then pipe the list into the backup command.

2. You can also backup your entire file system by i-node using the *Level* and *FileSystem* parameters.

Before a file system is backed up, you should unmount the file system. This will ensure that files being backed up are not in the process of being changed.The default backup device is /dev/rfd0 (or, your diskette drive). If flags are specified that are not appropriate for the specified backup device, the backup command displays an error message and continues with the backup. Note that a single backup can span multiple volumes.

The following command options will be extremely useful:

- -#: Level of backup (0=entire system)
- -f: Device to backup to
- -u: Update /etc/dumpdates
- -i: Backup by name

File types can be special files, regular files, or directories. When the file type is a directory, only the directory is backed up. The files under the directory are not backed up, unless they are explicitly specified:

1.   To backup all the files and subdirectories in the /home directory using full path names, enter

```
find /home -print | backup -i -f /dev/rmt0
```

The -i flag specifies that files will be read from standard input and archived by file name. The find command generates a list of all the files in the / home directory. The files in this list are full path names. The | (pipe symbol) causes this list to be read from standard input by the backup command. The -f flag directs the backup command to write the files to the / dev/rmt0 tape device. Because the files are archived using full path names, they will be written to the same paths when restored.

2.   To backup all the files and subdirectories in the /home/mike directory using relative path names, enter

```
cd /home/mike
```

```
find . -print | backup -i -v -q
```

Each file name in the list generated by the find command is preceded by ./ (dot, slash). Because the files are backed up using relative path names, they will be written to the current directory when restored. The -v flag causes the backup command to display additional information about the backup. The files are written to the default backup device /dev/rfd0.

3.   To backup the / (root) file system, enter

```
backup -0 -u -f /dev/rmt0 /
```

The 0 level specifies that all the files in the / (root) file system be backed up. The -u flag causes the backup command to update the /etc/dumpdates file for this backup.

restore Command

The restore command reads backup files created by the backup command and extracts the files stored on them. These backed up files can be in either file-name or file-system format. Backups can be stored on disk, diskette, or tape. Files must be restored using the same method by which they were backed up (so knowing whether relative path names or complete path names were used when backing up your files is important). The backed up format can be determined by examining the backed up volume header information that is displayed when using the -T flag. When using the -x, -r, -T, or -t flags, the restore command automatically determines the archive format.

The Command options include the following:

- -f: Device to restore from
- -T: Table of contents
- -r: Restores an entire file system
- -v: Verbose
- -x: Restores files specified, or all files if none specified

Individual files can be restored from either file-name or file-system archives by using the -x flag and specifying the file name. The file name must be specified as it exists on the archive. Files can be restored interactively from file-system archives using the -i flag. The names of the files on an archive can be written to standard output using the -T flag.

The diskette device, /dev/rfd0, is the default media for the restore command. To restore from standard input, specify a - (dash) with the f flag. You can also specify a range of devices, such as /dev/rmt0-2.

If you are restoring from a multiple-volume archive, the restore command reads the volume mounted, prompts you for the next volume, and waits for your response. After inserting the next volume, press the Enter key to continue restoring files.

If an archive, created using the backup command, is made to a tape device with the device block size set to 0, it may be necessary for you to have explicit knowledge of the block size that was used when the tape was created in order to restore from the tape.

Multiple archives can exist on a single tape. When restoring multiple archives from tape, the restore command expects the input device to be a no-retension-on-open, no-rewind-on-close tape device. Do not use a no-rewind tape device for restoring unless either the -B, -s, or -X flag is specified. For more information on using tape devices, see the rmt special file.

Note the following operations:

1. To list the names of files in either a file-name or file-system archive on the diskette device /dev/rfd0, enter

```
restore -Tq
```

The archive is read from the /dev/rfd0 default restore device. The names of all the files and directories contained in the archive are displayed. For file-system archives, the file name is preceded by the i-node number of the file as it exists on the archive. The -q flag tells the restore command that the first volume is available and is ready to be read. As a result, you are not prompted to mount the first volume.

2.   To restore a specific file, enter:

```
restore -xvqf myhome.bkup system.data
```

This command extracts the file system.data into the current directory from the archive myhome.bkup. The archive in this example is in the current directory. File and directory names must be specified as they are displayed when using the -T flag. The -v flag displays additional information during the extraction. This example applies to both file-name and file-system archives.

3.   To restore a specific directory and the contents of that directory from a file-name archive, enter

```
restore -xdvqf /dev/rmt0 /home/mike/tools
```

The -x flag tells restore to extract files by their file name. The -d tells restore to extract all the files and subdirectories in the /home/mike/ tools directory. File and directory names must be specified as they are displayed when using the -T flag. If the directories do not exist, they are created.

How to backup and restore through SMIT

SMIT provides you with a menu-driven method of backup and restoring AIX files or the entire rootvg volume group. Unmount a file system prior to backup to ensure data integrity. After you have unmounted the file system, enter smitty on the command line. Select

- Physical and Logical Storage
- File Systems
- Backup Files in a File System (smit backup)
- Backup the System (smit mksysb)

The Backup the System option will prompt you for the pathname of the directory you want to back up as well as the backup device.

To restore files, mount the file system you want to restore data to and enter:

- Physical and Logical Storage
- File Systems
- Restore Files in a File System

After the files have been restored, use SMIT and select the Verify a File System option. This option uses the fsck command to check the integrity of the file systems after you have restored them.

mksysb Command

The mksysb command creates a backup of the operating system (that is, the root volume group). This backup can be used to reinstall a system to its original state after it has been corrupted. If the backup is created on tape, the tape is bootable and includes the installation programs needed to install from the backup.

The file-system image is in backup-file format. The tape format includes a boot image, a bosinstall image, and an empty table of contents followed by the system backup (root volume group) image. The root volume group image is in backup-file format, starting with the data files and then any optional map files.

The mksysb command also creates the /bosinst.data file from the system default file if the /bosinst.data file does not exist. To generate a system backup to a tape device named /dev/rmt1, enter

```
mksysb /dev/rmt1
```

CHAPTER
9

- Why Should I Care About Speaking Your Language?

- I'm Convinced! How Do I Get AIX to Speak My Language?

- This is Interetsting! Tell Me More!

- References

AIX Speaks Your Language: Internationalization

Just the way you expect to be able to look up a person's name and number in a phone book, you expect the computer to do things in a way that makes sense. You expect the computer to be able to display and process the letters in your alphabet; you expect it to give understandable messages. Although an error message of "Invalid offset" may not help much, you certainly would not expect the computer to come back with the following:

無効なオフセットです。

You expect your computer to be a useful and usable tool. Since AIX users throughout the world feel the same way, AIX has been designed to be easily configured to "do the right thing" for over forty different "locales."

In AIX, a "locale" is an environment that you specify that tells AIX which language and cultural conventions you want to use. AIX Version 4 supports over forty of these. Some of them are defined in Table 9–1.

If you want AIX to display messages in Japanese, it will! If you want to see date and time displayed in the German format, you can! If you want to enter and print Chinese characters, you can! If you want to use French accent characters in your files, no problem!

Figure 9–1 is a brief example of how the operation of AIX changes depending on the "locale."

To be a little bit more technical, AIX internationalization is based on the industry standard X/Open Portability Guide Version 4 (known as XPG4) model which was created by industry standard gurus at X/Open with help from other industry standard gurus from throughout the world. For what it's worth this is also

Table 9–1   Did Somebody Say Locale?

Locale	Description
C	This is for Unix programmers anywhere!
POSIX	Same as C
ar_AA	Arabic
bg_BG	Bulgarian in Bulgaria
ca_ES	Catalan in Spain
cs_CZ	Czech in Czechoslovakia
da_DK	Danish in Denmark
de_CH	German in Switzerland
de_DE	German in Germany
el_GR	Greek in Greece
en_GB	English in Great Britain
en_US	English in the United States
es_ES	Spanish in Spain
fi_FI	Finnish in Finland
fr_BE	French in Belgium
fr_CA	French in Canada
fr_CH	French in Switzerland
fr_FR	French in France
hr_HR	Croatian in Croatia
hu_HU	Hungarian in Hungary
is_IS	Icelandic in Iceland
it_IT	Italian in Italy
iw_IL	Hebrew in Israel
ja_JP	Japanese in Japan
ko_KR	Korean in Korea
mk_MK	Macedonian in Macedonia
nl_BE	Dutch in Belgium
nl_NL	Dutch in the Netherlands
no_NO	Norwegian in Norway
pl_PL	Polish in Poland
pt_BR	Portuguese in Brazil
pt_PT	Portuguese in Portugal
ro_RO	Romanian in Romania

Table 9-1   *(Continued)*

Locale	Description
ru_RU	Russian in the Soviet Union
sh_SP	Serbian Latin in Serbia
sk_SK	Slovak in Slovakia
al_SI	Slovene in Slovenia
ar_SP	Serbian Cyrillic in Serbia
sv_SE	Swedish in Sweden
tr_TR	Turkish in Turkey
zh_CH	Simplified Chinese in China
zh_TW	Traditional Chinese in Taiwan

```
[trent@musashi] /u/trent > export LANG=En_US
[trent@musashi] /u/trent > date
Mon Jan  1 12:30:42 CST 1996
[trent@musashi] /u/trent > cat foo
cat: 0652-050 Cannot open foo.

[trent@musashi] /u/trent > export LANG=Ja_JP
[trent@musashi] /u/trent > cat foo
cat: 0652-050 fooがオープンできません。

[trent@musashi] /u/trent > export LANG=es_ES
[trent@musashi] /u/trent > date
Lu  1 Ene 12:31:30 1996
[trent@musashi] /u/trent > cat foo
cat: 0652-050 No se puede abrir foo.
```

Figure 9-1   AIX Locale Example

the same model used in industry standard POSIX P1003.2 from the IEEE Computer Society. This model contains six categories of information that tend to vary from country to country and from language to language. The purpose of defining these categories is to provide a foundation for a database of cultural conventions that users can easily pick and choose from. Oh, by the way, people who do internationalization for a living find the word internationalization is too long to type, too cumbersome to read, and certainly too much of a tongue twister to say. Thus they tend to type "i18n", and say I-eighteen-N, since there are 18 characters between the I and the N.

The first category is known as "LC_CTYPE". X/Open describes this as, "Character classification and case conversion." This category specifies what characters you can use, which are uppercase, which are lowercase, which are alphabetic, which are numeric, which are control, and . . . well, I think you get the picture. This category also specifies how case conversion is done; that is to say, there is a list of all lowercase characters, and which uppercase characters they can be mapped to, and vice versa.

The second category is known as "LC_COLLATE". X/Open describes this as "Collation order." Information in this category specifies exactly how words should be sorted. This is much more complicated and interesting than one might suppose. Many languages have their own special rules regarding sorting that are just as important as placing Apple before Zebra in an English sort. For instance, Spanish has "multicharacter collating symbols" such as "ch", "cz", and "ll". "ch" must collate between c and d, unless it is in the middle of a word, in which case it collates after "cz" and before d. Got that? We may have a pop quiz on this . . . Just kidding. Seriously, computers are supposed to keep track of details like this so that YOU don't have to.

The third category is known as "LC_TIME." X/Open describes this as, "Date and time formats." Each country and language tends to have their own words for days of the week and names of months. Often there are special formatting requirements for different countries on how dates and times should be displayed. These kind of things are specified in this category. (Time zones are handled with the TZ environment variable, and can be specified in SMIT rather than in this category.)

The fourth category is known as "LC_NUMERIC." X/Open describes this as, "Numeric, non-monetary formatting." This category just contains a couple of pieces of information: which character to use as the decimal point, which character to use to group, and how to group digits. That is, do you want to see 1,500.1 or 1500.1 or 1.500,1 or 1500,1?

The fifth category is known as "LC_MONETARY." X/Open describes this as, "Monetary formatting." This category contains information similar to

LC_NUMERIC. Since this is for formatting currency figures, it also includes which symbol to use (i.e., $ in the U.S., the yen symbol in Japan, and so on). It also specifies exactly how to format the number. That is, where exactly should the minus sign be placed? The plus sign? The currency symbol?

The sixth category is known as "LC_MESSAGES." X/Open describes this as, "Formats of informative and diagnostic messages and interactive responses." This category tells AIX two things: which language you want messages displayed in, and what it should consider a "yes" or a "no" response to a yes/no question.

I know all these different categories seem complicated, but trust me, generally you don't need to worry about it. Usually it is sufficient to simply specify a single locale that you wish to use, and AIX understands that you want the overall behavior specified by all of these different categories. The advantage of all these different locale categories is that by setting only LC_COLLATE to German, you can do things like sort a list of data in German, but if you don't actually speak German, you can have program prompts and messages displayed in English. Nifty isn't it?

Why Should I Care About Speaking Your Language?

If you only speak one language, and your customers only speak your language, and if you think this will never change, then you probably don't need to care, and you can skip to the next chapter.

If you would like to have AIX operate in a language other than English, or if you have customers that would like information processed in some way other than the "United States" way, then you should care deeply.

For what it's worth, large computer software and hardware companies make more than 50% of their profit from customers outside of the United States. Savvy programmers and hardware manufacturers design their products so that they work well in as many countries as possible. In fact, it is not enough to have a separate version localized for each country. For both scales of economy and ultimately customer satisfaction, it is best to ship a single product world-wide that can be easily configured by the user to adapt to any locale. This is the goal of both the XPG locale model, and its AIX implementation.

I'm Convinced! How Do I Get AIX to Speak My Language?

The first step is to ensure that the right pieces of AIX were installed on your system. Since this was all covered in the chapter on installing your system, this should not be a problem.

Manage Language Environment

☐ Change/Show Primary Language Environment

☐ Add Additional Language Environments

☐ Remove Language Environments

☐ Change/Show Language Hierarchy

☐ Change/Show Applications for a Language

☐ Convert System Messages and Flat Files

Figure 9–2   Manage Language Environment SMIT Screen

Before we get started we need to define a few terms you will see as we use SMIT to configure your system. A *codeset* is simply the name for the set of characters that a language uses. IBM-850 was the default English codeset in AIX 3.2. ISO8859-1 is the default English codeset in AIX Version 4. Both are based on ASCII. Other codesets are used as defaults for other languages. The term *cultural convention* refers to how you want your computer to behave when it sorts, displays dates, and so on. In fact the term cultural convention includes all of the categories discussed above except for the message translation used. *Language translation* specifies which language you want AIX to display messages in. Since AIX supports a variety of keyboards for each country, there is also an option to specify what kind of *keyboard* you are using.

Alright, let's use SMIT to configure system language defaults. Once this is complete, you can configure user defaults, or even change things on the fly! First start SMIT as root and select "System Environments." Next select "Manage Language Environment" (Figure 9–2). This is where all the action takes place for configuring your system to speak different languages.

Now select "Change/Show Primary Language Environment" (Figure 9–3). Next select "Change/Show Cultural Convention, Language, or Keyboard" (Figure 9–4).

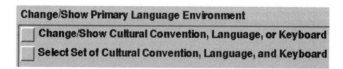

Change/Show Primary Language Environment

☐ Change/Show Cultural Convention, Language, or Keyboard

☐ Select Set of Cultural Convention, Language, and Keyboard

Figure 9–3   Change/Show Primary Language Environment SMIT Screen

Primary CULTURAL convention	ISO8859-1 C (POSIX) [C]	List
Primary LANGUAGE translation	ISO8859-1 C (POSIX) [C]	List
Primary KEYBOARD	ISO8859-1 C (POSIX) keyboard. [C]	List
INPUT device/directory for software	/dev/cd0	List
EXTEND file systems if space needed?	yes	List ▲ ▼

Figure 9–4   Change/Show Cultural Convention,
Language, or Keyboard SMIT Screen

To keep things simple, press the LIST button to the right of "Primary CUL-
TURAL convention" and select either the country you are in or the conventions
you wish to use. This will specify all of the locale category behavior information
we just discussed. Figure 9–5 is a partial list of cultural conventions.

Now select the LIST button to the right of "Primary LANGUAGE translation",
and select the language you wish to see messages in. Then select the LIST button
to the right of "primary KEYBOARD" and select the value that corresponds to
the keyboard you have on your system. Next, select the "INPUT device". This
should be the device that has your AIX install media, probably /dev/rmt0 if you
used a tape or /dev/cd0 if you used a CD-ROM to install. I recommend selecting
"yes" for the question, "EXTEND file systems if space needed?" Now SMIT will
install and configure your request. After this is done, shutdown your computer.
When you reboot, your computer will be speaking your language!

For the curious among us, Figure 9–6 shows what the Manage Language Environment smit menu looks like in Japanese. Figure 9–7 shows what the same
menu looks like in German.

The screens in Figures 9–6 and 9–7 were created simply by typing, "LANG=ja_JP
smit lang" and, "LANG=de_DE smit lang" from the desktop on a system that
had Japanese and German message translations installed. It's that easy!!

This is Interesting! Tell Me More!

Here are some nifty tidbits. If you forget what language you are using, you can
use the locale command to see what it is:

Figure 9–5   Partial List of Cultural Conventions

Figure 9–6   Japanese Manage Language Environment SMIT Screen

Figure 9-7   German   Manage   Language   Environment
SMIT Screen

```
[trent@musashi] /u/trent > locale

LANG=Ja_JP

LC_COLLATE="Ja_JP"

LC_CTYPE="Ja_JP"

LC_MONETARY="Ja_JP"

LC_NUMERIC="Ja_JP"

LC_TIME="Ja_JP"

LC_MESSAGES="Ja_JP"

LC_ALL=
```

This example shows that we are using the Japanese locale. OK, suppose you want to know what other locales can you use? Try typing "locale -a". This will list all of the locales installed on your system. You might see something like this:

```
    [trent@musashi] /u/trent > locale -a
C
POSIX
Sv_SE
Da_DK.IBM-850
De_CH.IBM-850
De_DE.IBM-850
En_GB.IBM-850
En_US.IBM-850
Es_ES.IBM-850
Fi_FI.IBM-850
Fr_BE.IBM-850
Fr_CA.IBM-850
Fr_CH.IBM-850
Fr_FR.IBM-850
Is_IS.IBM-850
It_IT.IBM-850
```

```
Pt_PT
Nl_BE.IBM-850
Nl_NL.IBM-850
No_NO.IBM-850
Pt_PT.IBM-850
Sv_SE.IBM-850
No_NO
Nl_NL
Nl_BE
It_IT
Is_IS
Fr_FR
Fr_CH
Fr_CA
Fr_BE
Fi_FI
Es_ES
En_US
En_GB
De_DE
De_CH
Da_DK
Ja_JP
Ja_JP.IBM-932
zh_TW
ar_AA.ISO8859-6
bg_BG.ISO8859-5
cs_CZ.ISO8859-2
da_DK.ISO8859-1
de_CH.ISO8859-1
de_DE.ISO8859-1
el_GR.ISO8859-7
en_GB.ISO8859-1
en_US.ISO8859-1
es_ES.ISO8859-1
fi_FI.ISO8859-1
fr_BE.ISO8859-1
fr_CA.ISO8859-1
fr_CH.ISO8859-1
fr_FR.ISO8859-1
hr_HR.ISO8859-2
hu_HU.ISO8859-2
is_IS.ISO8859-1
it_IT.ISO8859-1
iw_IL.ISO8859-8
ja_JP.IBM-eucJP
ko_KR.IBM-eucKR
mk_MK.ISO8859-5
```

```
nl_BE.ISO8859-1
nl_NL.ISO8859-1
no_NO.ISO8859-1
pl_PL.ISO8859-2
pt_PT.ISO8859-1
ro_RO.ISO8859-2
ru_RU.ISO8859-5
sl_SI.ISO8859-2
sk_SK.ISO8859-2
sh_SP.ISO8859-2
sr_SP.ISO8859-5
sv_SE.ISO8859-1
tr_TR
tr_TR.ISO8859-9
zh_TW.IBM-eucTW
pt_BR.ISO8859-1
sv_SE
sr_SP
sl_SI
sk_SK
sh_SP
ru_RU
ro_RO
pt_PT
pt_BR
pl_PL
no_NO
nl_NL
nl_BE
mk_MK
ko_KR
ja_JP
iw_IL
it_IT
is_IS
hu_HU
hr_HR
fr_FR
fr_CH
fr_CA
fr_BE
fi_FI
es_ES
en_US
en_GB
el_GR
de_DE
de_CH
```

```
da_DK
cs_CZ
bg_BG
ar_AA
Iw_IL
Ar_AA.IBM-1046
Iw_IL.IBM-856
Ar_AA
```

You notice how some of these have a dot and some text added? This tells you exactly what codeset this locale uses. Notice that we have four Japanese locales. Ja_JP and Ja_JP.IBM-932 are really the same, they both use IBM-932 as the codeset. (This is also known as Shift-JIS.) ja_JP and ja_JP.IBM-eucJP are also the same. They use IBM-eucJP (also known as Japanese EUC) as the codeset. You can temporarily change your language on the fly by changing the LANG environment variable to one of those values.

To set your language to English (with ksh or bsh) type

```
export LANG=en_US
```

If you use csh type

```
setenv LANG=en_US
```

To set your language to German (with bsh or ksh) type

```
export LANG=de_DE
```

or for csh:

```
setenv LANG=de_DE
```

If you wish to change your language permanently, the chlang command is a good way to do this. For example this would change your default language to German, effective next time you log in:

```
chlang de_DE
```

OK, now for something really out of the ordinary. Suppose you want to see what kind of information is actually IN the locale. This can be done with the locale command. Try this:

```
[trent@musashi] /u/trent > locale -ck LC_TIME

LC_TIME

abday="Sun";"Mon";"Tue";"Wed";"Thu";"Fri";"Sat"

day="Sunday";"Monday";"Tuesday";"Wednesday";"Thursday";
"Friday";"Saturday"

abmon="Jan";"Feb";"Mar";"Apr";"May";"Jun";"Jul";"Aug";"Sep";
"Oct";"Nov";"Dec"
```

```
    mon="January";"February";"March";"April";"May";"June";
"July";"August";"September";"October";"November";"December"

    d_t_fmt="%a %b %e %H:%M:%S %Z %Y"

    d_fmt="%m/%d/%y"

    t_fmt="%H:%M:%S"

    am_pm="AM";"PM"

    era=""

    era_d_fmt=""

    era_year=""

    t_fmt_ampm="%I:%M:%S %p"

    era_t_fmt=""

    era_d_t_fmt=""

    alt_digits=""
```

If you should find yourself needing to actually do programming related to internationalization or if you have an insatiable curiosity about this, check out some of the references below.

References

1. IBM International Technical Support Centers, *AIX Version 3.2 for RISC System/6000: National Language Support.* Order number GG24-3850-00

2. IBM Corporation. *AIX Version 3.2 for RISC System/6000: Internationalization of AIX Software—A Programmers' Guide.* Order number SC23-2431-00

3. X/Open Company Ltd. *Internationalization Guide Version 2.* U.K:. X/Open Company Ltd. ISBN: 1-85912-002-4

4. Ken Lunde. *Understanding Japanese Information Processing.* Sebastopol, CA: O'Reilly & Associates Inc., 1993. ISBN: 1-56592-043-0

CHAPTER 10

- Unlimited On-line Information

- 1-800-IBM-4FAX—Lots of Information for FREE!

- POWER Team Developer Support (1-800-627-8363)

- AIX and RS/6000: Resources on the Net

- AIX News Groups

- RS/6000 Talk Radio

All the Help
You Need

Now that you have your AIX system up and running; have loaded a cool backdrop, window, and icon colors; run a few commands and written a few shell scripts; set up your printer and CDROM drive; and backed up your system for the day—you're ready to access help and information from InfoExplorer, the Internet and multiple IBM resources. So what is and where is all of this help, documentation, and information?

- On-line help and documentation is accessed through InfoExplorer.

  InfoExplorer is a hypertext information retrieval system that enables you to browse 50,000 pages of AIX hardcopy information by topic. InfoExplorer contains information on how to use, manage, and program AIX and AIX software applications.

- Fax information on any IBM product, service, and solutions for specific problems is accessible through 1-800-IBM-4FAX.

  1-800-IBM-4FAX is an automated document retrieval system. You can select documents to be faxed directly to you from a menu including RISC/6000, AIX, PowerParallel, personal computers, OS2, AS/400, networking, and IBM education information.

- POWER Team development equipment, support, education, technical support, and marketing aids.

  The POWER Team is a group within IBM's Solution Developer Organization that provides RS/6000 equipment through leases and discounts to AIX and RS/6000 developers; directs product developers to advertising discounts, catalogues and marketing relationships; and provides superior technical support.

- The Internet!

  We've included a list (and URL) of IBM resources, sites, and programs available through the Internet. Enjoy!

- AIX News Groups

- RS/6000 Talk Radio

Unlimited On-line Information

InfoExplorer enables you to access the entire AIX library. You can install InfoExplorer on your RS/6000 or you can mount the InfoExplorer CD-ROM. InfoExplorer contains information on how to use, manage, and program the operating system and other applications that run on AIX as well as reference information.

InfoExplorer articles provide conceptual overviews and step-by-step procedures for completing tasks related to a particular topic. InfoExplorer takes you through using, programming, and managing AIX through the use of navigation lists, concept articles, procedure articles, and reference articles, as illustrated in Figure 10–1:

- Navigation lists provide several ways to access information including contents, topic lists, and indexes.

- Concept articles provide background information needed to complete tasks and procedures discussed in procedural and reference articles.

- Procedure articles list the steps necessary for accomplishing a task.

- Reference articles describe commands, calls, subroutines, file formats, and functions. The command reference articles provide diagrams illustrating the command syntax and appropriate flags.

How Does InfoExplorer Present Information?

To help you quickly find the specific type of information you are interested in, InfoExplorer topics are divided into System Management, Programming, Using, and Problem Solving. When you start InfoExplorer, the Topic & Task Index (Figure 10–2) is activated enabling you to immediately access the most appropriate information. Just click on the topic you are interested in.

A variety of retrieval and navigation tools enable you to find information easily (see Table 10–1).

You can also view information on-line by using the Books list. The Books list enables you to find information using a Contents List, just like you would if reading or referencing a hardcopy book. By selecting the List of Books on the InfoExplorer startup interface and then selecting System Management Guide, you bring

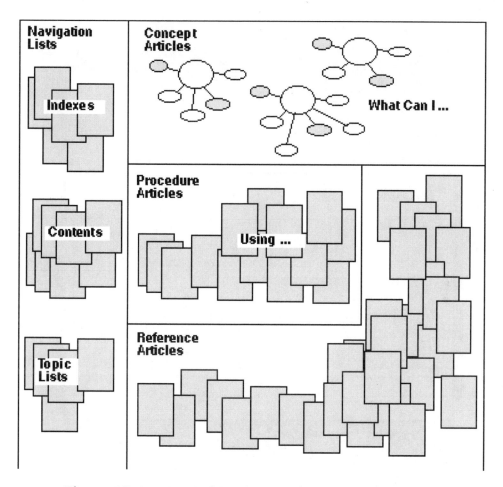

Figure 10–1   How InfoExplorer is Organized (Copied with Permission from IBM)

up the following Content List for the *AIX System User's Guide: Operating System and Devices* (Figure 10–3).

InfoExplorer Features

InfoExplorer provides several cool features:

*   List of Bookmarks

    You can create bookmarks for articles you consult frequently.

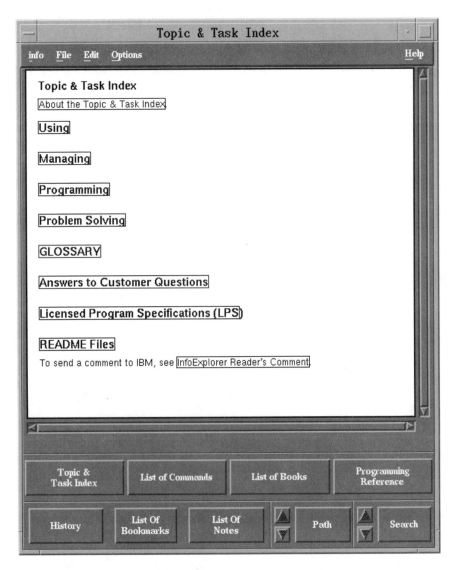

Figure 10–2   InfoExplorer Topic & Task Startup Screen

- History

    InfoExplorer keeps track of where you've linked to and creates a History file.

- List of Notes

    You can create margin notes in articles to add information, emphasize important tasks, or just doodle. Notes can be private, public, or system level and can be edited and saved.

Table 10–1   InfoExplorer Retrieval Methods (Copied with Permission from IBM)

TASK	RETRIEVAL METHOD
You know what you want to do, but not how to do it.	Topic & Task Index
You want to read about the command you used	List of Commands
You want to read everything about using communications	List of Books
You want to find information about a subject	Search
You want to go back to information you just read	History
You want to mark specific information for review	List of Bookmarks
You want to see only the information you have updated	List of Notes

- Path

  A Path button is provided on the InfoExplorer panel. You can select either the forward or backward arrow. Well, first you select the backward arrow to go back to where you've already visited; then you can select the forward arrow to drive back to where you just backtracked from—WHEW!

Starting InfoExplorer

To start InfoExplorer from the desktop, move the mouse pointer to the Application Manager icon and click the left mouse button twice. This brings up a window with several application groups, which represent directories. Click on the Information icon and then on the InfoExplorer icon.

You may also start InfoExplorer from an operating system command line in an AIX window. Type the following at the system prompt and press the Enter key:

```
info
```

The Welcome to the InfoExplorer Window Interface displays in the reading window and the Topic & Task Index displays in a navigation window. The welcome information explains how to do basic window operations and how to access Info-Explorer Help, copyrights, and trademarks.

Exiting InfoExplorer

You can stop the InfoExplorer program from any open InfoExplorer window. To exit the InfoExplorer program and save all bookmarks and notes, select the Quit option in the info pull-down menu from any InfoExplorer window. All open windows are closed and the program is exited.

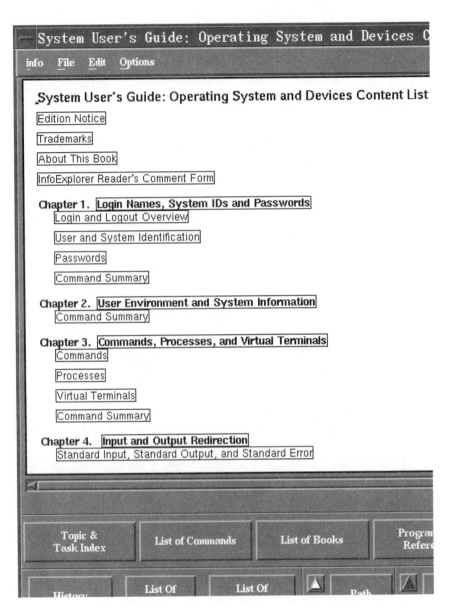

Figure 10–3 On-line Table of Contents

To exit the InfoExplorer program without saving all bookmarks and notes, select **Close** in the navigation window menu located to the left of the title bar. All open windows are closed and the program is exited.

1-800-IBM-4FAX—Lots of Information for FREE!

Tips and solutions for common AIX/6000 problems and questions asked by customers are available for FREE by dialing 1-800-IBM-4FAX. You will be asked to enter document numbers and your fax number—the documents you ordered are then faxed to your fax number. To obtain the faxes outside the U.S., call 415-855-4FAX.

Many faxes are available from this service, from product catalogs to service information. We've included the 12/19/95 list of AIX and RS/6000 faxes list at the end of this section. You can also access the AIX and RS/6000 faxes on the Internet by entering URL http://aix.boulder.ibm.com/pbin-usa/getobj.pl?/pdocs-usa/ tips_hints.html.

For example, an LED C31 during IPL on a RISC System/6000 in AIX 4.1 may be caused by an incorrect console configuration, by a corrupt ODM (Object Data Manager), or by a nonterminal device (such as a modem or printer) plugged into port 1 or 2. If LED C31 is flashing in your front panel window, you would call 1-800-IBM-4FAX and request fax document number 1991 be faxed to you. You would receive the following fax.

Example FAX 1991

To resolve the LED C31, check for a nonterminal device plugged into port 1 or 2. If that is not the problem, you will need to boot up in Service mode and change the console with the "chcons" command as follows:

1.   Check for a nonterminal device plugged into serial port 1 or 2. If there is not such a device, go to step 2. If there is one, unplug it or turn it off. Then reboot the machine with the key in Normal position. You do not need to continue with these steps.

2.   Turn the key to the Service position.

3.   With BOOTABLE MEDIA OF THE SAME VERSION AND LEVEL AS THE SYSTEM, boot the system.

      The bootable media can be ANY ONE of the following:

      • Bootable cdrom

      • Mksysb

      • Bootable Install Tape

      Follow the prompts to the "Welcome to Base OS" menu.

4.   Choose "Start Maintenance Mode for System Recovery" (Option 3). The Next screen would prompt the following Menu "Maintenance."

Choose "Access a Root Volume Group" (Option 1). At this stage the console would display information about rootvg, and also Display a Menu with 2 Options.

Choose "Access this volume group and start a shell" (Option 1). If you get errors from the above option, do not continue with the rest of this procedure. Correct the problem causing the error. If you need assistance correcting the problem causing the error, contact your local branch office, your local point of sale, or call 1-800-CALL-AIX (to register for fee-based services).

5.   Enter the following command:

```
ODMDIR=/dev/objrepos
```

6.   Change the system console with the following command. The change will take effect at the next startup of the system.

If your console is an lft (6091), run the following:

```
chcons -a login=enable /dev/lft/0
```

If your console is a tty (ibm3151), run the following:

```
chcons -a login=enable /dev/tty0
```

7.   With the key in Normal position, run

```
shutdown -Fr
```

8.   If the system does not stop at LED C31 during reboot, you do not need to continue with these instructions. If the system still stops on LED C31 during reboot, repeat steps 2-4 and then follow the following menu. Choose "Start Maintenance Mode for System Recovery" (Option 3). The Next Screen would prompt the following Menu "Maintenance."

Choose "Access a Root Volume Group" (Option 1). At this stage the console would display information about rootvg, and also Display a Menu with 2 Options. Choose "Access this volume group and start a shell before mounting the filesystems" (Option 2).

9.   Run the following commands, which will remove much of the system's configuration, saving it to backup directory:

```
mount /dev/hd4 /mnt
mount /dev/hd2 /usr
mkdir /mnt/etc/objrepos/bak
```

```
cp /mnt/etc/objrepos/Cu* /mnt/etc/objrepos/bak
cp /etc/objrepos/Cu* /mnt/etc/objrepos
/etc/umount all
exit
```

Determine which disk is the boot disk with the lslv command. The boot disk will be shown in the PV1 column of the lslv output:

```
lslv -m hd5
```

Save the clean ODM database to the boot logical volume. ('#' is the number of the fixed disk, determined with the previous command.)

```
savebase -d /dev/hdisk#
```

Continue with step 10.

10. Turn the key to Normal position and run

```
shutdown -Fr
```

11. If LED C31 still occurs when you reboot your system and you need further assistance with this problem, contact your local branch office, your point of sale, or call 1-800-CALL-AIX to register for fee-based services.

Available AIX and RS/6000 Faxes

AIX and RS/6000 faxes currently available include the following (among others):

Fax Number	Document Title
3140	7135 RAIDiant Array—Common Installation Issues
3119	7135 RAIDiant Array—UPDATED Installation Instructions
1829	About AIX Service Hints and Tips from 4FAX
3753	About Sparse Files (AIX 3.2)
4923	AIX 4.1.4 Release
1826	AIX Service Bulletin: Potential Security Exposure
1770	AIX Support Family—Gathering System Crash Information
1762	AIX Support Family—Sending Testcases
2482	Backup/Install—"Tape Not in Backup Format" Error
1293	Backup/Install—AIX 4.1 Installation Tips
2503	Backup/Install—All Files Owned by Root After mksysb
2685	Backup/Install—Backup and Restore ACLs During mksysb
2363	Backup/Install—Installing/Updating with Low Disk Space
1453	Backup/Install—LED 518 or Failed mksysb After Install

Fax Number	Document Title
2769	Backup/Install—Limitations of mksysb
2443	Backup/Install—Man Pages, Info Don't Work After Install
1456	Backup/Install—Paging Space Problems with mksysb Restoration
2702	Backup/Install—Relative and Absolute Backups
2561	Backup/Install—Restoring 0-Blocksize Tape
1959	Backup/Install—Restoring Multiple Tape Blocks
1294	Booting RS/6000 SP Node Via Manual Node Conditioning
4725	Configuring JetDirect Printer with BOOTP/TFTP Server
2263	Crash Command Information for TTY/Printer Subsystems
2737	Define Restricted Login Device for root
1499	Detection and Correction of Illegal Hard Links
2768	Determining Location and Cause of "core" File
4508	Determining Tape Block Size and Format
2461	Discussion of the Default Values in /etc/security/limits
2929	Disk Quota System—Setup and Use
1399	Dynamic Screen Utility (dscreen) Tips
1228	Electronic Fix Distribution for AIX
2609	Error Log Information and TTY Log Identifiers
1895	Fixed Disk—Removing/Replacing a Fixed Disk
3913	HACMP 3.1: Information Needed for Problem Resolution
2483	HACMP/6000 and I/O Pacing
2543	HANFS Helpful Information
1432	HCON—Creating Autolog Script Files
2703	High CPU Percentage for kproc Process 514/516
4925	How cron & at Commands Work
5102	How Manpages Work: Troubleshooting Tips
4510	How to Alter/Restore a Missing .fs.size.file
4618	How to Boot am SP2 Node into Maintenance Mode
4619	How to Install man pages for AIX 4.1
1073	How to Rebuild the Kerberos Database
1957	How to Resolve an X.25 'Device Busy' Condition

Fax Number	Document Title
2446	How to Set Up sar
4823	How to Setup Hayes Compatible Modem on RISC System/6000
2464	IBM AIX Support Family
1828	Introduction to Reading Dumps
3198	LV Prpblems After Migration fromAIX 3.2 to 4.1.2
3689	LVM—1016 Physical Partitions per Volume Group
3200	LVM—The Logical Volume Control Block
3690	LVM—The Volume Group Descriptor Area
2265	Making a Second Root User
1609	Managing File System Space
1296	Managing The Time Zone Variable
4254	Mirroring the rootvg Volume Group for AIX 4.1
2704	NAMED Configuration Help
1400	NetLS—Installing Nodelock and Floating Licenses
1697	NetLS—Planar Board Swapping Procedure
2701	NIS Configuration Tips
1537	Overview of AIX Support
4824	Overview of AIX System Security Audits
1075	Paging Space Tips for AIX 3.2 & 4.1
2770	Performance Tool Vulnerability—Information and Workaround
3199	Preparing Your AIX System for SATAN
2707	Preserve Login Session Information After Accounting
2809	Recovery from "Volume Group Locked" Error Message
2463	Recovery from a Corrupted Boot Logical Volume
4190	Recovery from LED 551, 555, or 557 in AIX 4.1
4825	Recovery From rm* From the Root (/) Directory
2565	Reducing Default Paging Space (hd6) For AIX 3.1—4.1
5101	Reducing File System Size in AIX 4.1
4724	Repairing File Systems with fsck in AIX 4.1
4253	Resetting File Permissions
2564	Resolving TTY "Respawning Too Rapidly" Errors

Fax Number	Document Title
1715	Service Director Download Instructions
2226	Setting Up an Auditing System to Monitor cron Events
5103	Setting up Man Pages & InfoExplored Using TECHLIB CDROM
1529	SNA Services/6000 Tuning and Performance Tips
1896	Tape Drive Densities and Special Files
2690	TCP/IP Over the X.25 Network Interface (XT)
1301	Tips for Network Communication Failure (Cannot "ping")
4620	Unable to Start Cluster Lock Manager on HACMP
1076	Using bootlist in Maintenance Mode in AIX 4.1
1845	Using iptrace to Track Remote Print Jobs
1760	Using Program Services
1470	Using the bootlist Command in Maintenance Mode
1909	UUCP (BNU) Helpful Information
1306	Xstation Problem Solving Hints
2541	Xstations and NIS

POWER Team Developer Support (1-800-627-8363)

The IBM Power Team provides development equipment through a developer discount program and a POWER lease program. It provides development support through newsgroups, product information and announcements, porting information and WorldWide Web Internet support. It provides education through the AIXpert magazine, newsletters, and technical conferences. It provides technical support through a 1-800 number, 24-hour electronic access to informational databases, consulting services, 90-day porting support, remote access to development equipment, and benchmarking. It also provides marketing aids through advertising discounts, direct mailing, marketing relationships, and the AIX POWER solutions catalog.

You can access the POWER Team homepage by starting up your Internet browser and opening URL http://www.austin.ibm.com/powerteam. The POWER Team home page is shown in Figure 10–4.

Developer discounts are available for both hardware and software.To qualify for a discount on both RS/6000 and Power Series hardware and AIX software, you must be a developer working on a product for commercial release on AIX (for either development or demonstration purposes). You are eligible for POWER

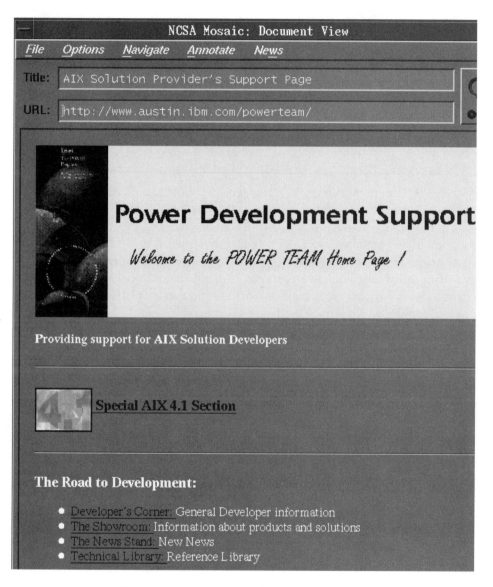

Figure 10–4   Power Team Home Page

leases if you are working on products for commercial release on AIX or if you are an industry remarketer.

To access development support on the Internet, start up your Internet browser and open URL http://www.austin.ibm.com/powerteam. You'll have immediate access to a "fix" database, technical tips and techniques, and how-to articles. Porting information (technical articles and white papers) is also available as well as newsgroups where you can communicate with other POWER Team members. After joining the POWER Team (free! just call 1-800-627-8363), you'll receive mailings designed to assist with product planning as well as customer support.

As a POWER Team member, you'll also receive *AIXpert*, a quarterly technical publication for software developers who write for the AIX platforms, port to AIX, or maintain software on AIX. Articles are written by both IBM employees and industry consultants. A POWER Team newsletter is available at URL http://www.austin.ibm.com/developer. IBM also sponsors technical conferences providing information on new technologies, support, and marketing programs. These conferences also give you an opportunity to meet, yell at, and pester IBM product architects, developers, and support team members.

Once you've got your product ready to sell, IBM can help you market the product. The AIX POWER Solutions catalog is distributed to over 50,000 AIX users worldwide. This catalogue is also available on-line at URL http://www.austin.ibm.com/powerteam. You can advertise your product in this catalogue as well as in the *AIXpert* magazine mentioned earlier. You can also list your software and services with the IBM National Solution Center. The National Solution Center maintains an on-line database used by IBM marketing representatives and business partners when they need to recommend a solution to a customer.

Other programs include an AIX Version 4 Certification Kit—you can request a royalty free "loan" copy of AIX Version 4 for application certification. The Developer Connection for AIX provides a CD including tools, demos, documentation, development kits, and sample code. IBM has a computer-based AIX/6000 education library and AIX professional certification. Solution Partnership Centers are available for developer marketing, recruiting, and porting activities. These centers are located in San Mateo and Boston.

AIX and RS/6000: Resources on the Net

AIXPort

http://aixport.sut.ac.jp

This website is maintained jointly by IBM and the Science University of Tokyo. It provides information on AIX in education and business, Advanced System, Networking, Education, and PTFs. It is available in either English or Japanese.

Developer Information for IBM AIX Version 4.1

`http://www.austin.ibm.com/services/vendors/aix41/aix41.html`

This site highlights AIX 4.1 features and also provides postscript versions of the AIX Version 4.1 Porting Guide and All About AIX Version 4.1.

AIXpert Home Page

`http://www.austin.ibm.com/powerteam/tech/aixpert/aixpert.html`

This provides an on-line *AIXpert* subscription form as well as on-line and printable versions of *AIXpert* back issues.

IBM Solution Developer Support Home Page

`http://www.developer.ibm.com/`

This home page provides information on developer news, events, and assistance available from IBM.

Object Oriented Technology Center

`http://mhvsoft.mcl.ibm.com/ootc`

This provides information, guidance and consulting services for your object-oriented projects.

IBM Object Technology

`http://www.torolab.ibm.com/objects`

This site serves as a starting point into the world of IBM object technology.

Open BluePrint

`http://www.torolab.ibm.com/openblue/OPENBLUE.HTM`

This page provides information on IBM's Open Blueprint, a comprehensive structure of the services required to support distributed client/server computing.

IBM Home Page

`http://www.ibm.com`

This home page offers links to IBM news, lead stories, products offerings, industry solutions, technology and research, and general IBM information. The IBM Home Page is depicted in Figure 10–5.

RS/6000 DIRECT

`http://www.issci.ibm.com/rsdirect/us`

This is the on-line version of the RS/6000 and AIX catalogue. It provides an on-line order form and configuration worksheet, promotions, and product descriptions.

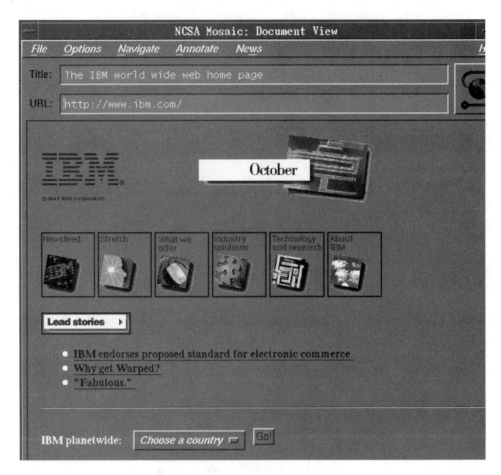

Figure 10–5   IBM Home Page

IBM Personal Computers Home Page

`http://www.pc.ibm.com`

This page links to the IBM Personal Computers desktop, ThinkPad, server, monitor, and options offerings. You can search through and download over 5,000 files for device driver, fixes, reference diskettes, and BIOS upgrades. The latest PC news is also available.

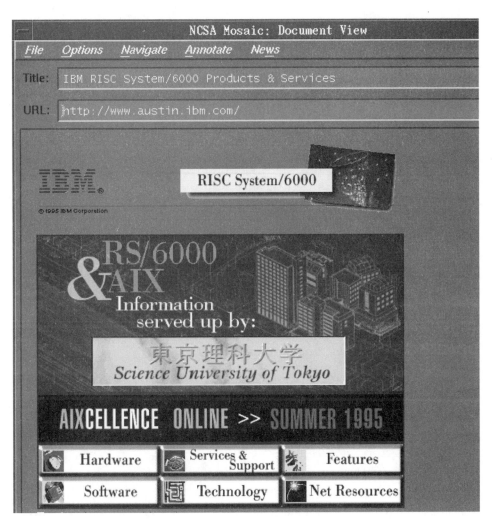

Figure 10–6   RS/6000 and AIX Home Page

IBM RISC System/6000 Products and Services

http://www.rs6000.ibm.com

A Comprehensive look at RS/6000 hardware, supported software, services and support, Internet Resources, and current plans/future activities is given here. This home page is shown in Figure 10–6.

AIX Support Network

http://service.boulder.ibm.com/www/support/aix

This is a full line of AIX services; from general Q&A to professional consulting services to custom offerings. Information offerings/services are determined by country or geography.

IBM Education—Global Campus

`http://webster.ibmlink.ibm.com:80/usedu`

Descriptions of and course catalogue of classes offered worldwide by the IBM Education group are listed here.

IBM RS/6000 Talk Radio—Home Page

`http://www.rs6000.ibm.com/talkradio`

This page tells you how to participate in RS/6000 Talk Radio—a weekly exchange of information between customers and IBM developers and specialists.

IBM Global Network

`http://www.ibm.com/globalnetwork/`

This feature links to the IBM Global Network services which include Internet services, network service, information on network outsourcing, e-mail, and electronic data interchange.

AIX and OS/2 Product and Services Database

`http://www.mfi.com/softwareguide`

This is a comprehensive resource for OS/2 and AIX software solution. It provides access to IAIX Software Solutions Product directory, OS/2 Software Solutions Product Directory, and Power Series solutions directory.

AIX CDE Desktop

`http://www.rs6000.ibm.com/software/OS/CDE/`

Information about what the CDE desktop is, and how to use it is provided here. It includes a frequently asked Questions List. It allows you to download the AIX WebExplorer. It also includes links to other sources.

AIX Welcome Center

`http://www.rs6000.ibm.com/support/welcome`

AIX 4.2 home pages offering a ton of local and internet links to AIX and IBM information. This home page is shown in Figure 10–7.

Figure 10-7   The AIX Welcome Center

AIX News Groups

comp.unix.aix

This posting contains frequently asked questions (FAQs) and answers about the IBM RS/6000 hardware and AIX. The posting is monitored by jwarring@aol.net.

This FAQ is available from: `<ftp://rtfm.mit.edu:/pub/usenet/news.answers/ aix-faq/part1>` `<ftp://mirrrors.aol.com:/pub/rtfm/usenet-by-hierarchy/comp/unix/ aix>` `<http://www.cis.ohio-state.edu:/hypertext/faq/usenet/aix-faq/top.html>`.

All entries are numbered with major and minor subject number (for example 2.11). If the subject is preceded by an asterisk, that entry has been changed or added since the last posting.

The comp.unix.aix group is for AIX on all IBM platforms—RT, PS/2, 370, RS/6000 and mainframes (ESA based on OSF/1), but the traffic has evolved to discuss predominantly AIX 3.x and the RS/6000. The newsgroups comp.sys.ibm.pc.rt and comp.sys.ibm.ps2.hardware cover the RT, mostly hardware and AOS 4.3, and on PS/2 hardware respectively.

RS/6000 Talk Radio

The RS/6000 Talk Radio show (Figure 10–8) is a weekly 60 minute audio teleconference that allows an exchange of information between AIX customers and IBM developers and specialists. Since it is a toll-free call, you can participate from the comfort of your own office. These lively shows keep you up-to-date on the latest AIX technology. You will receive the toll free phone number after enrolling, which doesn't cost any money! To enroll either call 1-800-289-0576 (or 1-913-661-0825), or point your web browser to http://www.rs6000.ibm.com/talkradio/.

Prior shows on audio cassette can be ordered by calling 1-800-222-4260 or 1-513-771-4244. Alternately, you can point your web browser to

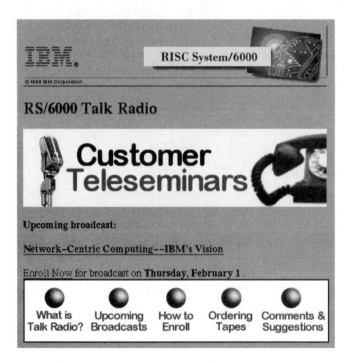

Figure 10–8   Talk Radio Home Page

http://www.rs6000.ibm.com/talkradio/tapes.final.html/. This is a partial list of available titles:

- PowerPC Update
- Advantages of Upgrading to SMPs
- SMP, Cluster, Scalable Positioning
- Storage Systems Solutions
- High Availability Offerings/Solutions
- What's New in AIX Version 4?
- RS/6000 Client/Server Strategies
- Distributed Systems Management
- Enterprise Connectivity
- Getting Started with New RS/6000
- DCE & Encina
- Massively-Parallel Application Solutions
- AIX Version 4 Technical Q&A Panel
- AIX PC Affinity
- Surfin' the Internet
- Why a Switch? Scaling and Investment, Protection in IBM RS/6000 SMPs
- Power Challenge: AIX vs. Windows NT
- RS/6000 Database Server Solutions
- High Availability Update and Competitive Positioning
- AIX Version 4.1 Update
- POWER Challenge: AIX vs. Windows NT in Server Events: A Technical View
- AIX Server Objects—CommonPoint Application System
- Integrating Workstations into Mainframe CAD/CAM Environments
- IBM Open Blueprint
- Interactive Voice Response Solutions
- Multi-vendor Client/Server Integration
- Mission-critical Transaction Processing with CICS for AIX
- Introduction to the RS/6000 and AIX
- High-Speed Clusters with High Availability

CHAPTER
11

- Performance Tools for System Management

- The AIX Development Environment

- Security and System Management

- FixDist—How to get the Latest Bug Fixes from the Internet

- AIX PitStop—How to Resolve Common AIX Problems

Gathering up the Pieces

I n this chapter we discuss performance tools for system management, the development environment, security, file systems, and useful tools to learn more about AIX.

Performance Tools for System Management

There are a number of questions that you may have about the state of your computer. This section will introduce you to some of the commands in the base operating system that will help you assess the state of your computer.

What is running right now? How much memory is it using?

To answer these questions use the ps commands (see Table 11–1).

How is memory is being used?

The vmstat command gives a lot of information about the status of a running AIX system. The output from this command falls into five categories: kernel threads, memory, paging, faults, and cpu usage (see Table 11–2).

How much of the disk is being used?

The iostat command can be used to monitor disk activity (see Table 11–3).

How much disk space is being used?

The df command shows how much disk space is used and available on each device (see Table 11–4). Disk space is displayed in 512-byte blocks. The Iused value refers to the number or percentage of i-nodes used. Each file takes up a certain number of inodes, and when there are no more inodes available, it is not possible to create new files even though there may be empty disk space open.

Table 11–1   Output from `ps ug`

USER	PID	%CPU	%MEM	SZ	RSS	TTY	STAT	STIME	TIME	CMMAND
root	516	98.5	0.0	0	4	-	A	Oct 12	269:15	kproc
trent	13676	1.9	1.0	304	592	pts/3	A	10:30:56	3:14	-ksh
trent	14564	0.0	0.0	132	224	pts/2	A	13:22:47	0:00	ps ug

USER
The name of the user associated with the process.
PID
The "Process ID". It identifies the number of the process running, and can be used as an argument to commands such as kill.
%CPU
The percentage of the CPU used by the process over its lifetime.
%MEM
The percentage of system memory used by the process over its lifetime.
SZ
The virtual size of the process or the total amount of paging space used by the program in kilobytes.
RSS
The resident set size of the process, or the total number of kilobytes of memory used by the program.
TTY
The terminal that is associated with the command. "-" means that there is no terminal associated with the command.
STAT
The current status of the process.
STIME
The time of day that the process started.
TIME
The total CPU time used by the process.
COMMAND
The name of the command that started this process.

What about paging space? How much of that do I have open?

The lsps command will show what the size of each disk based paging space is, along with the percentage available for use (see Table 11–5).

How can I increase my paging space?

The chps command can be used to increase the size of paging spaces. To increase the size of hd6 in the last example, you could use the following command, which must be run as root, and can be used repeatedly to further increase paging space:

```
$ chps -s'1' hd6
```

Table 11–2   Output from `vmstat`

kthr	memory		page						faults			cpu			
r b	avm	fre	re	pi	po	fr	sr	cy	in	sy	cs	us	sy	id	wa
0 0	4189	5533	0	0	0	0	0	0	117	15	19	0	1	98	0

Kernel Threads - r
The number of threads per second placed on the run queue during the observation period.

Kernel Threads - b
The number of threads per second placed on the wait queue during the observation period.

Memory - avm
The number of pages used in memory for paging.

Memory - fre
The number of real memory pages available.

page - re
The number of page reclaims during this period.

page - pi
The number of page-ins per second from paging space during the observation period.

page - po
The number of page-outs per second to paging space during the observation period.

page - fr
The number of pages per second freed during the observation period.

page - sr
The number of pages per second considered for freeing during the observation period.

page - cy
The number of times the paging space was entirely scanned for replacement during the observation period.

faults - in
The number of device interrupts per second during the observation period.

faults - sy
The number of system calls per second during the observation period.

faults - cs
The number of context switches per second during the observation period.

cpu - us
The percentage of CPU time used by the user during the observation period.

cpu - sy
The percentage of CPU time used by the system during the observation period.

cpu - id
The percentage of CPU time that was idle during the observation period.

cpu - wa
The percentage of CPU time that was spent in an I/O wait.

Table 11–3 Output from `iostat -d`

Disks:	% tm_act	Kbps	tps	Kb_read	Kb_wrtn
hdisk0	0.4	1.0	0.1	86557	76426
hdisk1	0.0	0.4	0.0	58031	36
cd0	0.0	0.0	0.0	0	0

% tm_act
Indicates the percentage of the time that the device was in use.

Kbps
Indicates the amount of data that was transferred to/from the device in kilobytes per second.

tps
Indicates the number of transfers per second.

KB_read
The total number of kilobytes read during the observation period.

KB_wrtn
The total number of kilobytes written during the observation period.

What about graphical user interfaces (GUIs) to do these kind of things?

Much of this information can be obtained through SMIT via "Performance & Resource Scheduling". Additionally, /usr/bin/X11/xload will show a graphical representation of CPU load. By using the -update option, you can specify exactly how often you want the graph to be updated. By installing the Performance Toolbox for AIX (LPP number 5696-900) you can use "xmperf", a GUI that displays

Table 11–4 Output from `df`

Filesystem	512-blocks	Free	%Used	Iused	%Iused	Mounted on
/dev/hd4	24576	15184	39%	1313	22%	/
/dev/hd2	983040	21864	98%	31121	26%	/usr
/dev/hd9var	8192	6032	27%	134	14%	/var
/dev/hd3	49152	22912	54%	567	10%	/tmp
/dev/hd1	8192	304	97%	171	17%	/home

Table 11–5   Output from `lsps -a`

Page Space	Physical Volume	Volume Group	Size	%Used	Active	Auto	Type
paging01	hdisk0	rootvg	4MB	82	yes	yes	lv
paging00	hdisk0	rootvg	4MB	82	yes	yes	lv
hd6	hdisk0	rootvg	64MB	13	yes	yes	lv

and monitors a variety of statistics including file system activity, and network activity, virtual memory usage.

The AIX Development Environment

This section describes some of the programs and tools that are available to use in the development of software on an AIX platform.

Compilers

Table 11–6 lists some of the compiler LPPs available from IBM.

Source Control (SCCS, CMVC, and RCS)

Source control packages allow teams of programmers to work on the same set of files over a period of time without having to worry about two people changing

Table 11–6   Compiler LPPs

LPP Name	Version	Number
C for AIX	3.1	5765-423
C Set++ for AIX	3.1	5765-421
COBOL Set for AIX	1.5	28H2176
XL Fortran for AIX	3.2	5765-176
XL Fortran Runtime Environment for AIX	3.2	5765-526
XL Pascal for AIX	2.1	5765-245
REXX/6000	1.1	5764-057

the same file at the same time. They also allow for a variety of features including version control, change tracking, ability to retrieve an old version, and in some cases provide extensive reporting and security mechanisms.

Two popular source control packages are available on AIX. The Source Code Control System (SCCS) is shipped as part of the base operating system in fileset bos.adt.sccs. SCCS allows basic source management. More information about SCCS can be found in the on-line documentation in InfoExplorer.

Another very powerful source management system available for AIX is Configuration Management Version Control (CMVC) which is based on SCCS. It can be ordered as LPP number 5765-207. CMVC is an extremely powerful system designed to work over a network in a client/server fashion. This allows users on clients to access the server to save, retrieve, and inquire about files. This model allows for extensive security and reporting. CMVC allows users to either use the command line or a powerful Graphical User Interface (GUI). CMVC runs on AIX as well as HP-UX, and SunOS.

Although AIX does not ship the Revision Control System (RCS) as part of the base operating system, RCS is available via anonymous ftp from prep.ai.mit.edu in directory /pub/gnu. The functionality the RCS provides is similar to that found with SCCS.

Programming for Internationalization

As described in the chapter on internationalization, AIX was designed to support a wide variety of countries and natural languages by using the XPG locale model. Programmers can make use of this in their programs by using the following key functions: setlocale(), nl_langinfo(), localeconv(), catopen(), catgets(), catclose(), iconv_open(), iconv(), iconv_close(), mblen(), mbtowc(), wctomb(). Information about these functions is available in InfoExplorer. Other useful references are found in the chapter on internationalization.

Performance Tools for Programmers

AIX provides several tools which can be used by programmers to analyze and assist in increasing program performance. Additional information on the usage of these commands can be found in InfoExplorer.

Prof and gprof are shipped as part of the base operating system in the bos.adt.prof fileset. Both of these tools require recompiling source code to include special routines that profile the program when it is running.

To use prof, compile your source code with the -p compiler option (cc -p test.c). When you run this program, a file called mon.out will be created which contains profiling data describing how much time was spent in each function used in your program, and how many times it was called. Using your program and the mon.out data file, prof will generate a human readable report containing this performance information.

To use gprof, compile your source code with the -pg compiler option (cc -pg test.c). When you run this program a file called gmon.out will be created which contains profiling data describing how much time was spent in each function used in your program. Using your program, and gmon.out as input, gprof command will display a list of how much time was spent in various functions, how many times each was called, along with a call graph that can be used to determine the flow of the program.

tprof is shipped in the perfagent.tools fileset and can be obtained by ordering the Performance Toolbox LPP (number 5697-900). Unlike prof and gprof, tprof does not require that source code be recompiled. tprof can be invoked by simply typing "tprof program_name", and it will generate a list where the cpu is spending its time. C programs can be recompiled with the -qlist compiler option to increase the usefulness of the output.

The dbx debugger

The most popular debugger shipped with AIX is probably dbx. It is straightforward to use. It is most useful when used with a program that has been compiled with the "-g" debugging option turned on, in which it allows stepping through executing code line by line, allowing variable tracking, modification, and so on. It is also of limited use with code that has not been compiled with "-g". For instance the "where" subcommand within dbx can show a programmer where a core dump was caused. Since this debugger is fairly intuitive, use the help command and experiment!

The adb debugger

Although the adb debugger is not as user friendly or sophisticated as dbx. it can be used to manipulate memory, set breakpoints, and so on. More information about this debugger can be found in InfoExplorer.

Make

AIX ships a standard version of the make command which is often used to automatically generate the necessary commands to compile complex software projects. For more information see either the InfoExplorer documentation on the make command, or the O'Reilly book *Managing Projects with make*.

Imake

Imake is similar to make, and is also a standard part of AIX. It is found in /usr/bin/X11/imake, and is documented in either InfoExplorer or the O'Reilly book on imake.

Security and System Management

AIX provides a number of tools and services that can make security management easier for system administrators. When most people hear the phrase "computer security", they probably think about hackers and computer break-ins. This is, however, only one part of the overall issue of security. The goal of computer security is to protect a computer system and its data from all manor of threats in such a way that the users can count on the software doing what they expect. Threats include things such as unauthorized access, acts of nature that could cause data loss (flood, fire), accidental erasure, malicious users, and so on.

AIX provides individual user accounts, file access control lists (ACL), error and command logging, a trusted computing base, trusted shells, enhanced password rules, extensive auditing capabilities, as well utilities to backup software to protect against data loss (backup, restore, tar, and pax commands).

A detailed coverage of security topics is well beyond the coverage of this book, so I would like to initially point out two good books on the subject:

1.   IBM, *Elements of Security: AIX 4.1*, (order number GG24-4433-00).

2.   Garfinkel, Simson, and Gene Spafford, *Practical Unix Security*, Sebastopol, CA: O'Reilly & Associates, Inc., 1993.

SMIT provides a simple interface to set up effective security. For instance, part of effective security is to use difficult-to-guess passwords, and change them at regular intervals. By selecting "Security & Users" from SMIT's main menu, then "Passwords", then "Change/Show Password Attributes", a system administrator can easily specify how long before a password will expire and must be changed, which words can NOT be used as passwords, and how many characters a password must be.

Some of the useful security related logs that AIX maintains are listed here:

•   **/var/adm/wtmp**   Contains a list of who logged on, when they did so, when they logged off, and where they logged in from. This information is viewable with the last command:

```
[trent@musashi] /u/trent/ > last | head -5

trent      pts/6                      Sat Oct 14 10:30 still logged in

trent      pts/6                      Fri Oct 13 15:20 - 15:47 (00:27)

trent      ftp    percy.austin.ibm   Fri Oct 13 14:07 - 14:07 (00:00)

trent      pts/12 sasaki.austin.ib   Thu Oct 12 23:14 - 23:18 (00:03)

trent      ftp    percy. austin.ibm  Thu Oct 12 16:45 - 16:46 (00:00)
```

• **/etc/utmp**   Contains information on each currently active user and
  processes. For users, such information as user name, terminal, logon date,
  and total time on are included. This information can be seen with the who
  command:

```
$ who

trent      pts/0      Oct 13 10:08      (musashi.austin.i)

trent      pts/1      Oct 14 14:45      (musashi.austin.i)
```

• **/var/adm/sulog**   Contains a human readable list of all attempts to use the su
  command. Since this is an ascii file, cat, vi or any other command can be used
  to look at it.

```
[trent:root@musashi] / # tail -3 /var/adm/sulog

SU 10/12 10:12 - pts/14 trent-root

SU 10/12 10:13 + pts/14 trent-root

SU 10/14 15:03 + pts/8  trent-root
```

  The plus in the fourth column indicates that the su command was successful;
  a minus in the same column indicates that the user provided the wrong password to su.

• **/etc/security/failedlogin**   This file contains a list of entries for all login failures. This information can be seen with the who command:

```
[trent:root@musashi] /var/adm # who /etc/security/failedlogin

UNKNOWN_      pts/10      Oct 04 19:37      (sitetest.austin.)

root          pts/10      Oct 04 19:40      (sitetest.austin.)
```

AIX's Trusted Computing Base (TCB)

AIX provides software that supports the concept of a trusted computing base,
which can be used to ensure that system commands have not been tampered
with. The heart of TCB is the tcbck command which is used to maintain data per-
taining to the trustworthiness of commands and files on the system. Other parts
of the trusted computing base include a limited shell called tsh. When used as a
login shell, it provides limited functionality so as to limit security risks. See Info-

Explorer or *Elements of Security: AIX 4.1* (IBM order number GG24-4433-00) for
more information on this topic.

FixDist—How to get the Latest Bug Fixes from the Internet

FixDist is a free user-friendly program that allows you to easily download the
latest bug fixes (called PTFs or APARs by IBM service folks) from the Internet.
FixDist also serves as an interface to a database of available fixes so that you can
see what kind of bugs are being reported and fixed. In the rare event that you
find a bug in AIX, you may be able to find a fix for it, and download it using
FixDist. Since FixDist supports both a graphics-based interface in addition to a
text-based interface, you will be able to use it in a variety of environments.

In order to use the FixDist tool, you will need to be running at least Version 3.2.4,
have your computer connected to the Internet, and of course have sufficient disk
space on your system. The FixDist tool may be obtained by getting file
/aix/tools/fixdist/fd.tar.Z via anonymous ftp from service.boulder.ibm.com (IP
address 189.17.57.66). Note this example:

```
$ cd /tmp/fixdist
$ ftp service.boulder.ibm.com
Connected to service.boulder.ibm.com.
Name (service.boulder.ibm.com:trent): anonymous
331 Send your complete e-mail address as password.
Password:
ftp> bin
ftp> cd /aix/tools/fixdist
ftp> dir
-rw-rw-r— 1 210          1          3487 Nov 13 09:03 README
-rw-rw-r— 1 210          1        183209 Nov 13 09:03 fd.ANS.tar.Z
-rw-r—r— 1 210           1        342705 Nov 13 09:03 fd.tar.Z
-rw-rw-r— 1 210          1         38001 Nov 13 09:03 fixdist.html
-rw-rw-r— 1 210          1         82021 Nov 13 09:03 fixdist.ps.Z
-rw-rw-r— 1 210          1         39404 Nov 13 09:03 fixdist.txt
ftp> get fd.tar.Z
ftp> get README
ftp> exit
$
```

In addition to the program (fd.tar.Z), and the README file which explains how to install the program, you may also want to retrieve the documentation file, by getting either the postscript version (fixdist.ps.Z) or the plain text version (fixdist.txt). Since the postscript manual (fixdist.ps.Z) is compressed, you will need to use the uncompress command before you will be able to view or print it.

After you have downloaded FixDist, you can install it by typing in the following as root ("as root" means you need to either log in as the root user, or type "su - root" and enter the root password):

```
cd /
zcat /tmp/fixdist/fd.tar.Z | tar -xpvf -
```

Now you can run the FixDist command by simply typing in "fixdist". When you do, you will see a screen like that in Figure 11–1 after you enter the server, target directory, select the database as 4.1, and press the download button.

At this point, I would recommend reading the FixDist documentation, however, I will explain a few of the features that you can use at this point. If you click on Maintenance Level, you will see a window (Figure 11–2) that will allow you to upgrade your machine to a certain level. You can download or view additional information about one of these by clicking on the appropriate line.

You can also select "Generally Available Fixes" from the main menu, to see a screen like the one shown in Figure 11–3. From this menu, you can view lists of either PTFs or APARs. In addition you can search by any text you wish. When you have found either the PTF or the APAR that you wish to download or view more information about, just click on it. See FixDist documentation for further information on installing the fixes after you have downloaded them.

AIX PitStop—How to Resolve Common AIX Problems

PitStop is a free graphics-based tool that is available over the Internet which allows AIX users to perform a variety of service related tasks such as these:

- Service faxes, tips, flashes, and news
- Runs service tools
- Links to internet web sites
- Creates a fastpath to the AIX support service center.

To obtain a copy of PitStop, point your web browser to http://service.boulder.ibm.com/www/support/aix/pitstop. You will see a page that looks something like the screen in Figure 11–4.

Figure 11-1   FixDist Main Screen

Figure 11-2   FixDist Maintenance Level Screen

Figure 11–3   FixDist PTF View Screen

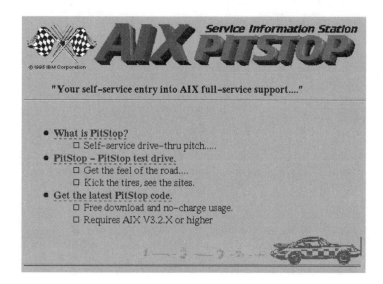

Figure 11–4   PitStop Home Page

Figure 11-5   PitStop ToolBar

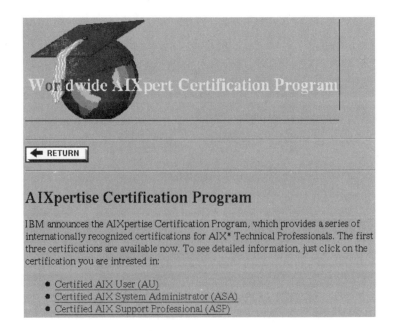

Figure 11-6   AIXpert Certification Program

Try the "What is PitStop" and "PitStop—PitStop test drive" options to get a better feel for the package, and when you are ready to download the package select "Get the latest PitStop code" option, and follow the directions on that page to download and install PitStop on your machine. After successful installation, just type "pitstop" to invoke this tool. You should see a tool bar like the one shown in Figure 11–5. Clicking on the icons will bring up the selected HTML page using your web browser without any need for Internet access since the data was all downloaded. You will find a wealth of interesting and useful information about AIX including, for instance the AIXpert Certification Program (Figure 11–6).

CHAPTER 12

- What is the IBM Developer Connection for AIX Program?

- CD-ROM Installation

- Contents of IBM Developer Connection for AIX CD-ROM

IBM Developer Connection for AIX CD-ROM

What is the IBM Developer Connection for AIX Program?

The IBM Developer Connection for AIX program has been set up to provide AIX developers throughout the world with quick and easy access to IBM technology and news by providing development tools, documentation, prerelease code, sample code, demo code, service, and support to subscribers. This subscription includes CD-ROMs, newsletters, and world-wide support. The newsletters include AIX news, future directions, new technologies, reviews, questions and answers, calendar of events, important telephone numbers, and so on. We are including a sample CD-ROM with this book to share with you the variety of information and programs available through this program. To subscribe in the U.S. call 1-800-633-8266 (1-800-6DEVCON) or fax 1-800-406-7129, or see the CD-ROM insert for more information. You can also check out the Developers Connection home page at Http://www.developer.ibm.com/sdp/DevCon.

CD-ROM Installation

In order to use the IBM Developer Connection for AIX CD-ROM, you will need a workstation that has AIX 4.1 or later installed with at least 16 megabytes of RAM and a CD-ROM drive that is supported by AIX. Follow these simple steps in order to install your CD-ROM (see the CD-ROM insert for the latest instructions):

1. Insert the CD-ROM into the CD-ROM drive and login as root.

2. Type the following on the AIX command line:

   ```
   mkdir -p /usr/DevCon
   ```

3. Allocate a CD-ROM file system. Type:

   ```
   smit storage
   ```

Select "File Systems"

Select "Add/Change/Show/Delete File Systems"

Select "CDROM File System"

Select "Add a CDROM File System"

Select the DEVICE name (i.e.: cd0)

Respond to the prompt for MOUNT POINT with

`/usr/DevCon`

Press enter to create, then F10 to exit

4. Mount the CD-ROM file system. Type:

    `smit mountfs`

    Select the FILE SYSTEM name (i.e.,: /dev/cd0)

    Select the DIRECTORY name (i.e.: /usr/DevCon)

    Select TYPE of filesystem (i.e.: cdrfs)

    Select mount as READ-ONLY system

    Press enter to mount, then F10 to exit

5. Type /usr/DevCon/dcsetup to install the IBM Information Presentation Facility/6000 (IPF) Viewer Component (this step can take a while).

6. Log out

7. Start the DevCon Demo program by typing:

    `/user/DevCon/devcon`

The Developer Connection for AIX contains a variety of documents in PostScript format. The catalog can display these documents for you if you have previously installed a PostScript viewer on your system. When you start the catalog, you will be prompted to identify the location of the PostScript viewer you would like to use. This willl be stored in the environment variable DEVCONPSVIEWER. You can set this environment variable now yourself, or let the catalog prompt you.

The Developer Connection for AIX contains a variety of documents in INF format. Step 5 above installs the viewer to display these files. This lets you view INF files (compiled IPF files) files on your system, either from the command line by typing xview<filename> or automatically from the Catalog. This installation is necessary to view the INF versions of the User's Guide and other IPF-based documents on the Devleeper Connection for AIX. If you choose not to install this IPF viewer, you will not be able to access all of the information. However, several

Figure 12–1 IBM Developer Connection for AIX Browser Screen

key files are also provided in ASCII format: the User's Guide is /usr/DevCon/usrguid.doc, the content list is /usr/DevCon/Welcome/aixcont.txt AIXCONT.TXT, and the welcome note is /usr/DevCon/Welcome/Welcome.txt.

When the demo browser is running, you will see a graphic screen something like the one in Figure 12–1. Use the mouse to click and explore!

Contents of IBM Developer Connection for AIX CD-ROM

(Contents subject to change with no notice, etc.)

Welcome

- Welcome note
- Contents of CD-ROM
- User's Guide

Technical Information: Papers

- Bidirectional Support in AIX
- Common Point* Application System
- PowerPC 601 Microprocessor
- PowerPC 603 Microprocessor
- POWER2 Microprocessor
- POWER2 Fixed-point Architecture
- POWER2 Floating-Point Architecture
- POWER2 Instruction Cache Unit
- POWER2 CPU Performance
- POWER2 Application Performance
- POWER2 Performance Monitor
- POWER2 TPC Performance
- Migration and Compatibility
- Compiler Performance Options
- ESSL
- Performance ToolBox Overview
- Distributed Performance Management
- PowerOPEN Environment Overview
- PowerOPEN Association Organization
- PowerOPEN Environment
- OpenDoc vs. OLE 2.0
- Bento—What is Bento?
- XDiary
- xgprof 2.4 User's Guide
- X-Recorder
- The Year 2000 and 2-digit Dates
- Zapp

Technical Information: Developer Connection AIX Newsletters

- Volume 2, No. 3, 1995
- Volume 2, No. 2, 1995
- Volume 2, No. 1, 1995
- Volume 1, No. 1, 1994

Technical Information: Books

- AIX 4.1 Porting Guide
- PowerPC Reference Platform Specification
- Encina Application Development Guide
- Encina Server Reference
- Encina Server Administration
- Encina PPC Executive Programer's Reference
- Encina Base Reference
- Encina Transactional-C Programmer's Guide and Reference
- Encina SFS Programmer's Guide and Reference
- Encina Monitor Programmer's Guide and Reference
- DCE Application Developer's Reference
- DCE makeDCE Application Developer's Guide

Technical Information: Red Books (HTML format)

- AIX Connections for Beginners
- AIX Version 4 Desktop Handbook
- Developing DCE Applications for AIX, OS/2, and Windows
- A Holistic Approach to AIX 4.1 Migration
- OPENDOC: An Introduction to Part Developers
- IBM DCE Cross-Platform Guide
- A Practical Introduction to SOM and DSOM

Technical Information: Manuals (compressed postscript)

- AIX SNA Server/6000: User's Guide
- AIX SNA Gateway/6000: User's Guide
- SNA Client Access for AIX V1R1: User's Guide
- AIX SNA Server/6000: Configuration Reference

- AIX SNA Server/6000: Command Reference
- AIX SNA Server/6000: Diagnosis Guide and Messages
- AIX SNA Server/6000: Transaction Program Reference
- Introduction to CPI-C Programming in an AIX SNA Server Version 2

Technical Information: Red Books (Postscript)

- AIX Connections for Beginners
- AIX Version 4 Desktop Handbook
- Developing DCE Applications for AIX, OS/2, and Windows
- The Distributed File System (DFS) for AIX/6000
- A Holistic Approach to AIX 4.1 Migration
- APPC Application Suite for AIX, User's Guide
- Guided Tour of ANS Server/6000 Version 2, Release 1

Technical Information: AIXpert Magazine

- August 1995
- May 1995
- February 1995

Software Development Tools and Applications

- MakeStack
- AIX SNA Server/6000, Version 2, Release 2
- AIX SNA Gateway/6000, Version 2, Release 2
- SNA Client Access for AIX, Version 1, Release 1
- SNA: APPC Application Suite
- SNA Programming Interface Development Tool
- SNA: X Based SNA Local Management Tool
- xgprof
- MASS Information
- IBM Information Presentation Facility/6000
- AIX Mosaic
- AIX Desktop GUI Builder
- AIX Desktop Data Type Tool
- X Magnifying Glass

- AIX Font Selection Tool
- X GC
- X CMStest
- X Recorder Information
- X Recorder Demo
- X-Window and Graphics Capture
- X Custom Resource Editor

System Administrators Tools

- AIX InfoExplorer
- AIX System Configuration Summary
- AIX User and Groups Manager
- AIX Device Manager
- AIX Install and Update Manager
- AIX Maintain Installed Software Manager
- AIX Storage (lvm) Manager
- AIX Print Manager
- Set Date and Time Manager

Productivity Tools

- AIX Desktop Calendar
- AIX Desktop Mail
- AIX Desktop Calculator
- AIX Desktop Icon Editor
- AIX Print Queue Info
- AIX Desktop Editor
- AIX Screen Saver Demos
- AIX Desktop Style Manager
- AIX Round Clock
- Simple File Editor
- X-Windows Audio CD Player
- X Lock Display

REXX/600

- Book—REXX/6000
- Install Information

AIX Device Driver Overview

- Overview Information
- Writing a DD for AIX 4.1 Samples
- PCMCIA Samples
- PMCIA Draft Information
- PMCIA Writing a PM Aware Device Driver
- Ethernet Device Driver
- ISA Samples
- Keyboard Device Driver
- Mouse Device Driver
- Diskette Device Driver
- Sample Streams tty Driver
- IBM 16/4 PowerPC Token-ring Driver
- Parallel Printer Device Driver

Microchannel WWD Samples

- Main WWD Sample Program
- Sample Interrupt Handler
- How to Access non-MCA I/O Space
- Configuration Method Examples
- Sets up DMA Master Transfer
- SCSI CDROM Device Driver
- SCSI LMS code
- SCSI Passthru Example
- IBM Ethernet Device Driver
- Graphics Device Driver
- IBM Filesystem Sample Program

AIXwindows Demos

- X Plaid
- X Ico
- X Maze Game
- X Muncher
- X Puzzle
- X Eyes
- X Gas
- X11 Performance Benchmarks (line)
- X11 Performance Benchmarks (rectangle)
- X11 Performance Benchmarks (circle)
- X11 Performance Benchmarks (triangle)
- X11 Performance Benchmarks (text)
- X11 Performance Benchmarks (move)
- X11 Performance Benchmarks (resize)

Performance Demos

- Performance Toolbox

Prerelease Code: OpenDoc Early Experience Package

- OpenDoc ReadMe
- OpenDoc Installation Guide

Prerelease Code: Program Visualizer

- Program Visualizer Information
- Install Information
- Paper—Program Visualization
- Paper—Multi-Layer Visualization
- Charts for Multi-Layer Visualization

Appendixes

AIX Man Pages

Appendix A   Directory Commands

mkdir—Makes one or more directories.

SYNOPSIS

mkdir [-mMode] [-p] Directory ...

DESCRIPTION

The mkdir command creates one or more new directories specified by the Directory parameter. You can specify the permissions for the new directories with the -m Mode flag. Using flag -p will create missing intermediate path name directories.

SEE ALSO

See the following commands: chmod, umask, rm, mkdir, rmdir.

cd—Changes the current directory.

SYNOPSIS

cd [directory]

DESCRIPTION

The cd command moves you from your present directory to another. You must have execute (search) permission in the specified directory. If you do not specify a directory, cd moves you to your login directory ($HOME). If the specified directory name is a full path name, it becomes the current directory.

EXAMPLES

1.   To change to your home directory:

     cd

2.   To change to an arbitrary directory:

     cd /etc

This changes the current directory to "/etc".

3.   To go down one level of the directory tree:

     cd uucp

If the current directory is "/etc" and if it contains a subdirectory named "uucp", then "/etc/uucp" becomes the current directory.

4.   To go up one level of the directory tree:

     cd ..

The special file name .. (dot-dot) refers to the directory immediately above the current directory. However, under symbolic links, .. (dot-dot) refers to the parent directory of the symbolic link, not to the directory above the current directory.

SEE ALSO

See the following command: pwd.

rmdir—Removes a directory.

SYNOPSIS

rmdir [-p] directory...

DESCRIPTION

The rmdir command removes a directory from the system. The directory must be empty before you can remove it. Use the ls -a command to see if the directory is empty.

The -p flag removes all directories along the path name specified by the Directory parameter.

EXAMPLE

To empty and remove a directory:

rm mydir/* mydir/.*

rmdir mydir

This removes the contents of "mydir", then removes the empty directory.

SEE ALSO

See the following commands: rm and ls.

mvdir—Moves (renames) a directory.

SYNOPSIS

mvdir directory1 directory2

DESCRIPTION

The mvdir command renames directories. The directory1 parameter must name an existing directory. If directory2 does not exist, directory1 is moved to directory2. If directory2 exists, directory1 becomes a subdirectory of directory2. Directory1 and directory2 may be the names of files. If directory2 is a file name, it is replaced with directory1.

EXAMPLE

To rename or move a directory to another location:

mvdir manpages aixbook

If "aixbook" does not exist, then this renames the directory "manpages" to "aixbook". You can also rename a directory with the mv command. If a directory named "aixbook" already exists, this moves "manpages" and its contents to "aixbook/ manpages". In other words, "manpages" becomes a subdirectory of "aixbook".

SEE ALSO

See the following commands: mkdir and mv.

ls—Lists the contents of a directory.

SYNOPSIS

ls [-1ACFLNRabcdefgilmnopqrstux] [File...]

DESCRIPTION

The ls command is the most commonly used command so it has many options! Try out some of these flags and combinations and find the set that you like the most. The ls command displays the contents of each specified directory or file, along with any other information you ask for with the flags. If you do not specify a file or directory, ls displays the contents of the current directory. By default, ls displays all information in alphabetic order by file name.

There are three main ways to format the output:

- List one entry per line by specifying the -1 or other flags.
- List entries in multiple columns by specifying either the -C or -x flags.
- List entries in a comma-separated series by specifying the -m flag.

The mode displayed with the -e and -l flags are as follows:

d   The entry is a directory.

b   The entry is a block special file.

c   The entry is a character special file.

l   The entry is a symbolic link.

p   The entry is a first-in first-out (FIFO) special file.

s   The entry is a local socket.

-     The entry is an ordinary file.

The next nine characters are divided into three sets of three characters each for owner, group, and other, respectively. The three characters in each set show read, write, and execute permission of the file. Permissions are indicated as follows:

r   Permission to read a file.

w   Permission to edit (write) a file.

x   Permission to search/execute the file.

-     No permission to a file.

When the size of the files in a directory are listed, the ls command displays a total count of blocks, including indirect blocks.

LS FLAGS

-A   Lists all entries except . (dot) and .. (dot-dot).

-a   Lists all entries in the directory, including the entries that begin with a . (dot).

-b   Displays nonprintable characters in an octal (\nnn) notation.

-c   Uses the time of last modification of the i-node for either sorting (when used with the -t flag) or for displaying (when used with the -l flag).

-C   Sorts output vertically in a multicolumn format. This is the default method when output is to a terminal.

-d   Displays only the information for the directory named. Directories are treated like files, which is helpful when using the -l flag to get the status of a directory.

-e   Displays the mode (including security information), number of links, owner, group, size (in bytes), time of last modification, and name of each file.

-f   Lists the name in each slot for each directory specified in the directory parameter. The order of the listing is the order in which entries appear in the directory.

-F   Puts a / (slash) after each file name if the file is a directory, an * (asterisk) if the file can be executed, an = (equal sign) if the file is a socket, a | (pipe) sign if the file is a FIFO, and an @ for a symbolic link.

-g   Displays the same information as the -l flag, except the -g flag suppresses-display of the owner and symbolic link information.

-i   Displays the i-node number in the first column of the report for each file.

-L   Lists the file or directory contents that the link references.

-l   (Lower case L) Displays the mode, number of links, owner, group, size (in bytes), and time of last modification for each file.

-m   Uses stream output format (a comma-separated series).

-n   Displays the same information as the -l flag, except that the -n flag displays the user and the group IDs instead of the user and group names.

-N   Does not follow symbolic links when determining the status of a file.

-o   Displays the same information as the -l flag, except the -o flag suppresses display of the group and symbolic link information.

-p   Puts a slash after each file name if that file is a directory.

-q   Displays nonprintable characters in file names as a ? (question mark).

-r   Reverses the order of the sort, giving reverse alphabetic or the oldest first, as appropriate.

-R   Lists all subdirectories recursively.

-s   Gives size in kilobytes (including indirect blocks) for each entry.

-t   Sorts by time of last modification (latest first) instead of by name.

-u   Uses the time of the last access, instead of the time of the last modification, for either sorting (when used with the -t flag) or for displaying (when used with the -l flag).

-x   Sorts output horizontally in a multicolumn format.

-1   Forces output into one-entry-per-line format.

EXAMPLES

1. To list all files in the current directory:

ls -a

This lists all files, including . (dot), .. (dot-dot), and other files with names beginning with a dot.

2. To display detailed information:

ls -l aixbook toc

This displays a long listing with detailed information about aixbook and .toc.

3. To display detailed information about a directory:

ls -d -l . aixbook aixbook/manpages

This displays a long listing for the directories . (dot) and aixbook, and for the file aixbook/manpages. Without the -d flag, this would list the files in . (dot) and aixbook instead of the detailed information about the directories themselves.

4. To list the files in order of modification time:

ls -l -t

This displays a long listing of the files that were modified most recently, followed by the older files.

SEE ALSO

See the following commands: chmod and find.

df—Reports information about space on file systems.

SYNOPSIS

df [-P] | [-IMitv] [-k] [-s] [filesystem ...] [file ...]

DESCRIPTION

The df command writes to standard output information about total space and available space on the specified file systems. filesystem can be the name of the device on which the file system resides or the directory on which it is mounted. If you specify file, then df will provide information about the filesystem file is located in. If you do not specify either file or filesystem, df provides information on all mounted file systems. File system statistics are displayed in units of 512-byte blocks by default.

FLAGS

-i   Displays the number of free and used i-nodes for the file system; this output is the default when the specified file system is mounted.

-I   Displays information on the total number of blocks, the used space, the free space, the percentage of used space, and the mount point for the file system.

-k   Displays statistics in units of 1024-byte blocks.

-M   Displays the mount point information for the file system in the second column.

-P   Displays information on the file system in POSIX portable format. When the -P flag is specified, the header line appears similar to:

Filesystem 512-blocks Used Available Capacity Mounted on

If the -k flag is specified in addition to the -P flag, the column heading 512-blocks is replaced by the heading 1024-blocks. File system statistics are displayed on one line in the following order:

FileSystem, TotalSpace, UsedSpace, FreeSpace, UsedPercentage, Mount-Point

-s   Gets file system statistics from the VFS specific file system helper instead of the statfs system call.

-t   Includes figures for total allocated space in the output.

-v   Displays all information for the specified file system.

EXAMPLE

To list information about all file systems:

df

SEE ALSO

See the following command: fsck.

Appendix B   File Manipulation Commands

cp—Copies files.

SYNOPSIS

cp [-fhip] [-r | -R] [- -] SourceFile target

cp [-fhip] [-r | -R] [- -] src1 ... srcN directory

DESCRIPTION

The cp (copy) command copies a source file or the files in a source directory to a target file or directory. If your output is to a directory, then the files are copied to that directory with the same file name.

FLAGS

-f   Specifies removal of the destination file if it can not be opened for write.

-h   Forces the cp command to copy symbolic links.

-I   Prompts for confirmation before overwriting any existing files.

-p   Preserves the modification times and modes of the source file for the copy.

-r   Copies each subtree rooted at the source file (recursive copy). Special files are created as regular files.

-R   Copies each subtree rooted at the source file (recursive copy). Special files are recreated as special files.

- -   Indicates that the arguments following this flag are to be interpreted as file names.

EXAMPLES

To make another copy of a file in the current directory:

cp book.txt book.bak

This copies "book.txt" to "book.bak". If the file "book.bak" does not already exist, then cp creates it. If it does exist, then cp replaces it with a copy of "book.txt".

To copy a file to another directory:

cp jones /u/trent/authors

This copies "jones" to "/u/trent/authors/jones".

To copy all the files in a directory to a new directory:

cp /u/trent/authors/* /u/trent/team

This copies the files and directories in the directory "authors" to the directory "team".

To copy a directory, its files, and its subdirectories to another directory:

cp -r /u/trent/authors /u/trent/team

This copies the directory "clients", its files, its subdirectories, and the files in the subdirectories to the directory "customers".

SEE ALSO

See the following command: mv.

mv—Moves and renames files.

SYNOPSIS

mv [-i | -f] [- -] src target

mv [-i | -f] [- -] src1 ... srcN TargetDirectory

DESCRIPTION

The mv command moves files and directories from one directory to another, or renames a file or directory. When you move a directory into an existing directory, the directory and its contents are added under the existing directory. When you use the mv command to rename a file or directory, the TargetDirectory parameter can specify either a new file name or a new directory path name.

FLAGS

-f   Does not prompt before overwriting an existing file.

-I   Prompts before moving a file or directory that would overwrite an existing file.

- -   Specifies that the following parameters are file names.

EXAMPLES

To rename a file:

mv manpgs manpages

This renames "manpgs" to "manpages".

To rename a directory:

mv book aixbook

This renames "book" to "aixbook".

To move a file to another directory, keeping the same name:

mv manpages aixbook

This moves "chap3" to "aixbook/chap3".

To move several files into another directory:

mv manpages overview aixbook

This moves "manpages" to "aixbook/manpages" and "overview" to "aixbook/overview".

SEE ALSO

See the following command: mvdir.

rm—Removes files or directories.

SYNOPSIS

rm [-firRe] [- -] File ...

DESCRIPTION

The rm command removes the specified files from a directory.

FLAGS

-e Displays a message after each file is deleted.

-f Does not prompt before removing a write-protected file.

-i Prompts you before deleting each file. When you use the -i and -r flags together, the rm command also prompts before deleting directories.

-r Causes recursive removal of directories and their contents when the File parameter is a directory. This flag is equivalent to the -R flag.

-R Causes recursive removal of directories and their contents when the File parameter is a directory. This flag is equivalent to the -r flag.

EXAMPLES

To delete a file:

rm myfile

To delete a file silently:

rm -f core

This removes core without asking any questions or displaying any error messages.

To delete files one by one with prompting:

rm -i mydir/*

This interactively asks you if you want to remove each file. After each file name is displayed, enter "y" to delete the file, or press Enter to keep it.

To delete a directory tree with prompting:

rm -ir aixbook

SEE ALSO

See the following command: õmdir

ln—Links files.

SYNOPSIS

ln [-fs] src [target]

ln [-fs] src1 ... srcN directory

DESCRIPTION

The ln command links the source file to the target file. If you are linking a file to a new name, you can specify only one file. If you are linking to a directory, you can list more than one file.

FLAGS

-f Causes ln to overwrite existing files without displaying an error message.

-s Creates a symbolic link to a file or directory.

EXAMPLES

To create another name (also called an alias) for a file:

ln chap1 overview

This links "chap1" to the new name "overview". Now "chap1" and "overview" are two file names that refer to the same file. Any changes made to one also appears in the other.

To create a symbolic link:

ln -s chap1 my_chap1

SEE ALSO

See the following commands: rm, mv, and cp.

cat—Concatenates or displays files.

SYNOPSIS

cat [-urSsq] [-n[b]] [-v[te]] [- I file ...]

DESCRIPTION

The cat command reads each file in sequence and writes it to standard output. If you do not specify file, or if you specify - (minus) instead of a file, cat reads from standard input.

FLAGS

-b   Omits line numbers from blank lines, when specified with the -n flag.

-e   Displays a $ (dollar sign) at the end of each line, when specified with the -v flag.

-n   Displays output lines preceded by line numbers, numbered sequentially from 1.

-q   Does not display a message if the cat command cannot find an input file. This flag is identical to the -s flag.

-r   Replaces multiple consecutive empty lines with one empty line. This flag is identical to the -S flag.

-s   Does not display a message if the cat command cannot find an input file. This flag is identical to the -q flag.

-S   Replaces multiple consecutive empty lines with one empty line. This flag is identical to the -r flag.

-t   Displays tab characters as ^I if specified with the -v flag.

-u   Does not buffer output.

-v   Displays nonprinting characters as visible characters.

-     Allows standard input to the cat command.

EXAMPLES

To display a single file at the work, i.e., station:

cat notes

To concatenate several files:

cat file1 file2 file3 >files

This creates a file named "files" that is a copy of "file1" followed by "file2" and "file3".

To append one file to the end of another:

cat file4 >>files

This appends a copy of "file4" to the end of "files". The ">>" is shell I/O redirection to append data to the end of "files".

SEE ALSO

See the following command: PG.

pg—Formats files to the work station.

SYNOPSIS

pg [-number][-p string][-cefns][+line][+/pattern/][file...]

DESCRIPTION

The pg command reads files and writes them to standard output, one screen at a time. If you specify file as - (minus) or run pg without arguments, pg reads standard input. Each screen is followed by a prompt. If you press the Enter key, another page is displayed. The pg command lets you back up to review a prior page. In the text below <number> simply means a number you type. Pattern generally refers to a string to search for.

SUBCOMMANDS

When pg pauses and issues its prompt, you can issue a subcommand. Some of these subcommands change the display to a particular place in the file, some search for specific patterns in the text, and others change the environment in which pg works.

The following commands display a selected place in the file:

page	Displays the specified page.
+<number>	Displays the page <number> pages after the current page.
-<number>	Displays the page <number> pages before the current page.
l	Scrolls the display one line forward.
<number>l	Displays a screen with the specified line number at the top.
+<number>l	Scrolls the display <number> lines forward.
-<number>l	Scrolls the display <number> lines backward.
d	Scrolls half a screen forward. Pressing Ctrl-D also does this.
-d	Scrolls half a screen backward. Pressing -Ctrl-D also does this.
Ctrl-L	Displays the current page again. A single period also does this.
$	Displays the last page in the file.

The following commands search for text patterns in the text:

[<number>]/pattern/	Searches for the <number>th occurrence of pattern. The default for <number> is 1.
<number>?pattern?	

<number>^pattern^   Searches backward for the <number>th occurrence of
                       pattern. The default for <number> is 1.

After searching, pg normally displays the line found at the top of the screen. You
can change this by adding m or b to the search command to leave the line found
in the middle or at the bottom of the window with all succeeding subcommands.
Use the suffix t to return to displaying the line with the pattern to the top of the
screen.

You can change the pg environment with the following subcommands:

[<number>]n   Begins examining the <number>th next file in the command
                 line. The default <number> is 1.

[<number>]p   Begins examining the <number>th previous file on the com-
                 mand line. The default <number> is 1.

[<number>]w   Displays another window of text. If <number> is present, sets
                 the window size to <number>.

s file   Saves the input in file. Only the current file being examined is
                 saved.

h   Displays an abbreviated summary of available subcommands.

q or Q   Quits pg.

!<shell-cmd>   Runs the specified shell command

FLAGS

-c   Moves the cursor to the home position and clears the screen be-
                 fore each page.

-e   Does not pause at the end of each file.

-f   Does not split lines. Normally, pg splits lines longer than the
                 screen width.

-n   Stops processing when a pg command letter is entered. Nor-
                 mally, commands must end with a newline character.

-p string   Uses string as the prompt. If the string contains a %d, the %d is
                 replaced by the current page number in the prompt The default
                 prompt is : (colon).

-s   Highlights all messages and prompts.

+<linenum>   Starts at <linenum>.

-<number>   Specifies the number of lines in the window.

+/pattern/   Starts at the first line that contains pattern.

SEE ALSO

See the following commands: cat and grep.

chmod - Changes permission codes.

SYNOPSIS

chmod [-Rfh]{u l g l o l a ...}{+ l - l =}{r l w l x l X l s l t ...} File ...

chmod [-Rfh] OctalNumber File ...

DESCRIPTION

The chmod command modifies the read, write, execute (file), or search (directory) permission codes of specified files or directories. You can use either symbolic or absolute mode (octal) to specify the desired permission settings.

FLAGS

-f　Suppresses all error reporting except invalid permissions and usage state-
　　ments.

-h　Suppresses a mode change for the file or directory pointed to by the encoun-
　　tered symbolic link.

-R　Descends directories recursively. The -R flag changes the file mode bits of
　　each directory and of all files specified.

SYMBOLIC MODE

When you use the symbolic mode to specify permission codes, the first set of
flags selects the permission field, as follows:

u　User (owner)

g　Group

o　All others

a　User, group, and all others (same effect as ugo). This is the default permis-
　　sion field.

The second set of flags selects whether permissions are to be taken away, added,
or set exactly as specified:

-　Removes specified permissions.

+　Adds specified permissions.

=　Clears the selected permission field and sets it to the code specified.

The third set of flags of the chmod command selects the permissions as follows:

r   Read permission.

w   Write permission.

x   Execute permission for files; search permission for directories.

X   Execute permission for files if the current (unmodified) mode bits have at least one of the user, group, or other execute bits set, otherwise the X flag is ignored.

s   SetUser-ID or set Group-ID permission. This permission bit sets the effective User-ID or Group-ID to that of the file whenever the file is run.

t   For directories, indicates that only file owners can link or unlink files in the specified directory. For files, sets the save-text attribute.

ABSOLUTE MODE (specify mode with octal numbers)

4000 Sets User-ID on execution.

2000 Sets Group-ID on execution.

1000 Sets the link permission to directories or sets the save-text attribute for files.

0400 Permits read by owner.

0200 Permits write by owner.

0100 Permits execute or search by owner.

0040 Permits read by group.

0020 Permits write by group.

0010 Permits execute or search by group.

0004 Permits read by others.

0002 Permits write by others.

0001 Permits execute or search by others.

EXAMPLES

1.   To add a type of permission to several files:

      chmod g+w chap1 chap2

      This adds write permission for group members to the files "chap1" and "chap2".

2.   To make several permission changes at once:

      chmod go-w+x mydir

This denies group members and others the permission to create or delete files in "mydir" ("go-w"). It allows them to search "mydir" or use it in a path name ("go+x"). This is equivalent to the command sequence:

chmod g-w mydir

chmod o-w mydir

chmod g+x mydir

chmod o+x mydir

3.   To use the absolute mode form of the chmod command:

chmod 644 text

This sets read and write permission for the owner, and it sets read-only mode for the group and others.

SEE ALSO

See the following commands: ls and umask.

cmp—Compares two files.

SYNOPSIS

cmp [-l] [-s] file1 file2

DESCRIPTION

The cmp command compares file1 and file2 and writes the results to standard output. If you specify a - (minus) for file1, cmp reads standard input. Under default conditions, cmp displays nothing if the files are the same. If they differ, cmp displays the byte and line number at which the first difference occurs. Normally, you use cmp to compare nontext files and the diff command to compare text files.

FLAGS

-l   Displays, for each difference, the byte number in decimal and the differing bytes in octal.

-s   Returns only an exit value. (0 indicates identical files; 1 indicates different files; 2 indicates inaccessible files or a missing argument.)

EXAMPLES

To determine whether two files are identical:

cmp prog.o.bak prog.o

This compares "prog.o.bak" and "prog.o". If the files are identical, then a message is not displayed. If the files differ, then the location of the first difference is displayed.

SEE ALSO

See the following command: diff.

diff—Compares text files.

SYNOPSIS

diff [-bcitw][[-C Lines | -D String | -e | -f | -n] | [-h]] File1 File2

diff [-bcilrstw][[-C Lines | -e | -f | -n] | [-h]][-S File] Directory1 Directory2

DESCRIPTION

The diff command compares file1 and file2 and writes to standard output information about what changes must be made to bring them into agreement. If you specify a - (minus) for file1 or file2, diff reads standard input. If file1 is a directory, then diff uses a file in that directory with the name file2. If file2 is a directory, then diff uses a file in that directory with the name file1.

The normal output contains lines of these three forms:

Lines Affected in file 1	Action	Lines Affected in file 2
num1	a	num2[,num3]
num1[,num2]	d	num3
num1[,num2]	c	num3[,num4]

These lines resemble ed subcommands to convert file1 into file2. The numbers before the action letters pertain to file1; those after pertain to file2. Thus, by exchanging a for d and reading backward, you can also tell how to convert file2 into file1. As in ed, identical pairs (where num1 = num2) are abbreviated as a single number.

Following each of these lines, diff displays all lines affected in the first file preceded by a <, then all lines affected in the second file preceded by a >.

An exit value of 0 indicates no differences, 1 indicates differences found, and 2 indicates an error.

FLAGS

-b	Ignores leading spaces and tab characters and considers other strings of spaces to compare as equal.
-C Lines	Produces a diff command comparison with a number of lines of context equal to the value specified by the Lines variable. The -C flag modifies the output slightly. The output begins with identification of the files involved and their creation dates. Each change is separated by a line with a dozen * (asterisks). The lines removed from File1 are marked with a - (minus sign) and those added to File2 are marked with a + (plus sign). Lines changed from one file to the other are marked in both files with an ! (exclamation point).
-c	Produces a diff command comparison with three lines of context. The -c flag modifies the output slightly. The output begins with identification of the files involved and their creation dates. Each change is separated by a line with a dozen * (asterisks). The lines removed from File1 are marked with a - (minus sign) and those added to File2 are marked with a + (plus sign). Lines changed from one file to the other are marked in both files with an ! (exclamation point).
-D [String]	Causes the diff command to create a merged version of File1 and File2 on the standard output. The C preprocessor controls are included so that a compilation of the result without defining String is equivalent to compiling File1, while defining String yields File2.
-e	Produces output in a form suitable for use with the ed editor to convert File1 to File2.
-f	Produces output in a form not suitable for use with the ed editor, showing the modifications necessary to convert File1 to File2 in the reverse order of that produced under the -e flag.
-h	Performs an alternate comparison which may be faster if the changed sections are short and well-separated.
-i	Ignores the case of letters.
-l	Long output format. Each result from the diff command text file comparison is piped through the pr command for pagination. Other differences are remembered and summarized after all text file differences are reported.

-n   Produces output similar to that of the -e flag, but in the opposite
            order and with a count of changed lines on each insert or delete
            command. This is the form used by the revision control system
            (RCS).

-r   Causes application of the diff command recursively to common
            subdirectories encountered.

-s   Reports files that are the same and otherwise not mentioned.

-S [File] Ignores files whose names collate before the file specified by the
            File variable when comparing directories.

-t   Expands tabs in output lines. Normal output or the -c flag output
            adds characters to the front of each line, which may affect indenta-
            tion of the original source lines and make the output listing diffi-
            cult to interpret. This flag preserves the original source's indenta-
            tion.

-w   Ignores all spaces and tab characters.

EXAMPLES

1. To compare two files:

    diff chap1.bak chap1

2. To compare two files, ignoring differences in the amount of white space:

    diff -w prog.c.bak prog.c

SEE ALSO

See the following commands: bdiff, cmp, comm, ed, and sdiff.

grep—Searches a file for a pattern.

SYNOPSIS

grep [-E | -F] [-c | -l | -q] [-insvxbhwy] [-p[parasep]] -e pattern_list...
    [-f pattern_file...] [file...]

grep [-E | -F] [-c | -l | -q] [-insvxbhwy] [-p[parasep]] [-e pattern_list...]
    -f pattern_file... [file...]

grep [-E | -F] [-c | -l | -q] [-insvxbhwy] [-p[parasep]] pattern_list [file...]

DESCRIPTION

This command is one of our favorites! Don't get overwhelmed with the number
of options and some of the syntax. The power of this command is the ability to
search through a bunch of files for a character string.

Commands of the grep family search input files for lines matching a pattern. Normally, they copy each line found to standard output. Three versions of the grep command permit you to express the matching pattern in varying levels of complexity:

grep   Searches for patterns which are basic regular expressions.

egrep   Searches for patterns which are extended regular expressions

fgrep   Searches for patterns that are fixed strings.

All versions of grep display the name of the file containing the matched line if you specify more than one file name. Characters with special meaning to the shell ("$ * [| ^ ( ) \") must be quoted when they appear in patterns. When the pattern is not a simple string, you usually must enclose the entire pattern in single quotation marks.

FLAGS

-b	Precedes each line by the block number on which it was found.
-c	Displays only a count of matching lines.
-E	Treats each pattern specified as an extended regular expression (ERE). The grep command with the -E flag is almost the same as the egrep command.
-e PatternList	Specifies one or more search patterns. This works like a simple pattern but is useful when the pattern begins with a - (minus). Patterns should be separated by a new-line character. (Hint, enclose the pattern list in single or double quotes.)
-F	Treats each specified pattern as a string instead of a regular expression. The grep command with the -F flag is almost the same as the fgrep command.
-f PatternFile	Specifies a file containing search patterns.
-h	Suppresses file name output when multiple files are specified.
-i	Ignores the case (uppercase or lowercase) of letters when making comparisons.
-l	Lists just the names of files (once) which contain matching lines.
-n	Precedes each line with the relative line number in the file.
-p[Separator]	Displays the entire paragraph containing matched lines. Paragraphs are delimited by either the Separator Pattern or by a blank line if a Separater isn't specified.

-q	Suppresses all writing to standard output, regardless of matching lines. Exits with a zero status if a pattern is found.
-s	Suppresses error messages ordinarily written for nonexistent or unreadable files.
-v	Displays all lines not matching the specified pattern.
-w	Does a word search.
-x	Displays lines that match the specified pattern exactly with no additional characters.
-y	Ignores the case of letters when making comparisons.

EXAMPLES

1. To search several files for a simple string of characters:

grep "strcpy" *.c

This searches for the string "strcpy" in all files in the current directory with names ending in ".c"

2. To count the number of lines that match a pattern:

grep -c "AIX" preface

This displays the number of lines in "preface" that contains the string "AIX".

3. To display the names of files that contain a pattern:

grep -l "strcpy" *.c

This searches the files in the current directory that end with ".c" and displays the names of those files that contain the string "strcpy".

cut—Writes out selected fields from each line of a file.

SYNOPSIS

cut {-b<list>[-n] | -c<list> | -f<list>[-d<char>][-s]} file ...

DESCRIPTION

The cut command cuts out columns from a table or cuts out fields from each line of a file and writes these columns or fields to standard output. If you do not specify a file, cut reads standard input.

You must specify either the -b, -c, or -f flag. The list parameter is a comma, blank, or hyphen separated list of integer numbers (in increasing order). The hyphen separator indicates ranges. Some sample lists are "1,4,7"; "1-3,8"; "-5,10" (short for "1-5,10"); and "3-" (short for third through last field).

FLAGS

-b List	Specifies byte positions.
-c List	Specifies character positions. For example, if you specify -c 1-40, the cut command writes out the first 40 characters in each line of the file.
-d Character	Uses the character specified by the Character variable as the field delimiter when you specify the -f flag.
-f List	Specifies a list of fields assumed to be separated in the file by a delimiter character, which is by default the tab character. For example, if you specify -f 1,7, the cut command writes out only the first and seventh fields of each line. If a line contains no field delimiters, the cut command passes them through intact (useful for table subheadings), unless you specify the -s flag.
-n	Suppresses splitting of multibyte characters. Only characters which are completely contained in the style list specified by the -f parameter will be displayed.
-s	Suppresses lines that do not contain delimiter characters. Use only with the -f flag.

EXAMPLE

To display several fields of each line of a file:

cut -f1,5 -d: /etc/passwd

This displays the login name and full user name fields of the system password file. These are the first and fifth fields ("-f1,5") separated by colons ("-d:"). So, if the /etc/ passwd file looks like this:

sys:*:3:3::/usr/src:

adm:*:4:4:System Administrator:/var/adm:/bin/sh

Cannon:*:200:200:Casey Cannon:/home/pierre:/bin/ksh

bentti:*:202:200:Davin Bentti:/home/joan:/bin/sh

then cut produces:

sys:

adm:System Administrator

Cannon:Casey Cannon

bentti:Davin Bentti

join—Joins data fields of two files.

SYNOPSIS

join [-a FileNumber | -v FileNumber][-e String][-o List][-t Character][-1 Field][-2 Field] File1 File2

DESCRIPTION

The join command reads the files specified by the File1 and File2 parameters, joins lines in the files according to the flags, and writes the results to standard output. The File1 and File2 parameters must be text files. Both File1 and File2 must be sorted on the field that they are being joined by before invoking the join command.

One line appears in the output for each identical join field appearing in both files. The join field is the field in the input files examined by the join command to determine what will be included in the output. The output line consists of the join field, the rest of the line from the file specified by the File1 parameter, and the rest of the line from the file specified by the File2 parameter. Specify standard input in place of either the File1 or File2 parameter by substituting a - (dash) as the file name.

Fields are normally separated by one or more space, tab character, or new-line characters.

FLAGS

-1 Field	Joins the two files using the field number specified by the Field variable in the File1 input file.
-2 Field	Joins the two files using the field number specified by the Field variable in the File2 input file.
-a FileNumber	Produces an output line for each line in the file specified by the FileNumber variable whose join fields do not match any line in the other input file. The output lines are produced in addition to the default output. The value of the FileNumber variable must be either 1 or 2, corresponding to the files specified by the File1 and File2 parameters, respectively.
-e String	Replaces empty output fields with the string specified by the String variable.
-o List	Constructs an output line to comprise the fields specified in the List variable.

One of the following forms applies to the List variable:

FileNumber.Field   Where FileNumber is a file number and Field is a decimal-integer field number. Separate multiple fields with a , (comma) or space characters with quotation marks around the multiple fields.

0 (zero)   Represents the join field. The -o 0 flag essentially selects the union of the join fields.

-t Character   Uses the character specified by the Character parameter as the field separator character in the input and the output. Every appearance of the character in a line is significant. The default separator is a space.

-v FileNumber   Produces an output line for each line in the file specified by the FileNumber variable whose join fields do not match any line in the other input file. Default output is not produced. The value of the FileNumber variable must be either 1 or 2, corresponding to the files specified by File1 and File2 parameters, respectively.

SEE ALSO

See the following commands: awk, sort, cut, and paste.

sort—Sorts or merges files.

SYNOPSIS

sort [-Abcdfimnru] [-o OutFile] [-t Character] [-T Directory] [-y [Kilobytes]] [-z RecordSize] ... [-k KeyDefinition] ... [File ...]

DESCRIPTION

Sort is a great command! It's easy to sort a file by name or number so that you can get information out of all that data! If the descriptions are too much for you, just go straight to the examples.

The sort command sorts lines in the files specified by the File parameter and writes the result to standard output. If the File parameter specifies more than one file, the sort command concatenates the files and sorts them as one file. A -(minus sign) in place of a file name specifies standard input. If you do not specify any file names, the command sorts standard input. An output file can be specified with the -o flag.

SORT KEYS

A sort key is a portion of an input line that is specified by a field number and a column number. Fields are parts of input lines that are separated by field separators. The default field separator is a sequence of one or more consecutive space or tab characters. A different field separator can be specified using the -t flag.

When using sort keys, the sort command first sorts all lines on the contents of the first sort key. Next, all the lines whose first sort keys are equal are sorted upon the contents of the second sort key, and so on. Sort keys are numbered according to the order they appear on the command line. If two lines sort equally on all sort keys, the entire lines are then compared based upon the collation order in the current locale.

When numbering columns within fields, the blank characters in a default field separator are counted as part of the following field. Leading blanks are not counted as part of the first field, and field separator characters specified by the -t flag are not counted as parts of fields. Leading blank characters can be ignored using the -b flag.

Sort keys can be defined using the following -k flag:

Sort Key Definition Using the -k Flag.   The -k KeyDefinition flag uses the following form:

-k [FStart [.CStart]] [Modifier] [, [FEnd [.CEnd]][Modifier]]

The sort key includes all characters beginning with the field specified by the FStart variable and the column specified by the CStart variable and ending with the field specified by the FEnd variable and the column specified by the CEnd variable. If Fend is not specified, the last character of the line is assumed. If CEnd is not specified the last character in the FEnd field is assumed. Any field or column number in the KeyDefinition variable may be omitted. The default values are as follows:

FStart   Beginning of the line

CStart   First column in the field

FEnd   End of the line

CEnd   Last column of the field

The value of the Modifier variable can be one or more of the letters b, d, f, i, n, or r. The modifiers apply only to the field definition they are attached to and have the same effect as the flag of the same letter. The modifier letter b applies only to the end of the field definition to which it is attached. For example,

-k 3.2b,3r

specifies a sort key beginning in the second nonblank column of the third field and extending to the end of the third field, with the sort on this key to be done in reverse collation order. If the FStart variable and the CStart variable fall beyond the end of the line or after the FEnd variable and the CEnd variable, then the sort key is ignored.

FLAGS

-A	Sorts on a byte-by-byte basis using ASCII collation order instead of collation in the current locale. This is the fastest way to sort.
-b	Ignores leading spaces and tabs to find the first or last column of a field.
-c	Checks that input is sorted according to the ordering rules specified in the flags.
-d	Sorts using dictionary order. Only letters, digits, and spaces are considered in comparisons.
-f	Changes all lowercase letters to uppercase before comparison.
-i	Ignores all nonprinting characters during comparisons.
-k KeyDefinition	Specifies a sort key. The format of the KeyDefinition option is:

[FStart][.CStart][Modifier][,[FEnd][.CEnd][Modifier]]

The sort key includes all characters beginning with the field specified by the FStart variable and the column specified by the CStart variable and ending with the field specified by the FEnd variable and the column specified by the CEnd variable. The value of the Modifier variable can be b, d, f, i, n, or r. The modifiers are equivalent to the flags of the same letter.

-m	Merges multiple input files only; the input is assumed to be already sorted.
-n	Sorts numeric fields by arithmetic value.
-o OutFile	Directs output to the file specified by the OutFile parameter instead of standard output. The value of the OutFile parameter can be the same as the File parameter.
-r	Reverses the order of the specified sort.
-t Character	Specifies Character as the single field separator character.

-u   Suppresses all but the first line in each set of lines that sort
                    equally according to the sort keys and options.

-T Directory   Places all temporary files that are created into the directory speci-
                    fied by the Directory parameter.

-y[Kilobytes]   Starts the sort command using the number of kilobytes of mem-
                    ory specified by the Kilobytes parameter and adds more as
                    needed.

-z RecordSize   Prevents abnormal termination if any of the lines being sorted are
                    longer than the default buffer size. RecordSize must designate a
                    value in bytes equal to or greater than the longest line to be
                    merged.

EXAMPLES

1.   To perform a simple sort in the file "fruits":

sort fruits

This displays the contents of "fruits" sorted in ascending lexicographic
order. This means that the characters in each column are compared one by
one, including spaces, digits, and special characters. For instance, if "fruits"
contains the text:

banana

orange

Persimmon

apple

%%banana

apple

ORANGE

then sort displays in the Clocale:

%%banana

ORANGE

Persimmon

apple

banana

orange

This order follows from the fact that in the ASCII collating sequence, "%" (percent sign) precedes the uppercase letters, which precede the lowercase letters.

2. To sort in dictionary order:

sort -d fruits

This sorts and displays the contents of "fruits", comparing only letters, digits, and blanks. If "fruits" is the same as in Example 1, then sort displays:

ORANGE

Persimmon

apple

%%banana

banana

orange

The "-d" flag tells sort to ignore the "%" character because it is not a letter, digit, or blank. This puts "%%banana" next to "banana".

3. To group lines that contain uppercase and special characters with similar lowercase lines:

sort -d -f fruits

This ignores special characters ("-d") and differences in case ("-f"). Given the "fruits" of Example 1, this displays:

apple

%%banana

banana

ORANGE

orange

Persimmon

4. To sort as in Example 3 and remove duplicate lines:

sort -d -f -u fruits

The "-u" flag tells sort to remove duplicate lines, making each line of the file unique. This displays:

apple

%%banana

orange

Persimmon

Note that not only was the duplicate "apple" removed, but "banana" and "ORANGE" as well. These were removed because the "-d" told sort to treat "%%banana" as if it were "banana", and the "-f" told it to treat "ORANGE" as "orange". Thus, sort considered "%%banana" to be a duplicate of "banana" and "ORANGE" a duplicate of "orange". Note: There is no way to predict which duplicate lines "sort -u" will keep and which it will remove.

SEE ALSO

See the following commands: comm, join, and uniq.

Appendix C   Backup Commands
compress—Compress and expand data.
SYNOPSIS

compress [-f] [-v] [-c] [-b bits] [name ...]

uncompress [-f] [-v] [-c] [name ...]

zcat [name ...]

DESCRIPTION

Compress reduces the size of the named files using adaptive Lempel-Ziv coding. Whenever possible, each file is replaced by one with the extension .Z, while keeping the same ownership modes, access, and modification times. If no files are specified, the standard input is compressed to the standard output. Compressed files can be restored to their original form using command uncompress or zcat.

The -f option will force compression. If -f is not given the user is prompted as to whether an existing name.Z file should be overwritten.

The -c ("cat") option makes compress/uncompress write to the standard output; no files are changed. The behavior of zcat is similar to that of uncompress -c.

The amount of compression obtained depends on the size of the input, the number of bits per code, and the distribution of common substrings. Typically, text such as source code or English is reduced by 50-60%. The -v option displays the percentage reduction of each file.

cpio—Copies files into and out of archive storage and directories.

SYNOPSIS

cpio -o[-acv][-BCvalue]

cpio -i[cdmrtuvfsSb6] [-BCvalue] [patterns ...]

cpio -p[adlmuv] directory

DESCRIPTION

The CPIO-O command reads file path names from standard input and copies these files to standard output along with path names and status information.

The CPIO-I command reads from standard input an archive file created by the cpio -o command and copies from it the files with names that match pattern. These files are copied into the current directory tree. You may list more than one pattern, using the file name notation described in the section on file globbing. Note, however, that in this application the special characters "*" (asterisk), "?" (question mark), and [" . . . "] (ellipse) also match the "/" (slash) in path names. The default pattern is "*" (select all files in the current directory).

The CPIO -P command reads file path names from standard input and copies these files into the named directory. The specified directory must already exist. If these path names include directory names and if these directories do not already exist, you must use the d flag to cause the directory to be created.

FLAGS

All flags must be listed together, without any blanks between them. Not all of the following flags can be used with each of the -o, -i, and -p flags.

a	Resets the access times of copied files to the current time.
b	Swaps both bytes and halfwords.
B	Performs block input/output, 512 bytes to a record.
c	Writes header information in ASCII character form.
Cvalue	Performs block input/output, value * 512 bytes to a record.
d	Creates directories as needed.
f	Copies all files except those matching pattern.
l	Links files rather than copies them, whenever possible.
m	Retains previous file modification time.
r	Renames files interactively.
s	Swaps bytes.

S   Swaps halfwords.

t   Creates a table of contents. This does not copy any files.

u   Copies unconditionally.

v   Lists file names.

6   Processes an old file (one written in UNIX Sixth Edition format).

EXAMPLES

1.   To copy files onto diskette:

cpio -ov <filenames >/dev/rfd0

This copies the files with path names that are listed in the file "filenames" onto the diskette. The v flag causes cpio to display the name of each file as it is copied. This command is useful for making backup copies of files. The diskette must already be formatted, but it should not contain a file system or be mounted.

2.   To copy files in the current directory onto diskette:

ls *.c | cpio -ov >/dev/rfd0

This copies all the files in the current directory whose names end with ".c".

3.   To copy the current directory and all subdirectories onto diskette:

find . -print | cpio -ov >/dev/rfd0

This saves the directory tree that starts with the current directory (.) and in-cludes all of its subdirectories and files. A faster way to do this is:

find . -cpio /dev/rfd0 -print

4.   To list the files that have been saved onto a diskette with cpio:

cpio -itv </dev/rfd0

This displays the table of contents of the data previously saved onto /dev/rfd0 in cpio format.

5.   To copy the files previously saved with cpio from a diskette:

cpio -idmv </dev/rfd0

This copies the files previously saved onto /dev/rfd0 by cpio back into the file system. The d flag allows cpio to create the appropriate directories as needed. The m flag maintains the last modification time that was in effect when the files were saved. The v flag causes cpio to display the name of each file as it is copied.

6.   To copy selected files from diskette:

cpio -i "*.txt" </dev/rfd0

This copies the files that end with ".txt" from diskette. Note that the pattern must be enclosed in quotation marks to prevent the shell from treating the "*" as a pattern-matching character.

SEE ALSO

See the following commands: ar, find, and ln.

tar—Manipulates archives.

SYNOPSIS

tar [-c -r -t -u -x] [-BFdhilmopsvw] [-number] [-ffile] [-bblocks] [-Sfeet] [-Sfeet@density] [-Sblocksb] [-LinputList] [-Nblocks] [-Cdirectory] [file directory]...

DESCRIPTION

The tar command writes files to or retrieves files from an archival storage medium. The tar command looks for archives on the default device (usually tape), unless you specify another device with the -f flag. File names must not be longer than 100 bytes and must not contain blanks.

FLAGS

You must supply one of the following five function flags to control the actions of tar:

-c   Creates a new archive and writes the file at the beginning of the archive.

-r   Writes the file at the end of the archive. This option will not work on tape devices.

-t   Lists the files in the order in which they appear in the archive.

-u   Adds files to the end of the archive only if not in the archive already or if they have been modified since written to the archive.This option will not work on a tape device.

-x   Extracts a file from the archive. If you specify a directory, tar extracts all files in that directory from the archive. If you do not specify a file or a directory, tar extracts all of the files from the archive.

-B   Forces blocking to 20 blocks per record.

OPTIONAL FLAGS

-bblocks	Specifies the number of 512-byte blocks per record. The default is 16, which is appropriate for tape records.
	The block size is determined automatically when tapes are read (function flags -x or -t). When archives are updated with the -u and -r functions, the existing record size is used. The tar command writes archives using the specified blocks value only when creating new archives with the -c flag.
-C directory	Causes tar to change to the specified directory. This flag must appear after all others and may be repeated and interspersed with file names.
-d	Makes separate entries for directories, blocks and character special files, and FIFOs. Normally, tar will not archive these files.
-F	Checks file type before archiving. SCCS, RCS, files named core, eirs, a, out, and files ending in .O are not archived.
-ffile	Uses file as the archive to be read or written. When this flag is not specified, tar uses the default file name /dev/rmto. If the file specified is "-" (minus), tar writes to standard output or reads from standard input.
-h	Forces tar to follow symbolic links. Normally tar does not do this.
-i	Ignores header check sum errors.
-Linput list	Writes the files listed in the inputlist file to the archive. The inputlist should contain one file name per line. These files are not treated recursively.
-l	Writes error messages to standard output if tar cannot resolve all of the links to the files archived.
-m	Uses the time of extraction as the modification time. The default is to preserve the modification time of the files.
-O	Provides backwards compatibility with older non-AIX versions of tar.
-N	Blocks uses the specified number of blocks when creating or reading an archive.
-P	Restores fields to original modes, ignoring present umask.
-S	Ttries to create symbolic link if tar is unsuccessful using regular link.

-S	<blocks>b
-S	feet
-S feet @density	Specifies the number of 512-byte blocks per volume (first format), independent of the tape blocking factor. You can also specify the size of the tape in feet by using the second form, and tar assumes a default density. The third form allows you to specify both tape length and density. Feet are assumed to be 11 inches long to be conservative.
-v	Lists the name of each file as it is processed. With the -t flag, -v gives more information about each entry.
-w	Displays the action to be taken followed by the file name, then waits for user confirmation.
-<number>	Uses /dev/rmt<number> instead of the default. For example, -1 is the same as -f/dev/rmt1.

EXAMPLES

1. To write chap1 and chap2 to a new archive on the default tape drive:

   tar -c chap1 chap2

2. To display the names of the files in the disk archive file book.tar on the current directory:

   tar -vtf book.tar

Backup—Backs up files and files systems.

SYNPOSIS

backup -i [-b Number] [-p [-e RegularExpression]] [-f Device] [-l Number] [-o] [-q] [-v]

backup [[-Level] [-b Number] [-c] [-f Device] [-u]] [FileSystem] | [-w | -W]

DESCRIPTION

The backup command creates copies of your files on a backup medium, such as a magnetic tape or diskette. The copies are in one of the two backup formats:

- Specific files backed up by name using the -i flag.
- Entire file system backed up by i-node using the Level and FileSystem parameters.

If you issue the backup command without any parameters, it defaults to a level 9 i-node backup of the root file system to the /dev/rfd0 device.

A single backup can span multiple volumes.

FLAGS

-b Number	For backups by name, specifies the number of 512-byte blocks; for backups by i-node, specifies the number of 1024-byte blocks to write in a single output operation. When the backup command writes to tape devices, the default value is 100 for backups by name and 32 for backups by i-node.
-c	Specifies that the tape is a cartridge, not a nine-track.
-e RegularExpression	Specifies that the files with names matching the regular expression are not to be packed.
-f Device	Specifies the output device. To send output to standard output specify a - (minus sign).
-i	Specifies that files be read from standard input and archived by file name.
-l Number	Limits the total number of blocks to use on the diskette device.
-o	Creates a Version 2-compatible backup by name.
-p	Specifies that the files be packed, or compressed, before they are archived. Only files of less than 24MB are packed.
-q	Indicates that the removable medium is ready to use. When you specify the -q flag, the backup command proceeds without prompting you to prepare the backup medium and press the Enter key to continue.
-u	Updates the /etc/dumpdates file with the raw device name of the file system and the time, date, and level of the backup.
-v	Causes the backup command to display additional information about the backup.
-w	Currently disabled. If the -w flag is specified, no other flags are applied.

-W   Displays, for each file system in the /etc/dumpdates file, the most recent backup date and level. If the -W option is specified, no other flags are applied.

-Level   Specifies the backup level (0 to 9). The default level is 9.

EXAMPLES

1. To backup all the files and subdirectories in the /home directory using full pathnames, enter:

   find /home -print | backup -i -f /dev/rmt0

   The -i flag specifies that files will be read from standard input and archived by file name. The find command generates a list of all the files in the /home directory. The files in this list are full path names. The -f flag directs the backup command to write the files to the /dev/rmt0 tape device.

2. To backup the / (root) file system, enter:

   backup -0 -u -f /dev/rmt0 /

   The 0 level specifies that all the files in the / (root) file system be backed up. The -u flag causes the backup command to update the /etc/dumpdates file for this backup.

3. To run the backup command using the System Management Interface Tool (SMIT), enter:

   smit backup

SEE ALSO

See the following command: restore.

restore—Copies back files created by the backup command

SYNOPSIS

restore -x [dMvq] [-b Blocks] [-f Device] [-s SeekBackup] [-X Number] [File ...]

restore -T [qv] [-b Blocks] [-f Device] [-s SeekBackup]

restore -r [Bqvy] [-b Blocks] [-f Device] [-s SeekBackup]

restore -R [Bvy] [-b Blocks] [-f Device] [-s SeekBackup]

restore -i [hmqvy] [-b Blocks] [-f Device] [-s SeekBackup]

restore -x [Bhmqvy] [-b Blocks] [-f Device] [-s SeekBackup] [File ...]

restore -t | -T [Bhqvy] [-b Blocks] [-f Device] [-s SeekBackup] [File ...]

DESCRIPTION

The restore command reads archives created by the backup command and extracts the files stored on them.

The diskette device, /dev/rfd0, is the default media for the restore command.

Use either the -x, -r, -R, or -i flag to restore archived files.

Use either the -T or -t flag to list archived files.

File-System Archives.   File-system archives are also known as i-node archives due
to the method used to archive the files. A file-system name is specified with the
backup command, and all files within that file system are archived.

File-Name Archives.   File-name archives are created by specifying a list of file
names to archive to the backup command.

FLAGS

-B	Specifies that the archive should be read from standard input. The archive is assumed to be in file-system format.
-b Blocks	Specifies the number of 512-byte blocks to read in a single input operation. The default value for the Blocks parameter is 100.
-d	Indicates that, if the File parameter is a directory, all files in that directory should be restored.
-fDevice	Specifies the input device. To receive input from standard input, specify a - (minus sign).
-h	Restores only the actual directory, not the files contained in it.
-i	Allows you to interactively restore selected files from a file-system archive. The subcommands for the -i flag are:

	cd Directory	Changes the current directory to the speci- fied directory.
	add [File]	Specifies that the File parameter is added to the list of files to extract.
	delete [File]	Specifies that the File parameter is to be removed from the list of files to be ex- tracted.
	ls [Directory]	Displays the directories and files con- tained within the Directory parameter.

	extract	Restores all the directories and files on the extraction list.
	pwd	Displays the full path name of the current directory.
	verbose	Causes the ls subcommand to display additional information about each file and directory.
	setmodes	Sets the owner, mode, and time for all directories added to the extraction list.
	quit	Causes restore to exit immediately without doing any more processing.
	help	Displays a summary of the subcommands.
-M		Sets the access and modification times of restored files to the time of restoration.
-m		Renames restored files to the file's i-node number as it exists on the archive.
-q		Specifies that the first volume is ready to use and that the restore command should not prompt you to mount the volume and hit Enter.
-r		Restores all files in a file-system archive.
-R		Requests a specific volume of a multiple-volume, file-system archive.
-s SeekBackup		Specifies the backup to seek and restore on a multiple-backup tape archive.
-t		Displays information about the backup archive.
-T		Displays information about the backup archive. Identical to -t flag for file-system format archives.
-v		Displays additional information when restoring.
-x		Restores individually named files specified by the File parameter. If the File parameter is not specified, all the archive members are restored. If the File parameter is specified, then those members will be restored.
-X VolumeNumber		Begins restoring from the specified volume of a multiple-volume, file-name backup.
-y		Continues restoring when tape errors are encountered.

EXAMPLES

1. To list the names of files in either a file-name or file-system archive on the diskette device /dev/rfd0, enter:

    restore -T

    The archive is read from the /dev/rfd0 default restore device. The names of all the files and directories contained in the archive are displayed.

2. To restore a specific file, enter:

    restore -xvf backupdata myfile

    This command extracts the file myfile into the current directory from the archive backupdata. The -v flag displays additional information during the extraction.

3. To restore an entire file-system archive, enter:

    restore -rvf /dev/rmt0

    This command restores the entire file system archived on the tape device, /dev/rmt0, into the current directory. This example assumes you are in the root directory of the file system to be restored.

SEE ALSO

See the following command: backup.

Appendix D   Miscellaneous Commands

crontab—Submits a schedule of commands to cron.

SYNOPSIS

crontab [-e | -l | -r | -v | File]

DESCRIPTION

The crontab command submits, edits, lists, or removes cron jobs. A cron job is a command run by the cron daemon at regularly scheduled intervals, all as specified via crontab file entries configued with the crontab command. The cron daemon mails you any command output or errors. If you specify a cron job incorrectly in your crontab file, the cron daemon does not run the job.

THE CRONTAB FILE ENTRY FORMAT

A crontab file contains entries for each cron job. Entries are separated by newline characters. Each crontab file entry contains six fields separated by spaces or tabs in the following form:

minute hour day_of_month month weekday command

These fields accept the following values:

minute	0 through 59
hour	0 through 23
day_of_month	1 through 31
month	1 through 12
weekday	0 through 6 for Sunday through Saturday
command	a shell command

You must specify a value for each field. Except for the command field, these fields can contain the following:

- A number in the specified range. To run a command in July, specify 7 in the month field.

- Two numbers separated by a dash to indicate an inclusive range. To run a cron job on Monday through Friday, place 1-5 in the weekday field.

- A list of numbers separated by commas. To run a command on the first and 15th day of a month, you would specify 1,15 in the day_of_month field.

- An * (asterisk), meaning all allowed values. To run a job every hour, specify an asterisk in the hour field.

FLAGS

-e   Edits a copy of your crontab file or starts an editing session if you don't already have a crontab file. When editing is complete, the entry is installed as your crontab file.

-l   Lists your crontab file.

-r   Removes your crontab file from the crontab directory.

-v   Lists the status of your cron jobs.

EXAMPLES

1.   To have the cron deamon use a file called myjobs, enter the following:

crontab myjobs

2.   To write the time to the console every hour on the hour, enter:

0 * * * * echo The hour is 'date' . >/dev/console

3.   **To run the** calendar command at 7:30 a.m. every Monday, Wednesday, and
      Friday, enter:

      30 7 * * 1,3,5 /usr/bin/calendar

4.   To define text for the standard input to a command, enter:

      30 17 15-31 12 5 /usr/bin/wall%HAPPY HOLIDAY!%Have a nice week-
      end.

      The text following the % (percent sign) defines the standard input to the
      wall command as follows to be displyed at 5:30 PM every Friday between
      December 15 and December 31:

      HAPPY HOLIDAY!

      Have a nice weekend.

FILES

/var/spool/cron/crontabs	Contains all user crontab files.
/var/adm/cron/cron.allow	Specifies a list of users allowed to use the crontab command.
/var/adm/cron/cron.deny	Specifies a list of users not allowed to use the crontab command.

Appendix E   Connectivity Commands

rcp Command

PURPOSE

Copies (transfers) files between a local and a remote host or between two remote
hosts.

SYNTAX

rcp [-p] { {User@Host:File | Host:File | File } { User@Host:File | Host:File | File
| User@Host:Directory | Host:Directory | Directory } | [-r] { User@Host:Direc-
tory | Host:Directory |Directory } { User@Host:Directory | Host:Directory | Di-
rectory } }

DESCRIPTION

The /usr/bin/rcp command is used to copy one or more files between the local
host and a remote host, between two remote hosts, or between files at the same
remote host.

Remote destination files and directories require a specified Host: parameter. If a remote host name is not specified for either the source or the destination, the rcp command is equivalent to the cp command. Local file and directory names do not require a Host: parameter.

If a Host is not prefixed by a User@ parameter, the local user name is used at the remote host. If the path for a file or directory on a remote host is not specified or is not fully qualified, the path is interpreted as beginning at the home directory for the remote user account.

Permissions. The user name entered for the remote host determines the file access privileges the rcp command uses at that host. Additionally, the user name given to a destination host determines the ownership and access modes of the resulting destination file or files. The remote host allows access if one of the following conditions is satisfied:

- The local host is included in the remote host /etc/hosts.equiv file and the remote user is not the root user.

- The local host and user name is included in a $HOME/.rhosts file on the remote user account.

For security reasons, any $HOME/.rhosts file must be owned by either the remote user or root user and should allow write access only by the owner.

FLAGS

-p   Preserves the modification times and modes of the source files in the copies sent to the destination only if the user has root authority or is the owner of the destination. Without this flag, the umask command at the destination modifies the mode of the destination file, and the modification time of the destination file is set to the time the file is received.

-r   Recursively copies, for directories only, each file and subdirectory in the source directory into the destination directory.

PARAMETERS

Host:File	Specifies the host name (Host) and file name (File) of the remote destination file, separated by a : (colon).
User@Host:File	Specifies the user name (User@) that the rcp command uses to set ownership of the transferred file, the host name (Host), and file name (File) of the remote destination file. The user name entered for the remote host determines the file access privileges the rcp command uses at that host.

File	Specifies the file name of the local destination file.
Host:Directory	Specifies the host name (Host) and directory name (Directory) of the remote destination directory.
User@Host:Directory	Specifies the user name (User@) the rcp command uses to set ownership of the transferred file, the host name (Host), and directory name (Directory) of the remote destination directory. The user name entered for the remote host determines the file access privileges the rcp command uses at that host.
Directory	The directory name of the local destination directory. The name of the local host is named in the file /etc/hosts.equiv at remotehost: for example, rcp myfile remotehost:/home/carolynj/boo

rexec Command

PURPOSE

Executes commands one at a time on a remote host.

SYNTAX

rexec [-d | -n] Host Command

DESCRIPTION

The /usr/bin/rexec command executes a command on the specified remote host. The rexec command provides an automatic login feature by checking for a $HOME/ .netrc file that contains the user name and password to use at the remote host.

FLAGS

-d   Enables socket-level debugging.

-n   Prevents automatic login. With the -n flag specified, the rexec command prompts for a user name and password to use at the remote host, rather than searching for a $HOME/.netrc file.

PARAMETERS

Command   Specifies the command, including any flags or parameters, to be executed on the remote host.

Host   Specifies in alphanumeric form the name of the host where the command is to be executed.

EXAMPLES

To execute the who command on a remote host, enter:

rexec musashi who

The output from the who command is now displayed on the local system.

If you do not have a valid entry in the $HOME/.netrc file for the remote host, you will be prompted for your login ID and password.

rexecd Daemon

PURPOSE

Provides the server function for the rexec command.

SYNTAX

/usr/sbin/rexecd [-s]

DESCRIPTION

The /usr/sbin/rexecd daemon is the server (background process) for the rexec command. This daemon processes commands issued by a foreign host and returns the output of those commands to that foreign host. The rexecd daemon sends and receives data over a Transmission Control Protocol/Internet Protocol (TCP/IP) connection.

The rexecd daemon is normally started by the inetd daemon. It can also be controlled from the command line, using SRC commands.

Changes to the rexecd daemon can be made using the System Management Interface Tool (SMIT) or System Resource Controller (SRC), by editing the /etc/inetd.conf or /etc/services file. Entering rexecd at the command line is not recommended.The rexecd daemon is started by default when it is uncommented in the /etc/inetd.conf file.

The inetd daemon gets its information from the /etc/inetd.conf file and the /etc/ services file. After changing the /etc/inetd.conf file, run the refresh -s inetd or kill -1 InetdPID command to inform the inetd daemon of the changes to its configuration file.

Service Request Protocol.   When the rexecd daemon receives a request, it initiates the following protocol:

1.   The server reads characters from the socket up to a null () byte and interprets the resulting string as an ASCII number (decimal).

2.   If the number received is nonzero, the rexecd daemon interprets it as the port number of a secondary stream to be used for standard error output. The rexecd daemon then creates a second connection to the specified port on the client machine.

3.   The rexecd daemon retrieves a null-terminated user name of up to 16 characters on the initial socket.

rlogin Command

PURPOSE

Remote logins, connects a local host with a remote host.

SYNTAX

rlogin RemoteHost [-e Character] [-8] [-l User]

DESCRIPTION

The /usr/bin/rlogin command logs into a specified remote host and connects your local terminal to the remote host. The remote terminal type is the same as that given in the TERM local environment variable. The Ctrl-S and Ctrl-Q key sequences stop and start the flow of information.

Remote Command Execution.   When using the rlogin command, you can create a link to your path using a host name as the link name. For example: ln -s /usr/bin/rsh HostName.

Entering the host name specified by the HostName parameter with a command at the prompt, automatically uses the rsh command to remotely execute the command specified on the command line of the remote host specified by the Host-Name parameter.

Entering the host name specified by the HostName parameter without an argument (command) at the prompt, automatically uses the rlogin command to log in to the remote host specified by the HostName parameter.

FLAGS

-e Character   Changes the escape character. Substitute the character you choose for Character. The default characters the tilde (~).

-l User   Changes the remote user name to the one you specify. Otherwise, your local user name is used at the remote host.

-8   Allows an 8-bit data path at all times. Otherwise may, the rlogin command only pass 7 bits.

SECURITY

The remote host allows access only if one or both of the following conditions is satisfied:

- The local host is included in the remote /etc/hosts.equiv file, the local user is not the root user, and the -l User flag is not specified.
- The local host and user name is included in the $HOME/.rhosts file in the remote user account.

For security reasons, any $HOME/.rhosts file must be owned by either the remote user or root and should allow write access only by the owner.

SRC Daemon

PURPOSE

Controls background daemons.

DESCRIPTION

The System Resource Controller (SRC) is used normally during system initialization to bring up background processes (daemons) such as telnetd and inetd.

COMMANDS

startsrc   starts a subsystem, group of subsystems, or a subserver

stopsrc   stop a subsystem, group of subsystems, or a subserver

lssrc   display start states which returns process name, ID, and state (active or inactive)

EXAMPLE

1. To start telnetd daemon, enter startsrc -t telnet
2. To force stop telnet, enter stopsrc -f -t -telnet

talk Command

PURPOSE

Converse with another user across the network.

SYNTAX

talk { User@Host | Host!User | Host.User | Host:User } [Tty] [Pty]

DESCRIPTION

The /usr/bin/talk command allows two users on the same host or on different hosts to have an interactive conversation. The talk command opens both a send window and a receive window on each user's display. Each user is then able to type into the send window while the talk command displays what the other user is typing.

To initiate a conversation, a local user executes the talk command and specifies a remote user's login ID. If the remote user is on a remote host, the name of the host must also be specified in one of the following ways:

User@Host Host!User Host.User Host:User

When using full domain names, the only valid form for specifying the user and host is User@Host.

When the local user initiates the conversation, a message is sent to the remote user, inviting a conversation. If the local user also specifies tty, the invitation message is sent only to the specified terminal. Otherwise, the invitation is sent to the remote user's login terminal.

To have the conversation, the remote user also has to execute the talk command from any terminal and specify the local user's account name and host name, if appropriate. When the remote user accepts the invitation, the talk command displays two windows on each user's terminal. One window displays what is typed by the local user; the other window displays what is typed by the remote user. To end the conversation, either user can press the Interrupt (Ctrl-C) key sequence and the connection is closed.

To disallow talk command invitations, the remote user can issue the mesg n command.

talkd Daemon

PURPOSE

Provides the server function for the talk command.

SYNTAX

/usr/sbin/talkd [-s]

DESCRIPTION

Note: The talkd daemon is normally started by the inetd daemon. It can also be controlled from the command line, using SRC commands.

The /usr/sbin/talkd daemon is the server that notifies a user (the recipient) that another user (the caller) wants to initiate a conversation. The daemon sets up the conversation if the recipient accepts the invitation. The caller initiates the conversation by executing the talk command specifying the recipient. The recipient accepts the invitation by executing the talk command specifying the caller.

Changes to all the ftp daemons can be made using the System Management Interface Tool (SMIT) or System Resource Controller (SRC), or by editing the /etc/inetd.conf or /etc/services file. Entering talkd at the command line is not recommended. The talkd daemon is started by default when it is uncommented in the /etc/inetd.conf file. After changing the /etc/inetd.conf or /etc/services file, run the refresh -s inetd or kill -1 InetdPID command to inform the inetd daemon of the changes to its configuration file.

Debugging messages are sent to the syslogd daemon.

FLAGS

-s   Turns on socket-level debugging.

telnet, tn, or tn3270 Command

PURPOSE

Connects the local host with a remote host, using the Telnet interface.

SYNTAX

{ telnet | tn | tn3270 } [-d] [-n TraceFile] [-e TerminalType] [Host [Port]]

DESCRIPTION

The telnet command, which is also referred to as the tn or tn3270 command, operates in two different modes: command mode and input mode.

Command Mode.   When the telnet command is issued without arguments, it enters command mode, as indicated by the telnet>, tn>, or the tn3270> prompt. A user can also enter command mode from input mode by pressing Ctrl-] for the telnet command, Ctrl-T for the tn command, or Ctrl-C for the tn3270 command. In command mode, subcommands can be entered to manage the remote system. Some of these subcommands return you to the remote session upon completion. For those subcommands that do not, pressing the Enter key returns you to the remote session.

If the client and the server negotiate to use a 3270 data stream, the keyboard mapping is determined by the following precedence:

$HOME/.3270keys   Specifies the user's 3270 keyboard mapping when the tn or telnet command is invoked. If you are using a color display, you can also change this file to customize the colors for 3270 displays.

/etc/map3270   Specifies the user's 3270 keyboard mapping when the tn3270 command is invoked. The /etc/map3270 file defines keyboard mapping and colors for the tn3270 command.

/etc/3270.keys   Specifies the base 3270 keyboard mapping for use with limited function terminals.

Environment Variables.   The following environment variables can be used with the telnet command:

EMULATE   Overrides terminal-type negotiation in the same way as the -e flag. If the value of the EMULATE environment variable is defined as vt100 or 3270, the telnet command emulates a DEC VT100 terminal or 3270 terminal, respectively.

TNESC   Specifies an alternate TELNET escape character, other than the default, Ctrl-] for the telnet command, Ctrl-T for the tn command, or Ctrl-C for the tn3270 command. To change the telnet escape sequence, set TNESC to the octal value of the character you want to use. Then export TNESC. For example, set TNESC to 35 to change the TELNET escape sequence to Ctrl-].

MAP3270   Specifies an alternate file that contains the user's 3270 keyboard mapping. The MAP3270 variable must contain the full path name to the alternate file. Create the alternate file using the same format as the default /etc/map3270 file.

FLAGS

-d	Turns debugging mode on.
-e TerminalType	Overrides terminal-type negotiation. Possible values are vt100, 3270, or none.
-n TraceFile	Records network trace information in the file specified by the TraceFile variable.

telnetd Daemon

PURPOSE

Provides the server function for the TELNET protocol.

SYNTAX

/usr/sbin/telnetd [-n] [-s]

DESCRIPTION

Note: The telnetd daemon is normally started by the inetd daemon. It can also be controlled from the command line, using SRC commands.

The /usr/sbin/telnetd daemon is a server that supports the Defense Advanced Research Product Agency (DARPA) standard Telnet Protocol (TELNET).

Changes to the telnetd daemon can be made using the System Management Interface Tool (SMIT) or System Resource Controller (SRC), by editing the /etc/inetd.conf or /etc/services file. Entering telnetd at the command line is not recommended. The telnetd daemon is started by default when it is uncommented in the /etc/inetd.conf file.

The inetd daemon get its information from the /etc/inetd.conf file and the /etc/services file. After changing the /etc/inetd.conf or /etc/services file, run the refresh -s inetd or kill -1 InetdPID command to inform the inetd daemon of the changes to its configuration file. Since the telnetd daemon allows the sending and receiving of 8-bit ASCII, NLS is supported.

The telnetd daemon supports the following TELNET options:

* Binary
* Echo/no echo
* Support SAK
* Suppress go ahead
* Timing mark
* Negotiate About Window Size (NAWS)

The telnetd daemon also recognizes the following options for the remote client:

- Binary
- Suppress go ahead
- Echo/no echo
- Terminal type

FLAGS

-n   Disables transport-level keep-alive messages. Messages are enabled by default.

-s   Turns on socket-level debugging.

tftp or utftp Command

PURPOSE

Transfers files between hosts using the Trivial File Transfer Protocol (TFTP).

SYNTAX

{tftp | utftp} {-g | -o | -p | -r | -w } LocalName HostPort RemoteName [netascii | image]

DESCRIPTION

The /usr/bin/tftp and utftp commands transfer files between hosts using the Trivial File Transfer Protocol (TFTP). Since TFTP is a minimal file transfer protocol, the tftp and utftp commands do not provide all of the features of the ftp command.

The remote host must have a tftpd daemon started by its inetd daemon and have an account defined that limits the access of the tftpd daemon.

Maximum Time-out Value.   The user can pick the maximum time-out value, but the initial time-out value for the first block is hardcoded. The user cannot pick the maximum time-out value for the server; the server times out after six retries with a maximum time-out value of 64 seconds.

Access Control.   The /etc/tftpaccess.ctl file is searched for lines that start with allow: or deny:. Other lines are ignored. If the file doesn't exist, access is allowed. The entries in the /etc/tftpaccess.ctl file must be absolute path names.

The /etc/tftpaccess.ctl file should be write-only by the root user and must be readable by all groups and others (that is, owned by root with permissions of 644). For more information, refer to the sample tftpaccess.ctl file, which resides in the /usr/ samples/tcpip directory. Further information and example configurations for Xstations, Diskless clients, and restricted entry can be found in the /usr/samples/tcpip/tftpaccess.ctl file.

The tftp and utftp commands and subcommands have two forms: interactive form and command-line form.

Interactive Form.   In the interactive form, the tftp and utftp commands are issued alone or with a Host parameter that specifies the default host to use for file transfers during this session. If you choose, you can also specify with the Port parameter which the tftp or utftp connection should use. When you enter the interactive form of either of these commands, the tftp> prompt is displayed.

When transferring data to a remote host, the transferred data is placed in the directory specified by the RemoteName parameter. The remote name must be a fully specified file name, and the remote file must both exist and have write permission set for others.

Command-Line Form.   The command-line forms of the tftp and utftp commands are equivalent, except that the utftp command does not overwrite a local file. The tftp command can overwrite a file, but prompts the user before doing so. Because it is not interactive, the command line form of the utftp command can be more useful than the tftp command in a pipe.

Subcommands

Subcommands Used in the Interactive Form.   Once the tftp> prompt is displayed, the following subcommands can be issued:

? [Subcommand]	Displays help information. If a Subcommand parameter is specified, only information about that subcommand is displayed.
ascii	Synonym for the mode ascii subcommand.
binary	Synonym for the mode binary subcommand. This subcommand is used in the interactive mode.
connect Host [Port]	Sets the remote host, and optionally the port, for file transfers.
get RemoteFile [LocalFile]	or get RemoteFile RemoteFile RemoteFile [RemoteFile . . .]

Gets a file or set of files from the remote host to the local host. Each of the RemoteFile parameters can be specified in one of the following two ways:

- As a file (File) that exists on the remote host if a default host has already been specified.

- As a host file (Host:File), where Host is the remote host and File is the name of the file to copy to the local system. If this form of the parameter is used, the last host specified becomes the default host for later transfers in this tftp session.

mode Type   Sets the type (Type) of transfer mode to either ascii or binary. A transfer mode of ascii is the default.

put LocalFile [RemoteFile]   or put LocalFile LocalFile LocalFile [LocalFile . . .]

RemoteDirectory   Puts a file or set of files from the local host onto the remote host. The RemoteDirectory and RemoteFile parameters can be specified in one of the following two ways:

- As a file or directory that exists on the remote host if a default host has already been specified.

- With Host:RemoteFile parameter, where Host is the remote host and RemoteFile is the name of the file or directory on the remote system. If this form of the parameter is used, the last host specified becomes the default host for later transfers in this tftp session.

In either case, the remote file or directory name must be a fully specified path name, even if the local and remote directories have the same name.

quit   Exits the tftp session. An End-Of-File key sequence also exits the program.

status   Shows the current status of the tftp program, including, for example, the current transfer mode (ascii or binary), connection status, and time-out value.

timeout Value   Sets the total transmission time out to the number of seconds specified by the Value parameter.

trace   Turns packet tracing on or off.

verbose   Turns verbose mode, which displays additional information during file transfer, on or off.

Subcommands Used in the Command Line Form

-w or -p   Writes (or puts) local data, specified by the LocalName parameter, to the file specified by the RemoteName parameter on the remote host specified by the Host parameter. If the LocalName parameter is a file name, the tftp command transfers the specified local file. If the LocalName parameter is specified as a - (dash), the tftp command transfers data from local standard input to the remote host.

-r or -g or -o   Reads (or gets) remote data from the file specified by the Remote-Name parameter at the remote host specified by the Host parameter and writes it to the file specified by the LocalName parameter. If the LocalName parameter is a file name, the tftp command writes the data to the specified local file. For the -r and -g actions, the tftp command prompts for verification before overwriting an existing local file. For the -o action, the tftp command overwrites an existing local file without prompting. If the LocalName parameter is specified as a - (dash), the tftp command writes the data to local standard output.

Since the tftp -g and tftp -r commands prompt before overwriting an existing local file, it may be impractical to use the tftp command in a pipe. The utftp command performs the same -r and -g actions as the tftp command, but simply stops before overwriting a local file. Thus, the utftp command may be more appropriate for use in a pipe.

For both of the following modes of file transfer, the RemoteName parameter is the name of a file that has write permission set for others.

The mode of transfer is one of the following:

netascii   Transfers the data as 7-bit ASCII characters in 8-bit transfer bytes. This is the default.

image   Transfers the data as 8-bit binary data bytes in 8-bit transfer bytes, with no conversion. image transfer can be more efficient than netascii transfer when transferring between two hosts. It is recommended that netascii be used when transferring ASCII files from a workstation to a different type of host.

ftp Command

PURPOSE

Transfers files between a local and a remote host.

SYNTAX

ftp [-d] [-g] [-i] [-n] [-v] [HostName [Port]]

DESCRIPTION

The ftp command uses the File Transfer Protocol (FTP) to transfer files between the local host and a remote host or between two remote hosts.

The FTP protocol allows data transfer between hosts that use dissimilar file systems. Although the protocol provides a high degree of flexibility in transferring data, it does not attempt to preserve file attributes (such as the protection mode or modification times of a file) that are specific to a particular file system.

If you are transferring files between systems and need to preserve file attributes or recursively copy subdirectories, use the rcp command.

Issuing Subcommands.   At the ftp> prompt, you can enter subcommands to perform tasks such as listing remote directories, changing the current local and remote directory, transferring multiple files in a single request, creating and removing directories, and escaping to the local shell to perform shell commands. See the "Subcommands" section for a description of each subcommand.

If you execute the ftp command and do not specify the HostName parameter for a remote host, the ftp command immediately displays the ftp> prompt and waits for an ftp subcommand. To connect to a remote host, execute the open subcommand. When the ftp command connects to the remote host, the ftp command then prompts for the login name and password before displaying the ftp> prompt again.

The command interpreter handles file name parameters according to the following rules:

- If a - (hyphen) is specified for the parameter, standard input (stdin) is used for read operations and standard output (stdout) is used for write operations.

- If the preceding check does not apply and file name expansion is enabled (see the -g flag or the glob subcommand), the interpreter expands the file name according to the rules of the C shell. When globbing is enabled and a pattern-matching character is used in a subcommand that expects a single file name, results may be different than expected.

Note: The ftp command interpreter does not support pipes. It also does not necessarily support all multibyte-character file names.

To end an ftp session when you are running interactively, use the quit or bye subcommand or the End of File (Ctrl-D) key sequence at the ftp> prompt. To end a file transfer before it has completed, press the Interrupt key (ctrl-c) sequence.

Security and Automatic Login.   If you execute the ftp command and specify the host name (HostName) of a remote host, the ftp command tries to establish a connection to the specified host. If the ftp command connects successfully, the ftp command searches for a local $HOME/ .netrc file in your current directory or home directory. If the file exists, the ftp command searches the file for an entry for the remote host. If the $HOME/.netrc file or automatic login entry does not exist or if your system has been secured with the securetcpip command, the ftp command prompts the user for a user name and password.

If the ftp command finds a $HOME/.netrc automatic login entry for the specified host, the ftp command attempts to use the information in that entry to log in to the remote host.

The HostName parameter is the name of the host machine to which files are transferred. The optional Port parameter specifies the ID of the port through which to transmit. (The /etc/services file specifies the default port.)

FLAGS

-d   Sends debugging information about ftp command operations to the syslogd daemon. If you specify the -d flag, you must edit the /etc/syslog.conf file and add one of the following entries:

user.info FileName

or

user.debug FileName

Note: The syslogd daemon debug level includes info level messages.

If you do not edit the /etc/syslog.conf file, no messages are produced. After changing the /etc/syslog.conf file, run the refresh -s syslogd or kill -1 SyslogdPID command to inform the syslogd daemon of the changes to its configuration file. For more information about debug levels, refer to the /etc/syslog.conf file and the debug subcommand.

-g   Disables the expansion of metacharacters in file names. Interpreting metacharacters can be referred to as expanding (sometimes called globbing) a file name. See the glob subcommand.

-i   Turns off interactive prompting during multiple file transfers. See the prompt, mget, mput, and mdelete subcommands for descriptions of prompting during multiple file transfers.

-n   Prevents an automatic login on the initial connection. Otherwise, the ftp command searches for a $HOME/.netrc entry that describes the login and initialization process for the remote host. See the user subcommand.

-v   Displays all the responses from the remote server and provides data transfer statistics. This display mode is the default when the output of the ftp command is to a terminal, such as the console or a display.

FTP Subcommands.   The following ftp subcommands can be entered at the ftp> prompt. Use double quotes (" ") to specify parameters that include blank characters.

![Command [Parameters]]   Invokes an interactive shell on the local host. An optional command, with one or more optional parameters, can be given with the shell command.

$Macro [Parameters]   Executes the specified macro, previously defined with the macdef subcommand. Parameters are not expanded.

?[Subcommand]   Displays a help message describing the subcommand. If you do not specify a Subcommand parameter, the ftp command displays a list of known subcommands.

account [Password]   Sends a supplemental password that a remote host may require before granting access to its resources. If the password is not supplied with the command, the user is prompted for the password.

append LocalFile [RemoteFile]   Appends a local file to a file on the remote host. If the remote file name is not specified, the local file name is used, altered by any setting made with the ntrans subcommand or the nmap subcommand. The append subcommand uses the current values for form, mode, struct, and type subcommands while appending the file.

ascii   Synonym for the type ascii subcommand.

bell   Sounds a bell after the completion of each file transfer.

binary   Synonym for the type binary subcommand.

block   Synonym for the mode block subcommand.

bye   Ends the file-transfer session and exits the ftp command. Same as the quit subcommand.

carriage-control   Synonym for the form carriage-control subcommand.

case   Sets a toggle for the case of file names. When the case subcommand is On, the ftp command changes remote file names displayed in all capital letters from uppercase to lowercase when writing them in the local directory. The default is Off (so the ftp command writes uppercase remote file names in uppercase in the local directory).

cd RemoteDirectory   Changes the working directory on the remote host to the specified directory.

cdup   Changes the working directory on the remote host to the parent of the current directory.

close   Ends the file-transfer session, but does not exit the ftp command. Defined macros are erased. Same as the disconnect subcommand.

copylocal   Toggles local copy. copylocal defaults to Off. An effort is made by ftp to make sure you do not zero out a file by ftp'ing it to itself (same hostname, same pathname). Turning copylocal ON bypasses this check.

cr   Strips the carriage-return character from a carriage-return and line-feed sequence when receiving records during ASCII-type file transfers. (The ftp command terminates each ASCII-type record with a carriage-return and line feed during file transfers.)

Records on non-AIX remote hosts can have single line feeds embedded in records. To distinguish these embedded line feeds from record delimiters, set the cr subcommand to Off. The cr subcommand toggles between On and Off.

delete RemoteFile   Deletes the specified remote file.

debug [0 | 1]   Toggles debug record keeping On and Off. Specify debug or debug 1 to print each command sent to the remote host and save the restart control file. Specify debug again, or debug 0, to stop the debug record keeping. The Ctrl-C key sequence also saves the restart control file.

dir [RemoteDirectory][LocalFile]   Writes a listing of the contents of the specified remote directory (RemoteDirectory) to the specified local file (LocalFile). If the RemoteDirectory parameter is not specified, the dir subcommand lists the contents of the current remote directory. If the LocalFile parameter is not specified or is a - (hyphen), the dir subcommand displays the listing on the local terminal.

disconnect   Ends the file-transfer session but does not exit the ftp command. Defined macros are erased. Same as the close subcommand.

ebcdic   Synonym for the type ebcdic subcommand.

exp_cmd   Toggles between conventional and experimental protocol commands. The default is off.

file   Synonym for the struct file subcommand.

form [carriage-control | non-print | telnet]   Specifies the form of the file transfer. The form subcommand modifies the type subcommand to send the file transfer in the indicated form. Valid arguments are carriage-control, non-print, and telnet.

carriage-control   Sets the form of the file transfer to carriage-control.

non-print   Sets the form of the file transfer to non-print.

telnet   Sets the form of the file transfer to Telnet. Telnet is a Transmission Control Protocol/Internet Protocol (TCP/IP) protocol that opens connections to a system.

get RemoteFile [LocalFile]   Copies the remote file to the local host. If the LocalFile parameter is not specified, the remote file name is used locally and is altered by any settings made by the case, ntrans, and nmap subcommands. The ftp command uses the current settings for the type, form, mode, and struct subcommands while transferring the file.

glob   Toggles file name expansion (globbing) for the mdelete, mget, and mput subcommands. If globbing is disabled, file-name parameters for these subcommands are not expanded. When globbing is enabled and a pattern-matching character is used in a subcommand that expects a single file name, results may be different than expected.

To preview the expansion of a directory name, use the mls subcommand:

mls RemoteFile

To transfer an entire directory subtree of files, transfer a tar archive of the subtree in binary form, rather than using the mget or mput subcommand.

hash   Toggles hash sign (#) printing. When the hash subcommand is on, the ftp command displays one hash sign for each data block (1024 bytes) transferred.

help [Subcommand]   Displays help information. See the ? subcommand.

image   Synonym for the type image subcommand.

lcd [Directory]   Changes the working directory on the local host. If you do not specify a directory, the ftp command uses your home directory.

local M   Synonym for the type local M subcommand.

ls [RemoteDirectory] [LocalFile]   Writes an abbreviated file listing of a remote directory to a local file. If the RemoteDirectory parameter is not specified, the ftp command lists the current remote directory. If the LocalFile parameter is not specified or is a - (hyphen), the ftp command displays the listing on the local terminal.

macdef Macro   Defines a subcommand macro. Subsequent lines up to a null line (two consecutive line feeds) are saved as the text of the macro. Up to 16 macros, containing at most 4096 characters for all macros, can be defined. Macros remain defined until either redefined or a close subcommand is executed.

The $ (dollar sign) and (backslash) are special characters in ftp macros. A $ symbol followed by one or more numbers is replaced by the corresponding macro parameter on the invocation line (see the $ subcommand). A $ symbol followed by the letter i indicates that the macro is to loop, with the $i character combination being replaced by consecutive parameters on each pass.

The first macro parameter is used on the first pass, the second parameter is used on the second pass, and so on. A symbol prevents special treatment of the next character. Use the symbol to turn off the special meanings of the $ and /. (backslash period) symbols.

mdelete RemoteFiles   Expands the files specified by the RemoteFiles parameter at the remote host and deletes the remote files.

mdir [RemoteDirectories LocalFile]   Expands the directories specified by the RemoteDirectories parameter at the remote host and writes a listing of the contents of those directories to the file specified in the LocalFile parameter. If the RemoteDirectories parameter contains a pattern-matching character, the mdir subcommand prompts for a local file if none is specified. If the RemoteDirectories parameter is a list of remote directories separated by blanks, the last argument in the list must be either a local file name or a - (hyphen).

If the LocalFile parameter is - (hyphen), the mdir subcommand displays the listing on the local terminal. If interactive prompting is On (see the prompt subcommand), the ftp command prompts the user to verify that the last parameter is a local file and not a remote directory.

mget RemoteFiles   Expands the RemoteFiles parameter at the remote host and copies the indicated remote files to the current directory on the local host. See the glob subcommand for more information on file name expansion. The remote file names are used locally and are altered by any settings made by the case, ntrans, and nmap subcommands. The ftp command uses the current settings for the form, mode, struct, and type subcommands while transferring the files.

mkdir [RemoteDirectory]   Creates the directory specified in the RemoteDirectory parameter on the remote host.

mls [RemoteDirectories LocalFile]   Expands the directories specified in the RemoteDirectories parameter at the remote host and writes an abbreviated file listing of the indicated remote directories to a local file. If the RemoteDirectories parameter contains a pattern-matching character, the mls subcommand prompts for a local file if none is specified. If the RemoteDirectories parameter is a list of remote directories separated by blanks, the last argument in the list must be either a local file name or a - (hyphen).

If the LocalFile parameter is - (hyphen), the mls subcommand displays the listing on the local terminal. If interactive prompting is on (see the prompt subcommand), the ftp command prompts the user to verify that the last parameter is a local file and not a remote directory.

mode [stream | block]   Sets file-transfer mode. If an argument is not supplied, the default is stream.

    block   Sets the file-transfer mode to block.

    stream   Sets the file-transfer mode to stream.

modtime   Shows the last modification time of the specified file on the remote machine. If the ftp command is not connected to a host prior to execution, the modtime subcommand terminates with an error message. The ftp command ignores parameter beyond the first parameter. If the FileName parameter is not specified, the ftp command prompts for a file name. If no file name is given, the ftp command sends a usage message to standard output and terminates the subcommand.

If the name specified by the FileName parameter exists on the remote host, and the name specifies a file, then the ftp command sends a message containing the last modification time of the file to standard output and terminates the subcommand. If FileName specifies a directory, the ftp command sends an error message to standard output and terminates the subcommand. Note: The modtime subcommand interprets metacharacters when allowed.

mput [LocalFiles]   Expands the files specified in the LocalFiles parameter at the local host and copies the indicated local files to the remote host. See the glob subcommand for more information on file name expansion. The local file names are used at the remote host and are altered by any settings made by the ntrans and nmap subcommands. The ftp command uses the current settings for the type, form, mode, and struct subcommands while transferring the files.

nlist [RemoteDirectory][LocalFile]   Writes a listing of the contents of the specified remote directory (RemoteDirectory) to the specified local file (LocalFile). If the RemoteDirectory parameter is not specified, the nlist subcommand lists the contents of the current remote directory. If the LocalFile parameter is not specified or is a - (hyphen), the nlist subcommand displays the listing on the local terminal.

nmap [InPattern OutPattern]   Turns the file name mapping mechanism On or Off. If no parameters are specified, file name mapping is turned Off. If parameters are specified, source file names are mapped for the mget and mput subcommands and for the get and put subcommands when the destination file name is not specified. This subcommand is useful when the local and remote hosts use different file naming conventions or practices. Mapping follows the pattern set by the InPattern and OutPattern parameters.

The InPattern parameter specifies the template for incoming file names, which may have already been processed according to the case and ntrans settings. The template variables $1 through $9 can be included in the InPattern parameter. All characters in the InPattern parameter other than the $ (dollar sign) and the \$ (backslash, dollar sign) define the values of the template variables. For example, if the InPattern parameter is $1.$2 and the remote file name is mydata.dat, the value of $1 is mydata and the value of $2 is dat.

The OutPattern parameter determines the resulting file name. The variables $1 through $9 are replaced by their values as derived from the InPattern parameter, and the variable $0 is replaced by the original file name. Additionally, the sequence [Sequence1,Sequence2] is replaced by the value of Sequence1, if Sequence1 is not null; otherwise, it is replaced by the value of Sequence2. For example, the subcommand:

nmap $1.$2.$3 [$1,$2].[$2,file]

would yield myfile.data from myfile.data or myfile.data.old, myfile.file from myfile, and myfile.myfile from .myfile. Use the \ (backslash) symbol to prevent the special meanings of the $ (dollar sign), [(left bracket),] (right bracket), and , (comma) in the OutPattern parameter.

non-print   Synonym for the form non-print subcommand.

ntrans [InCharacters [OutCharacters]]   Turns the file name character translation mechanism On and Off. If no parameters are specified, character translation is turned off. If parameters are specified, characters in source file names are translated for mget and mput subcommands and for get and put subcommands when the destination file name is not specified.

This subcommand is useful when the local and remote hosts use different file naming conventions or practices. Character translation follows the pattern set by the InCharacters and OutCharacters parameter. Characters in a source file name matching characters in the InCharacters parameter are replaced by the corresponding characters in the OutCharacters parameter.

If the string specified by the InCharacters parameter is longer than the string specified by the OutCharacters parameter, the characters in the InCharacters parameter are deleted if they have no corresponding character in the OutCharacters parameter.

open HostName [Port]   Establishes a connection to the FTP server at the host specified by the HostName parameter. If the optional port number is specified, the ftp command attempts to connect to a server at that port. If the automatic login feature is set (that is, the -n flag was not specified on the command line), the ftp command attempts to log in the user to the FTP server.

You must also have a $HOME/.netrc file with the correct information in it and the correct permissions set. The .netrc file must be in your home directory.

prompt   Toggles interactive prompting. If interactive prompting is on (the default), the ftp command prompts for verification before retrieving, sending, or deleting multiple files during the mget, mput, and mdelete subcommands. Otherwise, the ftp command acts accordingly on all files specified.

proxy [Subcommand]   Executes an ftp command on a secondary control connection. This subcommand allows the ftp command to connect simultaneously to two remote FTP servers for transferring files between the two servers. The first proxy subcommand should be an open subcommand to establish the secondary control connection. Enter the proxy ? subcommand to see the other ftp subcommands that are executable on the secondary connection.

The following subcommands behave differently when prefaced by the proxy subcommand:

- The open subcommand does not define new macros during the automatic login process.

- The close subcommand does not erase existing macro definitions.

- The get and mget subcommands transfer files from the host on the primary connection to the host on the secondary connection.

- The put, mput, and append subcommands transfer files from the host on the secondary connection to the host on the primary connection.

- The restart subcommand can be handled by the proxy command.

- The status subcommand displays accurate information.

File transfers require that the FTP server on the secondary connection must support the PASV (passive) instruction.

put LocalFile [RemoteFile]   Stores a local file on the remote host. If you do not specify the RemoteFile parameter, the ftp command uses the local file name to name the remote file, and the remote file name is altered by any settings made by the ntrans and nmap subcommands. The ftp command uses the current settings for the type, form, mode, and struct subcommands while transferring the files.

pwd   Displays the name of the current directory on the remote host.

quit   Closes the connection and exits the ftp command. Same as the bye subcommand.

quote String   Sends the string specified by the String parameter verbatim to the remote host. Execute the remotehelp or quote help subcommand to display a list of valid values for the String parameter. Note: "Quoting" commands that involve data transfers can produce unpredictable results.

record   Synonym for the struct record subcommand.

recv RemoteFile [LocalFile]   Copies the remote file to the local host. Same as the get subcommand.

reinitialize   Reinitializes an FTP session by flushing all I/O and allowing transfers to complete. Resets all defaults as if a user had just started an FTP session without logging in to a remote host.

remotehelp [Subcommand]   Requests help from the remote FTP server.

rename FromName ToName   Renames a file on the remote host.

reset   Clears the reply queue. This subcommand resynchronizes the command parsing.

restart get | put | append   Restarts a file transfer at the point where the last checkpoint was made. To run successfully, the subcommand must be the same as the aborted subcommand, including structure, type, and form. Valid arguments are get, put, and append.

rmdir RemoteDirectory   Removes the remote directory specified by the RemoteDirectory parameter at the remote host.

runique (ReceiveUnique)   Toggles the facility for creating unique file names for local destination files during get and mget subcommands. If this facility is Off (the default), the ftp command overwrites local files. Otherwise, if a local file has the same name as that specified for a local destination file, the ftp command modifies the specified name of the local destination file.

send LocalFile [RemoteFile]   Stores a local file on the remote host. Same as the put subcommand.

sendport   Toggles the use of FTP PORT instructions. By default, the ftp command uses a PORT instruction when establishing a connection for each data transfer. When the use of PORT instructions is disabled, the ftp command does not use PORT instructions for data transfers. The PORT instruction is useful when dealing with FTP servers that ignore PORT instructions while incorrectly indicating the instructions have been accepted.

site Args   Displays or sets the idle time-out period, displays or sets the file-creation umask, or changes the permissions of a file, using the chmod command. Possible values for the Args parameter are umask and chmod.

size   RemoteFile Displays the size, in bytes, of the remote file specified by the RemoteFile parameter.

status   Displays the current status of the ftp command as well as the status of the subcommands.

stream   Synonym for the mode stream subcommand.

struct [file | record]   Sets the data transfer structure type. Valid arguments are file and record.

file   Sets the data-transfer structure type to file.

record   Sets the data-transfer structure type to record.

sunique (Send/Store Unique)   Toggles the facility for creating unique file names for remote destination files during put and mput subcommands. If this facility is off (the default), the ftp command overwrites remote files. Otherwise, if a remote file has the same name as that specified for a remote destination file, the remote FTP server modifies the name of the remote destination file. Note that the remote server must support the STOU instruction.

system   Shows the type of operating system running on the remote machine.

telnet   Synonym for the form telnet subcommand.

tenex   Synonym for the type tenex subcommand.

trace   Toggles packet tracing.

type [ascii | binary | ebcdic | image | local M | tenex]   Sets the file-transfer type. Valid arguments are ascii, binary, ebcdic, image, local M, and tenex. If an argument is not specified, the current type is printed. The default type is ascii; the binary type can be more efficient than ascii.

ascii   Sets the file-transfer type to network ASCII. This type is the default. File transfer may be more efficient with binary-image transfer. See the binary argument for further information.

binary Sets the file-transfer type to binary image. This type can be more efficient than an ASCII transfer.

ebcdic Sets the file-transfer type to EBCDIC.

image Sets the file-transfer type to binary image. This type can be more efficient than an ASCII transfer.

local M Sets the file-transfer type to local. The M parameter defines the decimal number of bits per machine word. This parameter does not have a default.

tenex Sets the file-transfer type to that needed for TENEX machines.

user User [Password] [Account] Identifies the local user (User) to the remote FTP server. If the Password or Account parameter is not specified and the remote server requires it, the ftp command prompts for the password or account locally. If the Account parameter is required, the ftp command sends it to the remote server after the remote login process completes. Note: Unless automatic login is disabled by specifying the -n flag on the command line, the ftp command sends the User, Password, and Account parameters automatically for the initial connection to the remote server. You also need a .netrc file in your home directory in order to issue an automatic login.

verbose Toggles verbose mode. When the verbose mode is on (the default), the ftp command displays all responses from the remote FTP server. Additionally, the ftp command displays statistics on all file transfers when the transfers complete.

ftpd Daemon

PURPOSE

Provides the server function for the Internet FTP protocol.

SYNTAX

Note: The ftpd daemon is normally started by the inetd daemon. It can also be controlled from the command line, using SRC commands.

/usr/sbin/ftpd [-d] [-k] [-l] [-t TimeOut] [-T MaxTimeOut] [-s] [-u Octal-Val]

DESCRIPTION

The /usr/sbin/ftpd daemon is the DARPA Internet File Transfer Protocol (FTP) server process. The ftpd daemon uses the Transmission Control Protocol (TCP) to listen at the port specified with the ftp command service specification in the /etc/ services file.

Changes to the ftpd daemon can be made using the System Management Interface Tool (SMIT) or System Resource Controller (SRC), by editing the /etc/inetd.conf or /etc/services file. Entering ftp at the command line is not recommended. The ftpd daemon is started by default when it is uncommented in the /etc/inetd.conf file.

The inetd daemon gets its information from the /etc/inetd.conf file and the /etc/ services file. If you change the /etc/inetd.conf or /etc/services file, run the refresh -s inetd or kill -1 InetdPID command to inform the inetd daemon of the changes to its configuration files.

The ftpd daemon expands file names according to the conventions of the csh command. This command allows you to use such metacharacters as the * (asterisk), the ? (question mark), [ ] (left and right brackets), { } (left and right braces), and the ~ (tilde).

Before the ftpd daemon can transfer files for a client process, it must authenticate the client process. The ftpd daemon authenticates client processes according to these rules:

- The user must have a password in the password database, /etc/security/passwd. (If the user's password is not null, the client process must provide that password.)

- The user name must not appear in the /etc/ftpusers file.

- The user's login shell must appear in the shells attribute of the /etc/security/ login.cfg file.

- If the user name is anonymous or ftp, an anonymous FTP account must be defined in the password file. In this case, the client process is allowed to log in using any password. By convention, the password is the name of the client host. The ftpd daemon takes special measures to restrict access by the client process to the anonymous account.

File Transfer Protocol Subtree Guidelines. When handling an anonymous FTP user, the server performs the chroot command in the home directory of the FTP user account. For greater security, implement the following rules when you construct the FTP subtree:

~ftp   Make the home directory owned by root and mode r-xr-xr-x (555).

~ftp/bin   Make this directory owned by the root user and unwritable by anyone. The ls program must be present in this directory to support the list command. This program should have mode 111.

~ftp/etc   Make this directory owned by the root user and unwritable by anyone.

~ftp/pub   Make this directory mode 777 and owned by FTP. Users should then place files that are to be accessible through the anonymous account in this directory.

Note: The shell script /usr/samples/tcpip/anon.ftp uses the above rules to set up the anonymous FTP account for you.

The server must run as the root user to create sockets with privileged port numbers. The server maintains an effective user ID of the logged-in user, reverting to the root user only when binding addresses to sockets.

FLAGS

-l   Sends logging information about ftpd daemon operations to the syslogd daemon. If you specify the -l flag, you must edit the /etc/syslog.conf file and add the following entry:

daemon.info FileName

If you do not edit the /etc/syslog.conf file, no messages are produced. After changing the /etc/syslog.conf file, run the refresh -s syslogd command or kill -1 SyslogdPID command to inform the syslogd daemon of the changes to its configuration file. For more information about debug levels, refer to the /etc/syslog.conf file.

-t   TimeOut Logs out inactive sessions after the number of seconds specified by the TimeOut variable. The default limit is 15 minutes (900 seconds).

-T   MaxTimeOut Logs out inactive client sessions after a maximum number of seconds specified by the MaxTimeOut variable. The default limit is 2 hours (7200 seconds).

-s   Turns on socket-level debugging.

-u   OctalVal Sets the ftpd daemon's umask. The OctalVal variable must be specified as an octal value to define the umask. The default umask is an octal value of 027, which results in file permissions of rw-r———.

Index

KEEP UP TO DATE WITH THE LATEST TOOLS FOR AIX

The IBM Developer Connection, a sample of which is included with this book, contains all the latest tools and information on AIX.

The IBM Developer Connection is a subscription program that offers you four issues of the hottest tools for AIX and OS/2 development. Each CD is packed with the latest development toolkits, including OS/2 Warp, OpenDoc for OS/2, OpenDoc for AIX, LAN Systems, Pen, and SMP. The CDs also contain source code, utilities, productivity tools, documentation, and more! Be the first to find out what is happening in the AIX environment with a subscription to the IBM Developer Connection.

Order Numbers:

In the following countries:

Austria	0660 8705	
Canada	1-800-561-5293	1-905-821-1187 (fax)
Germany	0 130 812177	
Mexico	91-800-00316	
Mexico City (only)	525-627-1111	
United States	1-800-6DEVCON (633-8266)	1-800-406-7129 (fax)

In Latin and South America:

Argentina	01-313-0014	Bolivia	02-35 1840			
Brazil	0800-111205	Chile	02-633-4400	Colombia	01-257-0111
Costa Rica	223-6222	Dominican Rep.	566-5161	Ecuador	02-56 5100
El Salvador	02-98 5011	Guatemala	02-31 5859	Honduras	32-2319
Panama	02-639 977	Paraguay	021-444 094	Peru	014-36 6345
Uruguay	02-923 617	Venezuela	02-908-8901			

In Asia/Pacific:

The Developer Connection can be ordered in Asia/Pacific countries from IBM in Australia (61 is the country code). Please ensure that you dial the international access code applicable to your country before the listed phone or fax number. NOTE: 61 is the country code for Australia.

Phone	+61 2-354 7684	+61 2-354 7766 (fax)

In Europe and all other countries not listed above:
The Developer Connection can be ordered direct from IBM in Denmark (45 is the country code). Please ensure that you dial the international access code applicable to your country before dialing the appropriate phone or fax number. Operators speaking the following languages are available:

Danish	+45 4-810 1300	Dutch	+45 4-810 1400
English	+45 4-810 1500	French	+45 4-810 1200
Finnish	+45 4-810 1650	German	+45 4-810 1000
Italian	+45 4-810 1600	Norwegian	+45 4-810 1250
Spanish	+45 4-810 1100	Swedish	+45 4-810 1150
Fax	+45 4-814 2207		

Be sure to look us up on these important World Wide Web sites:
IBM Home Page: http://www.ibm.com
IBM Developer Connection Home Page:
          http://www.developer.ibm.com/devcon/
IBM Software Developer Support Home Page:
          http://www.developer.ibm.com
AIX Developer Support Home Page: http://aix.boulder.ibm.com/aixsupport/
OS/2 Warp Developer Support Home Page:
          http://www.austin.ibm.com/pspinfo/developer.html

THE IBM DEVELOPER CONNECTION CD-ROM

The companion CD-ROM contains the IBM Developer Connection for AIX.

Please note the separate page containing IBM Developer Connection license agreement. Please see preceding page for additional information and contacts regarding complete subscription available for the IBM Developer Connection.

Note: Aix Version 4.1 or later is required.

AIX DEVELOPER CONNECTION INSTALLATION:

To setup use of the AIX CD:

1. Insert the Developer Connection for AIX CD into the CD-ROM drive and login as 'root'.
2. At the AIX command line, type: "mkdir -p /usr/DevCon"
    NOTE: This procedure assumes the path "/usr/DevCon" for the DevCon directory. You can use a different path, but be sure to use that path whenever the procedure refers to "/usr/DevCon".
3. Allocate a CD-ROM file system as follows:
    a. Type: smit storage.
    b. Select 'File Systems'
    c. Select 'Add/Change/Show/Delete File Systems'
    d. Select 'CDROM File System'
    e. Select 'Add a CDROM File System'
    f. Select the Device name (for example, cd0).
    g. Respond to the prompt for 'Mount Point' with '/usr/DevCon'
    h. Press Enter to create, then F10 to Exit.
4. Mount the CDROM file system as follows:
    a. Type: "smit mountfs"
    b. Select the file system name (for example, "/dev/cd0")
    c. Select the directory name (for example, "/usr/DevCon")
    d. Select mount as READ-ONLY system
    e. Press Enter to mount, then F10 to Exit
5. You may now logout as 'root'.
6. Type "/usr/DevCon/devcon" to start the Developer Connection for AIX Catalog.
    The first time you open the catalog, the DevCon for AIX setup window is displayed automatically.
7. If any 'Viewer Paths' field in the setup window is empty or incorrect, type the path name of an appropriate file viewer or HTML (Web) browser for the corresponding file type. For example, type "/usr/bin/gostview" in the PostScript field if you have GhostView installed in that directory.
8. Select OK to complete the setup and close the setup window.

When the setup is complete, the Developer Connection for AIX Catalog opens and you can continue with the next section, "Using the Developer Connection for AIX Catalog."

Notes:
1. If you need to change your initial Developer Connection setup, use the command '/usr/Dev-Con/bin/dcsetup". to open the setup window again.
2. The IBM Information Presentation Facility/6000 (IPF) viewer component is required for you to view INF (compiled IPF) files and use the Developer Connection for AIX Catalog. The Catalog is essential for selecting products and viewing on-line documentation. You cannot use the Catalog if you deselect IPF/X in the DevCon Setup window. However, the following files are also provided in ASCII text so you can view them before setting up the Catalog: the User's Guide, 'usrguide.doc'; the content list, 'contents.aix'; and the welcome note, 'welcome.txt'.

3. The Developer Connection for AIX CD contains many documents in PostScript format. To view these, you must have a PostScript viewer installed on your system and use the setup window to specify its location. GhostView is a common PostScript file viewer.
4. If you specify an HTML viewer (also called a World Wide Web browser), you can double-click on any "http:..." link mentioned in the Catalog text to visit that Web site. Netscape Navigator and NCSA Mosaic are common Web browsers.

- **Hardware Requirements**

  - System Units: All system units supported by AIX–4.1 or higher

  - Memory Requirements: Minimum 16MB—recommended 32MB; memory requirements vary depending on workload

  - Disk Space Requirements: Disk space requirements vary depending on software installed, and user data

  - CD–ROM drive: A CD–ROM drive supported by AIX

  DevCon for AIX is designed to support POWER, POWER2, and PowerPC based hardware with AIX Version 4.1 and configured with at least one supported display with keyboard and mouse.

- **Software Requirements**

  - Installation and execution of programs contained on the CD(s) requires AIX 4.1 or higher. Additional or special requirements may be dictated by the specific program being installed and/or executed.

IBM DEVELOPER CONNECTION LICENSE AGREEMENT

End-User Promotion License

THIS IS A LEGAL AGREEMENT BETWEEN YOU (THE END USER) AND THE IBM CORPORA-TION. BEFORE USING THE CD-ROM PACKAGE, YOU SHOULD CAREFULLY READ THE FOL-LOWING TERMS AND CONDITIONS. USING THE CD-ROM PACKAGE INDICATES YOUR AC-CEPTANCE OF THESE TERMS AND CONDITIONS. IF YOU DO NOT AGREE TO THESE TERMS AND CONDITIONS, PROMPTLY RETURN THE CD-ROM PACKAGE TO THE IBM CORPORA-TION.

IBM END-USER PROMOTION LICENSE AGREEMENT FOR THE DEVELOPER CONNECTION

(The Developer Connection, including all object code, sample source code, publications, documenta-tion and other programs and products contained therein, are hereinafter referred to as "The Dev-Con").

I. GRANT OF LICENSE.   Subject to the terms and conditions of this Agreement, IBM grants to You a non-transferable, non-exclusive, non-assignable right to use one copy of The DevCon. You may only use this copy on one machine at any one time.

Α   You may not copy, modify or merge copies of The DevCon except as provided below. You may not reverse compile, reverse engineer or reverse assemble any products in, or accessed through, The DevCon that are provided in object code form. You may not rent, lease, sell, sublicense, as-sign or otherwise transfer The DevCon except as provided below.

II. ADDITIONAL RIGHTS AND RESTRICTIONS—notwithstanding anything to the contrary above, the following products contained in The DevCon have the following additional rights and restrictions:

A) Evaluation purposes: The following programs may be used for evaluation purposes only:

REXX/6000.

B) Demonstration purposes: The following programs may be used for demonstration purposes only:

AIXwindows Demos and Performance Toolbox.

C) The following AIX pre-release Code/Program/Material (DCE Tools, OpenDoc Early Experi-ence Package, and Program Visualizer) have the following additional rights and restrictions:

a) You may use the Code/Program/Material (and any copies of it) only for internal evalua-tion and testing purposes. You may make a reasonable number of copies of the Code/Program/Material in support of such evaluation and testing. You agree to repro-duce the copyright notice and any other legend of ownership on each copy or partial copy.

b) You hereby assign to IBM all right, title, and interest (including ownership of copyright) in any data, suggestions, and written materials You provide to IBM. If IBM requires it, You agree to sign an appropriate document to assign such rights.

c) You agree to 1) maintain a record of all copies of the Code/Program/Material and 2) en-sure that anyone who uses the Code/Program/Material does so only for Your autho-rized use and complies with this Agreement. IBM will not provide program services or technical support, unless IBM specifies otherwise.

D) IBM grants to You a non-exclusive, non-assignable, non-transferable right, under the applica-ble IBM copyrights, to use one copy of the enclosed AIX device driver sample code on a sin-gle computer for the sole purposes of designing, developing and testing derivative work(s) which are device drivers for the AIX program (the "AIX Device Driver").

In addition, IBM grants to You the non-exclusive, non-assignable, non-transferable right, under the applicable IBM copyrights, to reproduce and distribute, in object code form only, the AIX device driver sample code and/or the permitted derivative work thereof, but only in conjunction with and as part of the AIX Device Driver and only if You; a) does not make any statements to the effect or which imply that the AIX Device driver is "certified" by IBM or that its performance is guaranteed by IBM and b) agree to indemnify, hold harmless and defend IBM and its subsidiaries and their suppliers from and against any and all claims, legal proceedings, liabilities, damages, costs and expenses, including attorney's fees, arising out of or in connection with Your distribution of the AIX device driver sample code and/or the AIX Device Driver.

You must reproduce any copyright notice(s) on each copy, or partial copy, of the AIX device driver sample code.

III. COPYRIGHT. The DevCon is owned by IBM and its suppliers and is protected by United States copyright laws. The DevCon is licensed not sold. In addition to the rights granted above, You may make one copy of The DevCon solely for backup or archival purposes.

IV. TERM AND TERMINATION. Unless notified earlier by IBM, Your license for The DevCon terminates 120 days after receipt of this issue of The DevCon or upon receipt of the next issue of The DevCon, whichever occurs sooner. Not withstanding the above, if IBM makes the AIX pre-release Code/Program/Material generally available prior to the above date of termination Your license to such Code/Program/Material shall terminate 10 days after IBM makes them generally available. Prior to the above dates of termination, (1) You may terminate Your license at any time by destroying all of Your copies of The DevCon and (2) IBM may terminate Your license if You fail to comply with all the terms and conditions of this Agreement. Upon termination, You agree to destroy all Your copies of The DevCon or the applicable Code/Program/Material.

V. DISCLAIMER OF WARRANTY. The DevCon includes products which contain pre-release material and may be modified substantially before general availability. These pre-release material may not be at the level of performance or compatibility of generally available IBM products. IBM does not guarantee that any of the pre-release material contained in The DevCon will ever be made generally available.

The DevCon is provided "AS-IS". IBM makes no warranties of any kind, either express or implied, with respect to The DevCon. IBM expressly disclaims the implied warranties of merchantability and fitness for a particular purpose and any warranty of non-infringement. The entire risk arising out of use or performance of The DevCon remains with you.

In no event will IBM and/or its suppliers be liable for any damages whatsoever including, but not limited to, indirect, incidental, or consequential damages, or any damages claimed by You based on any third party claim, even if IBM, or its authorized supplier, has been advised or is aware of the possibility of such damages.

Some jurisdictions do not allow the exclusion of implied warranties or the exclusion or limitation of consequential or incidental damages, so the above provisions relating thereto may not apply to You.

VI. GENERAL. If You use The DevCon in the United States or Puerto Rico, this license is governed by the substantive laws of the State of New York (excluding choice of law rules). If You use The DevCon in Canada, this license is governed by the laws of the Province of Ontario. Otherwise, this license is governed by the laws of the country in which You use The DevCon.

* IBM, and AIX are registered trademarks of International Business Machines Corporation.
**OpenDoc is a trademark of Apple Computer, Inc.
**Other products and brand names may be trademarks or registered trademarks of their respective owners.

Important Notice:

The CD-ROM contains licensed materials. Please read the preceeding license agreements for the terms and conditions for using the programs and books on the CD-ROM. By accessing, using, or copying the programs and books, you agree to the terms and conditions of the license agreements. If you do not agree, please return the package to IBM.